Dr Kathleen Rankin, née Lilley (1928–2018), was a graduate of Queen's University, Belfast where she completed her Ph.D. on the In-service Education of Teachers with particular reference to science. For many years she was involved with the organisation of both Chemistry and Biology courses for teachers at the Queen's University Teachers' Centre. In addition she was a graduate of Trinity College, University of Dublin where she obtained an M.Litt. in Education. Dr Rankin was the daughter of the late Herbert R. Lilley, a well known linen designer, and from retirement as a lecturer in Lisburn Institute, she was involved with Living Linen, an organisation associated with the gathering of information on the Irish Linen industry in the twentieth century.

Kathleen Rankin published several books on a range of subjects, mostly concerning Irish linen. They include *Linen Houses of the Lagan Valley, the story of their families*, and on the same theme, *Linen Houses of the Bann Valley, the story of their families*.

Kathleen Rankin was appointed MBE in the 2010 New Year's Honours List.

A river in the Glens of Antrim
Herbert R. Lilley
From a Private Collection

The LINEN HOUSES
of COUNTY ANTRIM AND NORTH COUNTY DOWN

The story of their families

KATHLEEN RANKIN

ULSTER HISTORICAL
FOUNDATION

Dedicated

to

Living Linen

*which has done so much to ensure that
Irish linen heritage is not forgotten*

First published in 2012
by the Ulster Historical Foundation
www.ancestryireland.com

Except as otherwise permitted under the Copyright, Designs and Patents Act 1988, this publication may only be reproduced, stored or transmitted in any form or by any means with the prior permission in writing of the publisher or, in the case of reprographic reproduction, in accordance with the terms of a licence issued by The Copyright Licensing Agency. Enquiries concerning reproduction outside those terms should be sent to the publisher.

© Kathleen Rankin, 2012

Printed by Lightning Source in 2023
Design and production, Dunbar Design

ISBN 978-1-913993-45-0

CONTENTS

ACKNOWLEDGEMENTS   ix
LIST OF ABBREVIATIONS   x
PREFACE   xi
INTRODUCTION   xiii

1
ENVIRONS OF BELFAST

Greeves Family Tree		2
The Greeves Family of Belfast		3
Greeves	Lismachan, Strandtown, Belfast	5
Greeves	Tweskard, Strandtown, Belfast	7
Greeves	Bernagh, Strandtown, Belfast	8
Greeves	Altona, Strandtown, Belfast	9
The Ewart Family of Belfast		11
Ewart Family Tree		14
Ewart	Glenmachan, Strandtown, Belfast	15
Ewart	Glenbank House, Ballysillan, Belfast	18

2
NEWTOWNABBEY

Mackie Family Tree		22
The Mackie Family of Belfast		23
Mackie	Hazelbank House, Whitehouse, Newtownabbey	27
Mackie	Ringdufferin House, County Down	30
Mackie	Meroc, Greenisland, Newtownabbey	33
Campbell Family Tree		35
The Campbell Family of Mossley		36

Campbell	Mossley House, Whiteabbey	39
Campbell	Rathfern, Whiteabbey	41
Campbell	Lorne, Craigavad	43

The Henshall Family   46

Henshall	Lonsdale, Newtownabbey	48

Philip Johnston & Sons   49

Johnston	Dalriada, Newtownabbey	50
Johnston	Three Acres, Dunmurry	52

Valentine Family Tree   54
The Valentine Family   55

Valentine	Glenavna House, Whiteabbey	57
Valentine	The Moat, Strandtown	59
Robinson	Abbeydene, Newtownabbey	61
Owden	Seapark House, Carrickfergus	64

3
SOUTH COUNTY ANTRIM

Cunningham Family Tree   70

Cunningham	Crookedstone, Aldergrove	71
MacClure	Islandreagh House, Dunadry	73
Cowdy	Clady House, Dunadry	75
Webb	Clady Cottage, Dunadry	77

Chaine Family Tree   80
The Chaine Family of South Antrim   81

Chaine	Ballycraigy House, Muckamore	83
Chaine	Glenhurst, Muckamore	86
Chaine	Moylena, Muckamore	87
York Street Flax Spinning Co.	Firgrove House, Muckamore	90
McMeekin	Invermuir House, Doagh	92

4
MID COUNTY ANTRIM

Webb Family Tree		96
The Webb Family of Randalstown		97
Webb	Knockvare, Randalstown	99
Webb	Redlands, Randalstown	100
Gotto	Briarfield, Randalstown	101
Webb	Barney's Brae, Randalstown	102
Webb	Drummaul House, Randalstown	104
Dickey	Hollybrook House, Randalstown	105
Young Family Tree		107
The Young Family of Ballymena		108
Young	Galgorm Castle, Ballymena	110
Young	Fenaghy House, Cullybackey	113
Cunningham	Ardvernis House, Galgorm	115
Cunningham Family Tree		116

5
MAIN VALLEY
WEST COUNTY ANTRIM

Patrick Family Tree		120
The Patrick Family of Dunminning and Ballymena		121
Patrick	Dunminning House, Glarryford	122
Patrick	Dunminning Cottage, Glarryford	124
Cunningham	Duneoin, Cullybackey	125
Frazer	Hillmount House, Cullybackey	127
Haughton	Harperstown House, Cullybackey	130
Haughton	Red Cottage, Cullybackey	132
Haughton	Kilconway, Cullybackey	133
Robinson Family Tree		134
Robinson	Dromona, Cullybackey	135
Reade Family Tree		137
Reade	Carncairn Lodge, Broughshane	138
Millar	Valley Cottage, Crevilly Valley	140
Hanna	Kildrum House, Kells	142
Dinsmore	Greenfield House, Kells	144
Flax Spinners Annual Dinner photograph		146

6
NORTH EAST COUNTY DOWN

Andrews Family Tree		151
The Andrews Family of Comber		152
Andrews	Maxwell Court, Comber	154
Andrews	Ardara, Comber	156
Andrews	Ballywilliam House, Comber	159
Walker	Regent House, Newtownards	161
Bradshaw	Milecross Lodge, Newtownards	163
Johnston	Glen House, Newtownards	165
Mulholland Family Tree		167
The Mulholland Family of Belfast		168
Mulholland	Ballywalter Park, Ballywalter	171
Mulholland	Craigavad House, Holywood	175
Crawford	Mount Randal, Belfast	177
Mitchell Family Tree		181
Mitchell	The Grey House, Craigavad	182
Hurst Family Tree		185
The Hurst Family of Drumaness		186
Hurst	The Hill, Drumaness, Ballynahinch	188
Hurst	Harmony Hill, Drumaness	189
BIBLIOGRAPHY		191
INDEX		195

ACKNOWLEDGEMENTS

A book of this nature requires an input of knowledge from a considerable number of sources.

I would like to take this opportunity to thank the many people who have helped to make this work possible, in particular John R. Cowdy for his very extensive knowledge of the owners of 'Linen Houses', Peter J. Rankin OBE for architectural advice and details of his own ancestral family involvement in linen manufacture, and J. Fred Rankin for photographing the majority of the houses involved in this publication. I am deeply indebted to the owners of the many houses who have allowed photographs to be taken, and also, in some cases, provided family photographs. They often contributed information concerning the history of their houses, and this has been of great assistance. My thanks are also due to Samantha Curry, at Mossley Mill, Newtownabbey Borough Council, who provided helpful advice and a photograph of Hazelbank, 1958, the first Town Hall for Newtownabbey. I would also like to thank Mrs Julie Mackie, again for a photograph of Hazelbank, which does not now exist, and extensive information and photographs involving the Mackie family. Photographs of members of the Young family of Galgorm Castle were kindly provided by Ballymena Museum.

Where possible modern photographs of the houses have been used and, on occasion, an older photograph included for comparison. Unfortunately a considerable number of the 'Linen Houses' no longer exist, and photographs have had to be sourced from former owners or local museums and libraries. This book endeavours, wherever possible, to give some idea of the lifestyle of the people who lived in the 'Linen Houses'. Many of their descendants are still alive and my thanks are due in very great measure to them for photographs of houses and their residents. I am grateful to the following for photographs: J. Anthony D. Greeves, Keith Haines, (Archivist, Campbell College), Anthony Wilson, James Henshall, Donald Macleay (Australia), A.J.H. Cunningham, Mrs Joan Emerson, Richard Reade DL, Mervyn Gilfillan, Frank Pettigrew, Mrs Maud Hamill, (Abbey Historical Society), Richard Graham, Derek Martin, William Dunlop, (Scrabo Golf Club), Neil Gordon, (The Grey House), Brian Metcalfe, (Photograph of Spinners' Dinner, 1958), Lord and Lady Dunleath, Ballywalter Park, Dr Trevor McCavery, (Principal, Regent House School), Dr William Roulston, John M.J. Andrews for Andrews Family information, and photographs.

Acknowledgement must also be made to the various institutions that assisted with archive material and photographic research, and that have kindly given permission for photographs to be reproduced from their collections: the Public

Record Office of Northern Ireland (PRONI), the Monuments and Buildings Record (MBR), Built Heritage, Northern Ireland Environment Agency (NIEA), the Trustees of the National Museums and Galleries of Northern Ireland: Ulster Museum (UM) and Ulster Folk and Transport Museum (UFTM), the Controller of her Majesty's Stationery Office on behalf of the Ordnance Survey of Northern Ireland.

Lastly, I owe a very great debt to my husband, Fred, who entered into the project with great enthusiasm, and is responsible for the majority of the photographs in this book. With the inclusion of many illustrations it became clear that sponsorship support was required from outside bodies. I am extremely grateful to those listed for their generous contributions:

Living Linen
The Esmé Mitchell Trust
Northern Ireland Environment Agency (NIEA)
Belfast Natural History and Philosophical Society

ABBREVIATIONS

BNL	*Belfast Newsletter*
BT	*Belfast Telegraph*
LL	Living Linen
MBR	Monuments and Buildings Record of Northern Ireland
PRONI	Public Record Office of Northern Ireland
NMGNI UFTM	Ulster Folk & Transport Museum
NMGNI UM	Ulster Museum
JFR	J.F. Rankin

PREFACE

The Living Linen project was set up in 1995 in order to record as an Oral Archive the knowledge of the linen industry still available within a nucleus of people who were formerly working in the industry in Ulster. Over the period 1870 to 1970 the north east of Ireland was the world's leading linen producing area. Ulster manufacturers produced three quarters of the United Kingdom's output, specialising in the medium and fine end of the market. Concern has been expressed regarding the fact that despite the linen industry underpinning the local economy no comprehensive history of the industry over three centuries has been written. Nevertheless, considerable studies on the Irish linen industry in the eighteenth and nineteenth centuries have been published, but very little has been done in the last one hundred years to emphasise the world wide nature of this trade in that period.

A very important feature of the linen industry in Ireland has been the resilience of the small or medium size private family firm. Although in the aftermath of the First World War, the difficulties of trade in the 1930s, and the Second World War, many of these companies were forced to close, a considerable number survived into the 1970s. However, by the close of the twentieth century there had been a very great reduction in numbers with less than twenty companies continuing to operate. Therefore, with the Irish linen trade in very steep decline, there appeared to be an urgent necessity to gather information while it was still available. The Living Linen project, in Phase I, was set up to gather knowledge quickly, which was held by many of the former owners and managers of the industry, since there was a wealth of information not put in writing. Nevertheless, there was also oral knowledge which could be recorded, from the representatives of the linen trade who travelled world wide, and from pockets of highly skilled people living in manufacturing areas. This second group of recordings, with the work supported financially by the Heritage Lottery Fund from 1999 to 2002, constituted Phase II of the project, and all Living Linen recordings were placed in the Ulster Folk & Transport Museum, Cultra, County Down.

Initially, in Phase I, various Living Linen committee members made, in the main, recordings of the owners and managers of the old linen industry. With others, I had the privilege of invitations to homes of linen merchants where, in some cases, records of their lifestyle, including portraits and photographs, going back over many years, were held. Many of the linen merchants built new properties or improved existing ones with the large growth of the linen industry in the latter half of the nineteenth century in the greater Belfast area, in County

Antrim along the Six Mile Water and the River Main, and finally in north County Down. It therefore appeared appropriate to compile a book concerned with an historical and architectural study of these houses as with the companion volumes for the Lagan Valley and the Upper Bann Valley. Although this book makes use of information and photographs gathered in the Living Linen project, it has had to draw on the considerable records of the Public Record Office of Northern Ireland, the Linen Hall Library, Belfast, the Ulster Folk & Transport Museum, Newtownabbey Council Museum, and the Mid-Antrim Museum, Ballymena.

INTRODUCTION

In Ireland, during the eighteenth century, the spinning of linen yarn was carried out by women in their cottages, which were scattered throughout the countryside. Irish Linen developed and specialised in the production of extremely fine yarns, which were woven into damasks and cambrics, unmatched in quality world wide. However, in England, within twenty years of the successful mechanisation of the spinning of cotton yarn a beginning had been made with the power spinning of flax. John Marshall of Leeds and his associates opened the first spinning mill in 1790 as a result of the inventions of John Kendrew and Thomas Porthouse of Darlington. From Yorkshire power spinning of flax was taken up in the linen manufacturing districts of the east of Scotland, where it soon became an important industry. The English and Scottish industries manufactured mainly coarse linens, for which the yarn produced by the primitive mill spindles was considered satisfactory. In Ireland, the linen industry remained almost untouched by these changes since it concentrated on fine cloth made from locally produced yarns. However, by the beginning of the nineteenth century, outside the traditional centres of the Ulster industry in Lurgan, Portadown, Banbridge, and Lisburn, the cottage spinning of yarn and weaving of cloth did begin to decrease and considerable quantities of flax were exported from Ulster to Britain for dry spinning. In 1825 James Kay of Preston invented a wet spinning process in that he discovered that a thorough soaking in cold water made flax fibres more slippery so that they could be drawn by machinery into a really fine yarn.

In 1828, two events marked a change of the most revolutionary kind in the Irish linen industry. McCutcheon states:

> The story of one important Belfast mill, that of the brothers Thomas and Andrew Mulholland in Henry Street, off York Street, illustrates many of the points which characterised the great industrial upheaval of these formative years. The Mulholland brothers established a large cotton spinning mill in Henry Street in 1822 which was driven by a steam engine. Unfortunately, in June 1828 this mill was gutted by fire and the brothers decided to rebuild the mill for flax spinning.

The Mulholland's wet spinning mill opened for production in the spring of 1830, so introducing flax spinning by power on a large scale for the first time. The movement begun by the Mulholland brothers in the York Street mill proceeded rapidly, which is shown by the fact that by 1838 there were fifteen flax spinning mills in Belfast, and the number increased to twenty-eight by 1852, eight of them on the Falls Road. The fact that the York Street mill consumed 3,000 tons of coal in a year is sufficient explanation for industrial flax spinning not spreading far inland. Usage of imported coal, and large quantities of imported flax kept the flax spinning industry in and around Belfast, with the commercial importance of Belfast developing rapidly. E.R.R. Green, writing about the industrial revolution in the linen industry states:

> The Mulholland's great York Street mill employed 800 workers and had 16,000 spindles, spinning 700 tons of flax into yarn in the year. In 1856, there were 25,000 spindles and a power-loom factory. The Falls Road flax mill of Charters, Coats and Gamble had 8,400 spindles and employed 650 people.

William Ewart & Son, about the year 1840, secured extensive ground, with water rights, on the Crumlin Road, Belfast, where they built their first spinning mill, and in 1850 a power loom weaving factory was added. Additionally, in 1852, the firm purchased the bleach works at Glenbank, Ligoniel, from Mackie and Charters. By 1850 the steam engine occupied a prominent position in Ulster industry, which meant that with the relatively late introduction of power loom weaving many of the new weaving factories were built in Belfast. However, there was also an expansion in provincial towns long associated with the linen trade, where the expanding railway network could ensure ease of coal import. At the time of the American Civil War, 1861–65, when the demand for linen was high, John Andrews & Co. built a new flax spinning mill in Comber in 1863–64. Edmund Grimshaw at Whiteabbey converted the Mossley print works to flax spinning. In February 1859 an agreement was signed between the Ulster Bank and Gunning and Campbell for the property at Mossley, this being the beginning of the firm of Henry Campbell. The mill was greatly enlarged and two steam engines with boilers were installed, having the advantage of being close to the Belfast to Ballymena railway, and within easy reach of Ballynure Road Station for the transport of coal.

This situation was replicated in Belfast where the brothers, John and Thomas Malcomson Greeves whose family had been in the linen industry in Dungannon for many years, in 1862 took over a mill on the Falls Road previously occupied by McConnell, Kennedy & Co., and set up the large Forth River flax spinning mills. The demand for linen soared during the American Civil War, giving rise to a great increase in the capacity for both spinning and weaving. Emily Boyle, writing in *Belfast, The Making of the City* states:

> The number of flax spinning spindles operating in and around Belfast increased from less than 500,000 in 1862, to 724,000 in 1868, and the number of power looms rose from under 3,000 to nearly 9,000. Seven new weaving factories were opened, including Lawnbrook, Bain's Place, Loopbridge, Cupar Street and Brookfield.

Many firms expanded integrating their spinning and weaving concerns, William Ewart & Son even adding a new mill and weaving factory to their works on the Crumlin Road. In the late nineteenth century west Belfast, principally the Falls Road, Shankill Road, Crumlin Road, and their connecting streets contained a considerable number of flax spinning mills and weaving factories, along with rows of terrace houses to accommodate the growing number of workers required for the trade. Emily Boyle again reports:

> The profits made by the Belfast linen lords in these years were vast. One contemporary spoke of 'profitable returns of well nigh fabulous percentage', and claimed that for two years running one firm's profits 'equalled the value of the entire premises and plant'. Certainly, Gunning and Campbell, flax spinners of Mossley Mill just outside Belfast, saw their profits rise from under £7,000 in 1861, to over £21,000 in 1864.

By 1873 Belfast was the largest linen producing centre in the world, a position retained by the city until the outbreak of the First World War. Unfortunately trade fell in the latter part of the nineteenth century and there were a significant number of bankruptcies, but many linen companies survived well into the twentieth century.

The bleachers were also affected by the introduction of power spinning, with small bleach greens being bought up by larger concerns. McCutcheon states:

> While bleaching and finishing by independent firms on a contract basis was important there was by now a fair degree of vertical grouping within the industry, and about half the bleach works already formed part of larger units comprising spinning mills, weaving factories and bleachworks.

William Ewart & Son were one of the first firms to achieve vertical integration, having opened the Glenbank Bleach works on the Ligoneil Road in 1852. By 1900, of the eight bleachworks operating in and around Belfast all but one were located in the industrial sector of west Belfast. Nearby, in the Lagan Valley, Richardson, Sons & Owden had much earlier in the 1830s opened their very considerable bleach green at Glenmore.

In County Antrim there was a remarkable concentration of bleach greens in the valley of the Six Mile Water, largely dependent on water power and on an adequate supply of river water for processing. During the late eighteenth and early nenteenth centuries the Six Mile Water, and its tributaries the Clady, Four Mile Burn, and Doagh Stream, had a considerable number of mills on their banks. Three families, the Thompsons, Chaines and Refords, appear to have dominated the linen and bleaching trade. William Chaine (1778–1862), who came to Muckamore in 1797, gradually built up his linen business in the Antrim area, buying up bleach greens and making it into a very well run business which employed between 300 and 500 people at any one time. His grandson, James Chaine, MP, DL (1841–85), sold the majority of his bleach greens and properties in 1883 to the York Street Flax Spinning Co., Ltd., so enabling them to finish considerable quantities of brown linen at Muckamore. McCutcheon has written:

INTRODUCTION

Thus, of the forty or so bleachworks in existence in 1900 over thirty were outside Belfast and of these about 60 per cent were independent contract bleachers and finishers. Of these contract bleachers a large number were by now handling a substantial business in the bleaching and finishing of cotton fabrics woven in the north of England. The high reputation of the textile finishing trade in the north of Ireland made it possible for these bleachworks to compete successfully with English firms despite the substantial transport costs involved.

Frazer & Haughton were very significant independent contract bleachers and finishers at Cullybackey in County Antrim. Again at Cullybackey on the River Main the company known as Dromona & Maine were independent bleachers, dyers and finishers, carrying out a considerable trade in dyeing. The Old Bleach Linen Company Ltd. at Randalstown, County Antrim, carried out bleaching, dyeing and finishing for themselves, using the River Main.

While many of the very successful linen manufacturers had their businesses in Belfast a considerable number preferred to live outside the city. Perhaps the most significant of these would be Andrew Mulholland, proprietor of the York Street Flax Spinning Mill, Belfast, who in 1846 bought Springvale, an estate on the eastern side of the Ards peninsula in north County Down, adjacent to the village of Ballywalter, and after considerable additions to the property renamed it Ballywalter Park. In the latter part of the nineteenth century the Ewart family and the Greeves family both built luxurious mansions on the wooded Sydenham hillside, overlooking Belfast Lough, and off the Belmont Road. Henry Campbell, owner of the very successful Mossley Mill, Whiteabbey, County Antrim, built a new house named Lorne at Craigavad, County Down, in 1865.

However, many of the enterprising linen manufacturers and bleachers operating outside Belfast bought distinguished old homes or built new ones close to their work place in the nineteenth and twentieth centuries, both in County Antrim and in north County Down. Although almost all linen manufacture in Northern Ireland has ceased a considerable number of the linen houses remain. This book aims to provide an illustrated and informed commentary on the major linen families and their houses, with exterior views of the actual houses, some unfortunately demolished, and portraits of their owners, many selected from private collections of the families themselves. The format of the book is similar to *The Linen Houses of the Lagan Valley*, and *The Linen Houses of the Bann Valley*, with short family histories and family trees for major linen families, which have, of necessity, been limited to the male members of a family, who have, for several generations, been involved in some aspect of the linen industry.

The identification of these houses, some of which are very old, with the entrepreneurs of the Irish linen industry, will also serve to show the importance of that industry to the growth of Ulster over a period of three hundred years.

OPPOSITE: Belfast Docks, 1912
Herbert R. Lilley
From a Private Collection

1
Environs of BELFAST

GREEVES FAMILY TREE

The Greeves Family Tree only shows male members of the family involved in J. & T. M. Greeves, Ltd.

Thomas Greeves = Rachel Malcomson
1792–1852   1795–1871

John Greeves = Elizabeth Pim Jackson
1831–1917   1837–1924
LISMACHAN, Belmont

Thomas Malcomson Greeves = Georgiana E. Jackson
1835–1924   1835–1925
TWESKARD, Belmont

Joseph Malcomson Greeves
1858–1925
BERNAGH

George Ridgeway Greeves
1861–1942

Arthur Greeves
1865–1934
ALTONA

Thomas Jackson Greeves
1872–1939

Owden Valentine Greeves
1874–1959

Malcolm Macgregor Greeves
1863–1941

Alfred Greeves
1865–1948

Fergus Macgregor Greeves
1866–1956

John Ronald Howard Greeves
1900–1988

Alfred William Greeves
1899–1956

Norman Greeves
b. 1905

THE GREEVES FAMILY
OF BELFAST

The Greer family, of which one branch changed their name to Greeves, is very extensive and originally came from Alnick, Northumberland. Henry Greer arrived in Ireland in 1653, settling at Redford, near Grange, County Tyrone, and became an early member of the Society of Friends *c.* 1660. In the eighteenth century a number of the Greer families lived in the area between Dungannon and Moy, and were highly esteemed linen merchants, so much so that John Greer, of The Grange, County Tyrone, became Inspector General of the Linen Trade in Ulster. Over a period of one hundred years the members of the Greer family involved in the linen industry became very numerous, and a grandson of Robert Greer (1660–1730) adopted the name Greeves at the time of his marriage in 1744, to Mary Morton. It was descendants of this branch of the family who were to continue in the nineteenth century their involvement with the mechanised linen industry. This was the period of the diminution of the domestic linen industry with a great decrease in linen woven by farmers at their homes, and the movement to towns where mills and factories were set up for the industrial manufacture of linen.

The brothers, John and Thomas Malcomson Greeves, sons of Thomas and Rachel Greeves of Fernshaw, Dungannon, moved to Belfast, and set up J. & T.M. Greeves & Co. in 1862, later incorporated as J. & T.M. Greeves, Ltd. 1899, flax spinners, Forth River Mills, Belfast. Additionally, two sons of John Greeves (1831–1917), Thomas Jackson Greeves (1872–1939) and Owden Valentine Greeves (1874–1959) set up the Portadown Weaving Company, and were followed in their business by their nephew, William Edward Greeves and also by their sons. Prior to their move to Belfast, John and Thomas M. Greeves had been in the linen industry for some time, serving apprenticeships and becoming managers appropriately with the Richardsons, who were one of the oldest of the linen families and also Quakers. John Greeves trained in the spinning mill in Bessbrook, Newry, owned by John Grubb Richardson, and Thomas Malcomson Greeves in J.N. Richardson, Sons & Owden at Glenmore, Lisburn.

In 1862 the Greeves brothers established J. & T.M. Greeves & Co. taking over a mill on the Falls Road previously occupied by McConnell, Kennedy & Co., who had been flax spinners. They greatly improved the premises, installing a large number of spindles, and, according to J.B.H. Metcalfe, (LL1 R98/17), at the turn of the century the mill had 82,000 spindles, which was nearly ten per cent of the total spindles in the trade. They produced very, very fine yarn, and were renowned in America for the fineness and quality of their yarn (W. Phenix LL2 R00/87), being specialist cambric yarn spinners. Mr Phenix has also recorded that J. & T.M. Greeves was quite a progressive and go ahead company, being assisted in this by the Eves family, who were both intellectually and hands-on practical engineers.

John Greeves of Lismachan
COURTESY OF THE GREEVES FAMILY

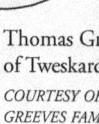

After becoming a limited company, John Greeves was chairman from 1899 to his death in 1917, and he was followed by Thomas Malcomson Greeves as chairman from 1917 to 1924, their sons also being directors of J.& T.M. Greeves. In addition to the Forth River Mill the Greeves also had a newer mill at Cupar Street, the two mills being linked by an overhead avenue. The sons of Thomas M. Greeves successively became chairmen of the company, the last chairman being Lieutenant Colonel J.R.H. Greeves, a grandson of John Greeves. As the linen trade decreased in the 1950s demand for fine yarns also decreased and in late 1959 J. & T.M. Greeves was taken over by Herdmans Ltd., Sion Mills. Denys H.L. Jemphrey, OBE, stated in 1995 that J.R.H. Greeves was put on the Board of Herdmans since they had their own yarn connections. (LL1 R95/5).

Trevor Eves
COURTESY OF THE GREEVES FAMILY

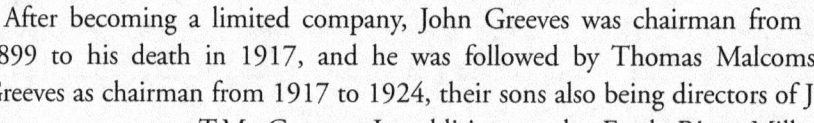

Thomas Greeves of Tweskard
COURTESY OF THE GREEVES FAMILY

LISMACHAN
STRANDTOWN, BELFAST

BACK ROW FROM LEFT: Rachel, Joseph, Jackson, George, Arthur
FRONT ROW FROM LEFT: Greta, John Greeves, Owden, Lily, Bertha

COURTESY OF THE GREEVES FAMILY

Lismachan is situated at 378 Belmont Road, Belfast, and was originally built in 1870, for James Shaw, the architect being Thomas Jackson. However, by 1878 the house was occupied by John Greeves, his wife and family, as shown by the Street Directory of that date. Dean states:

> One of many large villas in the Glenmachan area by Thomas Jackson, architect to rich merchants and Quakers.

A report on 'Villa at Strandtown near Belfast' In the *Irish Builder* of 1st January 1870, states:

> The villa which is the subject of our illustration in this number, is to be erected for Mr James Shaw, at Ballymaclean, about three miles from Belfast. — This gentleman is landlord of several townlands in the district, and has given encouragement to build, by granting long leases at moderate rentals.

Strandtown Villa will comprise two front sitting rooms, each 24 ft. by 18 ft., exclusive of the bay projections; two smaller sitting rooms, each 16 ft. square; ample hall and staircase, and back stairs; eight bed rooms and dressing rooms; convenient kitchen, culinary apartments, &c., &c. Attached to the villa there are about thirty acres of land.

Lismachan gate lodge
JFR

Lismachan is a two-storey house in the Italianate style, with single storey east wing, standing on a hillside, and originally would have commanded extensive views of Belfast Lough and the Antrim Hills. The roofs are hipped and slated, with modillioned eaves, cornices and tall chimneys. The walls are smooth rendered with heavily moulded details. The front of Lismachan is of five bays with round headed windows, having scrolled keystones on the ground floor. A platband separates the ground floor from the top floor, and the house has raised quoins shown particularly on the projecting three-storey tower, centrally positioned on the main block and containing the porch which has a round headed doorway. Lismachan has a gate lodge, which, according to Dean, is in informal Italianate style and designed by Thomas Jackson's son.

John Greeves lived at Lismachan until his death in 1917, his wife having pre-deceased him in 1895. After his death their daughters, the Misses Lillian, Rachel, Bertha and Margretta continued to live at Lismachan.

Gordon Ewart with his bride Lily Greeves, 14 December 19
COURTESY OF THE GREEVES FAMILY

Lismachan with Altona in the background
COURTESY OF THE GREEVES FAMILY

Thomas Malcomson Greeves with his wife Georgina Greeves née Jackson, December 1901

COURTESY OF THE GREEVES FAMILY

TWESKARD

STRANDTOWN, BELFAST

Tweskard, the home of Thomas Malcomson Greeves and his wife, was on the opposite side of the Belmont Road, Strandtown, to Lismachan. The house was built about 1875 to a design by the architect Thomas Jackson, who was the father of Mrs Georgina Greeves. Tweskard was a two-storey gabled house plus attic with a side entrance sheltered by a small porch. The windows, topped by flat arches were recessed, sashed and silled. The roof was slated with deep eaves, and the decorative chimneys had recessed panels, while the house walls were smooth rendered. Tweskard was built in considerable grounds but the building has since been demolished and the area now contains a number of modern houses.

Tweskard

Thomas M. Greeves lived at Tweskard until his death in 1924, followed by that of his wife in 1925. Keith Haines, archivist to nearby Campbell College, has recorded that Tweskard, house, stables, and grounds, were rented, initially for two years, as accommodation for an intermediate school between the junior forms at Cabin Hill and the senior forms at Campbell College, and opened in September 1926. However, Ormiston, a larger and more suitable property, was purchased from Harland & Wolff by the school early in 1927, and by September of that year catered for fifty boys in all. Subsequently, Tweskard was occupied in turn by various families but was eventually demolished to make way for new housing.

BERNAGH
STRANDTOWN, BELFAST

Bernagh
COURTESY MR ANTHONY WILSON

Bernagh was situated on Circular Road, off Belmont Road, Strandtown, and was built about 1890 for Joseph Malcomson Greeves, eldest son of John Greeves, and a director of J. & T.M. Greeves. This was a substantial, two-storey with attic, red brick Victorian villa, the façade of which was balanced by bay windows on either side of the entrance. The windows were recessed, sashed and silled, a string course running above the ground floor windows. The entrance was set within an arch which had a moulded surround, and the roof was slated. Bernagh was latterly known as Red Hall, and became the property of the South and East Belfast Health Trust. However, it became surplus to requirements, and was demolished, to be replaced by a block of flats.

Bernagh was the childhood home of Arthur Greeves, fourth son of Joseph M. Greeves. He was a life-long friend of the famous author C.S. Lewis, whose home, Little Lea, was nearby on Circular Road. Lewis returned annually to Northern Ireland as an adult and, following his father's death in 1929, he would stay with Arthur Greeves at Bernagh.

Joseph Malcomson Greeves and family
COURTESY OF THE GREEVES FAMILY

Altona
COURTESY OF THE GREEVES FAMILY

ALTONA

STRANDTOWN, BELFAST

Altona is situated on the Glenmachan Road, Belmont, and is set in two and a half acres of wooded hillside. The house was built in 1864, not far from Glenmachan House, by the architect Thomas Jackson for his own use. This is a two-storey L-shaped house with bay windows, built in hand made red brick, with walls which have raised quoins. The roof is hipped and slated, having tall chimney stacks. The windows are recessed, sashed and silled, and topped by a flat arch in brick. There is a single storey projecting entrance porch with a matching side window. Photographs taken in the latter half of the twentieth century show the walls of the house smooth rendered and painted cream, but it has now been restored to the original brick. There is a considerable conservatory to the front of Altona, and, nearby, a stable block with slated hipped roof.

An interesting description of Altona is given by Hugh Dixon in an article entitled 'Honouring Thomas Jackson, 1807–90 (Architect)' and dated 10th December, 1974. This states:

> Altona, the house he designed for himself, which is still occupied by his descendants, is a model of convenience combined with that characteristic restraint which sets Jackson's work aside from that of the majority of mid-Victorian architects. Designed in 1864 to stand in ample gardens, it was just a small part of a grand design for developing the Sydenham hillside with a series of tangent demesnes, really big wooded gardens for successful industrialists.

J.R.H. Greeves with his wife at Altona
COURTESY OF THE GREEVES FAMILY

Altona, 2011
JFR

J.R.H. Greeves, the last chairman of J. & T.M. Greeves and a grandson of John Greeves, lived with his wife and family in Altona, as did his father, Arthur Greeves, also a director of the company. There was a close connection between the nearby Quaker families in that two of Thomas Jackson's daughters married into the Greeves family: Elizabeth Pim Jackson marrying John Greeves of Lismachan, and Georgiana Eliza Jackson marrying Thomas Malcomson Greeves of Tweskard.

THE EWART FAMILY
OF BELFAST

THOMAS EWART was granted the lease of a farm of twenty acres in the townland of Carnreagh, Annahilt, near Hillsborough, in 1716. At that time the Linen Board was assisting farmers to procure handlooms of the most modern design and the weaving of damask spread, particularly from Lisburn to Hillsborough and Waringstown. In 1746 the Carnreagh lease was renewed to another Thomas Ewart and in the following generation, 1759, William Ewart (1) was born. Under his leadership the firm grew from parochial in nature to one with world wide connections. The Ewarts first bought locally spun yarns from the cottagers around Hillsborough, and distributed them to the neighbouring cottage weavers, the resulting cloth being sold to the bleachers.

However, William Ewart (1) had ambitions beyond those of his father and grandfather and about 1790 he moved to Ballymacarrett, then a country village well outside the town of Belfast, where female labour was plentiful. He installed looms and taught the people how to weave linen, purchasing yarn in the surrounding yarn markets. Later he began to finish and sell his own cloth.

During this period William Ewart kept in touch with Hillsborough and for many years sent a van there every week to collect cloth. With developing sales he appointed agents in various cross-channel centres, his proximity to Belfast facilitating the shipping of his goods. By 1814 William Ewart (1) (1759–1851) had taken his eldest son, William (2) (1789–1873) into partnership, and the firm of William Ewart & Son was established with a town office and warehouse in Rosemary Street, Belfast.

William Ewart (2) developed the firm into one with world wide connections, bought and perfected bleach works, built and bought spinning mills, weaving factories, and warehouses in order to meet the requirements of an ever growing trade. About the year 1840 the firm secured the extensive ground, with water rights, on the Crumlin Road, Belfast, where they built their first spinning mill, and in 1850 a power loom weaving factory was added. In 1852 the firm purchased the bleach works at Glenbank, Ligoneil, from Mackey and Charters, and William (2) went to live at Glenbank House, later moving to Sydenham Park where he died. William Ewart (3) (1817–89) was taken into partnership in 1843, so that for some years the partners were father, son and grandson. Glenbank House was home to three generations of the Ewart family, the last being Lavens Mathewson Ewart, JP.

William Ewart (1) 1759–1851, came to Belfast from Annahilt about 1790, Artist unknown.
PRIVATE COLLECTION

William Ewart (3) became one of the outstanding figures in Belfast, marrying in 1840 Isabella Kelso, daughter of Lavens Mathewson of Newtownstewart, County Tyrone, and having a family of nine sons and five daughters. He was Mayor of Belfast in 1859 and 1860, and also represented the City in Parliament at Westminster from 1878 to 1889, being created a Baronet in 1887. The firm enjoyed large sales during the boom years which the linen trade experienced during the American Civil War (1861–65), the profits made being devoted to the permanent consolidation of William Ewart & Son. In 1883 Sir William Ewart turned his firm into a Limited Liability Company, with a capital of £500,000. The first directors were Sir William Ewart and his six sons who were:

1 Sir William Quartus, DL, MA, (1844–1919) who succeeded his father in 1889.

2 Lavens Mathewson, (1845–98) of Glenbank House, Ligoneil – an Alderman of Belfast and a distinguished antiquary.

3 Richard Hooker (1848–1918), went as a young man to the American branch of the firm in New York.

4 James Mathewson (1854–98) joined his brother Richard in the firm in New York.

5 George Herbert, MA, (1857–1924) of Firmount, Belfast. He was a prominent churchman and worked in the interests of the Foster Green Hospital and of the Maternity Hospital.

THE EWARTS OF BELFAST

8 August 1961
The Queen is welcomed by the chairman, Mr V.F. Clarendon, CBE, DL. The Duke of Edinburgh is shaking hands with Sir Ivan Ewart, Bt, DSC, director, and chairman of the Flax Spinners Association.

BELFAST TELEGRAPH

6 Frederick William, DL, MA, (1858–1934) Barrister-at-law, of Derryvolgie, Lisburn. He was for many years a District Inspector of the Royal Irish Constabulary.

In the twentieth century Ewarts was one of the largest manufacturers and exporters of Irish linen in the western world. Recognition of this was given on 8th August 1961, when, on her visit to Northern Ireland, Her Majesty Queen Elizabeth, with His Royal Highness The Duke of Edinburgh, toured the warehouse of William Ewart & Son, Ltd., Belfast.

The linen trade worldwide decreased very substantially in the late 1960s and early 1970s, with the result that Ewarts came to an agreement with Vantona, an English textile manufacturer, for the takeover of the company in 1973, and a joint operation with Liddells of Donaghcloney, also owned by Vantona. Many members of the family were recruited into the firm but the last to head Ewarts was Sir W. Ivan C. Ewart, a great-grandson of Sir William, the first Baronet, and the eighth generation from Thomas Ewart of Carnreagh.

Visit of
Her Majesty the Queen
and His Royal Highness
the Duke of Edinburgh to
William Ewart & Son Ltd
Belfast

EWART FAMILY TREE

The Ewart Family Tree only shows male members of the family involved in William Ewart & Son Ltd.

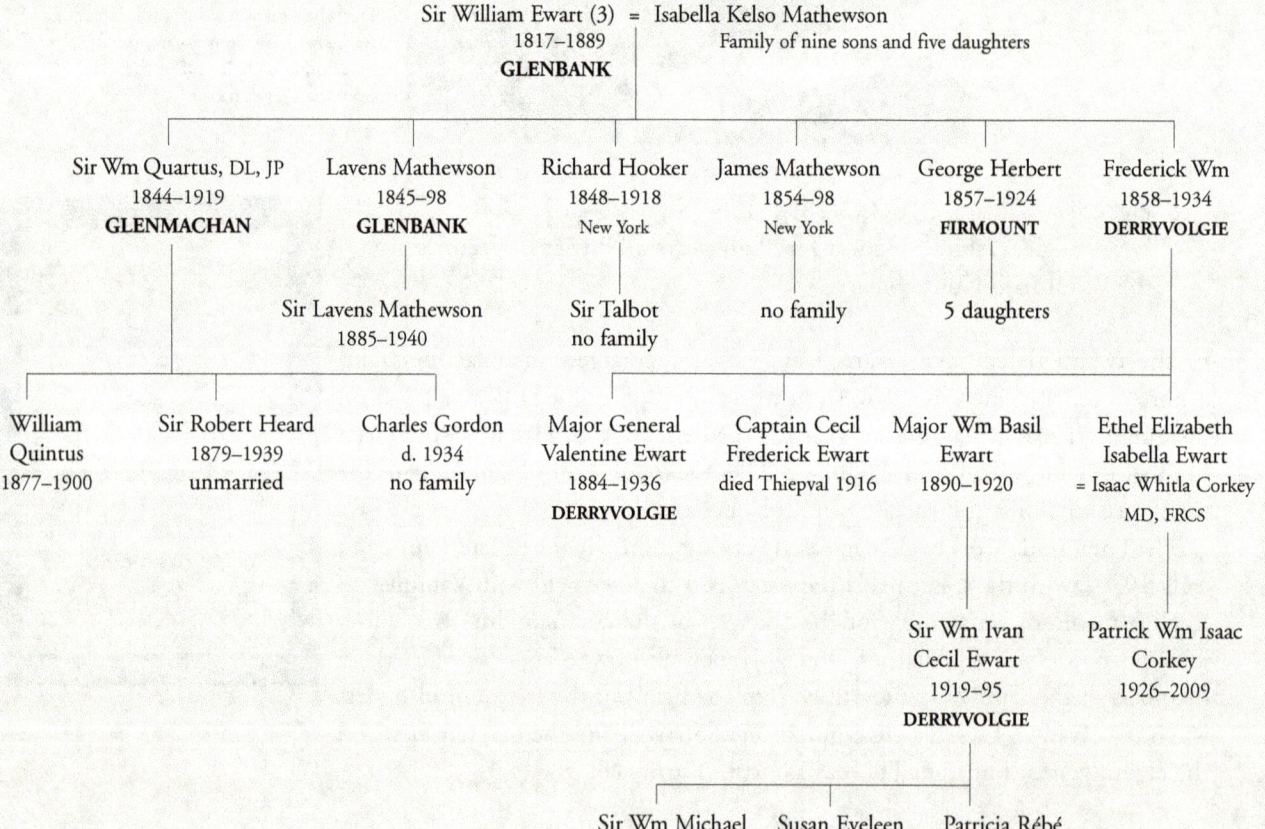

GLENMACHAN
STRANDTOWN, BELFAST

Glenmachan House was designed by the architect Thomas Jackson in 1862 for Sir William Ewart, and was the beginning of Jackson's plans for the Sydenham hillside. In the *Heritage Newsletter*, Spring 1984, published by the Ulster Architectural Heritage Society, it states:

> In the mid and late 19th century, Belfast was a wealthy city whose merchants could afford luxurious mansions. In our own century many of these have been torn down to make way for roads or housing estates, and one of the last of the really big houses still to be privately occupied was Glenmachan House on the Old Holywood Road.

Unfortunately the house has since been demolished, but up to 1979 it was lived in by Mrs Forrest, a grand-daughter of Sir William Ewart who built Glenmachan House. Apparently, according to the UAHS *Heritage Newsletter*, she retained the elegance and splendour of the Victorian interiors, and kept the surrounding estate well maintained.

The original Glenmachan House was a three bay, two-storey stuccoed house, with shallow bays on either side of an imposing front entrance. The house built on a hillside had a semi-basement, and on one side there was a courtyard leading to a stable block. The windows were sashed and silled with the upper storey

Sir William Ewart, Bt., 1817–89
Head of William Ewart & Son, flaxspinners and linen merchants; Mayor of Belfast 1859–61; President of the Belfast Chamber of Comerce 1863; MP for Belfast 1878–85, Belfast North 1885–9.
BELFAST CITY HALL

Glenmachan House 1862

Tennis at Glenmachan, 1911

Arthur Greeves (back left) and C.S. Lewis (back right) together at Glenmachan. C.S. Lewis spent a great deal of his childhood at Glenmachan, his cousins' grand house near to his home at Little Lea. Glenmachan has long since been demolished.

PRONI D4185/A/1/11

Lady Ewart with Lily Ewart and Warren Lewis on the steps of Glenmachan, *c.* 1919.

PRONI D4185/A/1/6

Glenmachan House with additions, 1903

windows being round headed with a keystone. The roof was hipped and slated having moulded eaves and cornice, and the front of the house was quoined. There was a single storey entrance porch which was also quoined, and there was a recessed doorway.

Glenmachan was considerably enlarged in keeping with the original house c. 1903–04 by Sir William Quartus Ewart, the extensions being built over the original courtyard. The UAHS *Newsletter* of 1984 reported that the house was a vast two-storey stucco building rambling round an internal courtyard. This formed the setting for a stupendous conservatory whose cast-iron barley-sugar columns doubled as down pipes. After the death of Mrs Forrest the house was considerably vandalised and was eventually demolished.

Glenbank house and gardens: the house was demolished in the mid-1920s when the gardens were laid out as Glenbank Park.

NMNI

GLENBANK HOUSE
BALLYSILLAN, BELFAST

Lavens Mathewson Ewart

Glenbank House was home to three generations of the Ewart family, the last being Lavens Mathewson Ewart, JP, (1845–98), who enlarged the property and, according to Dean, built a gate lodge *c.* 1875. In 1920, G. Herbert Ewart, (1857–1924), then chairman of William Ewart & Son, Ltd., offered Belfast Corporation the 'house and grounds of about seven and a half acres known as Glenbank House, for use as a public park'. According to Robert Scott:

> Mrs Herbert Ewart officially handed over the property on 18 August 1923 and the new park was declared open by the Lady Mayoress. A proposal to demolish Glenbank House was passed a month later. The building had been vacant for some years and was in need of structural repair.

Glenbank House was a five bay, two storied Georgian residence with a hipped slated roof, which was built in 1825, but enlarged for Lavens M. Ewart, prior to his marriage to Mary Elizabeth Clarendon in 1873. The windows, which were sashed and silled, had moulded architraves. Glenbank House also had an imposing single storey Ionic portico with fluted columns, and there was a recessed extension added to the side of the building.

In 1852 Glenbank Bleach Green and adjoining lands, situated on the banks of the Forth River, together with Glenbank House were purchased by William Ewart & Son from Mackey and Charters. In a speech delivered by Mr Reid, on

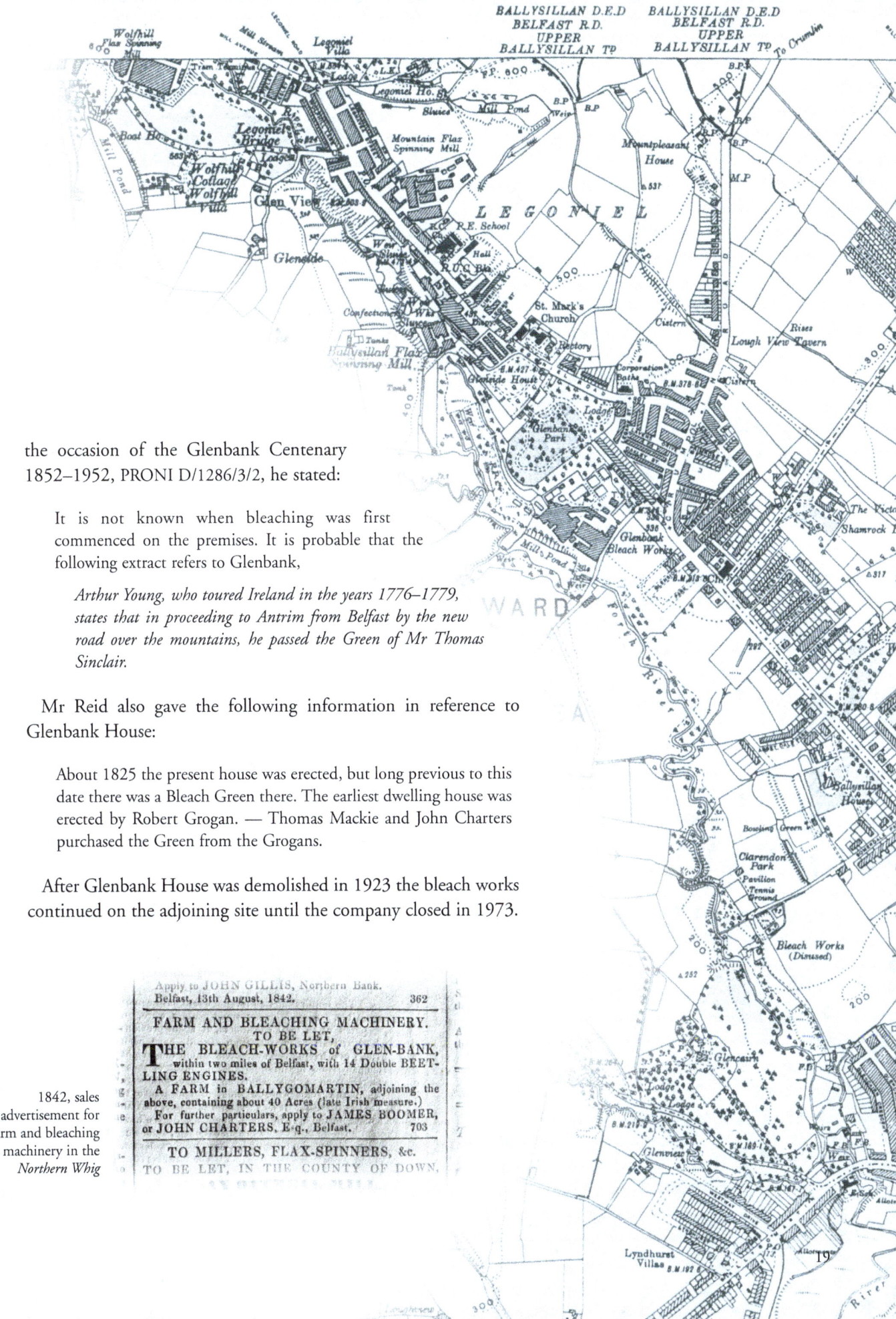

the occasion of the Glenbank Centenary 1852–1952, PRONI D/1286/3/2, he stated:

> It is not known when bleaching was first commenced on the premises. It is probable that the following extract refers to Glenbank,
>
> > *Arthur Young, who toured Ireland in the years 1776–1779, states that in proceeding to Antrim from Belfast by the new road over the mountains, he passed the Green of Mr Thomas Sinclair.*

Mr Reid also gave the following information in reference to Glenbank House:

> About 1825 the present house was erected, but long previous to this date there was a Bleach Green there. The earliest dwelling house was erected by Robert Grogan. — Thomas Mackie and John Charters purchased the Green from the Grogans.

After Glenbank House was demolished in 1923 the bleach works continued on the adjoining site until the company closed in 1973.

1842, sales advertisement for farm and bleaching machinery in the *Northern Whig*

2
NEWTOWNABBEY

MERVILLE, AS SEEN FROM THE SHORE
engraved by E.K. PROCTOR

LINEN HALL LIBRARY

MACKIE FAMILY TREE

The Mackie Family Tree only shows male members of the family involved in James Mackie & Sons, Ltd., Belfast

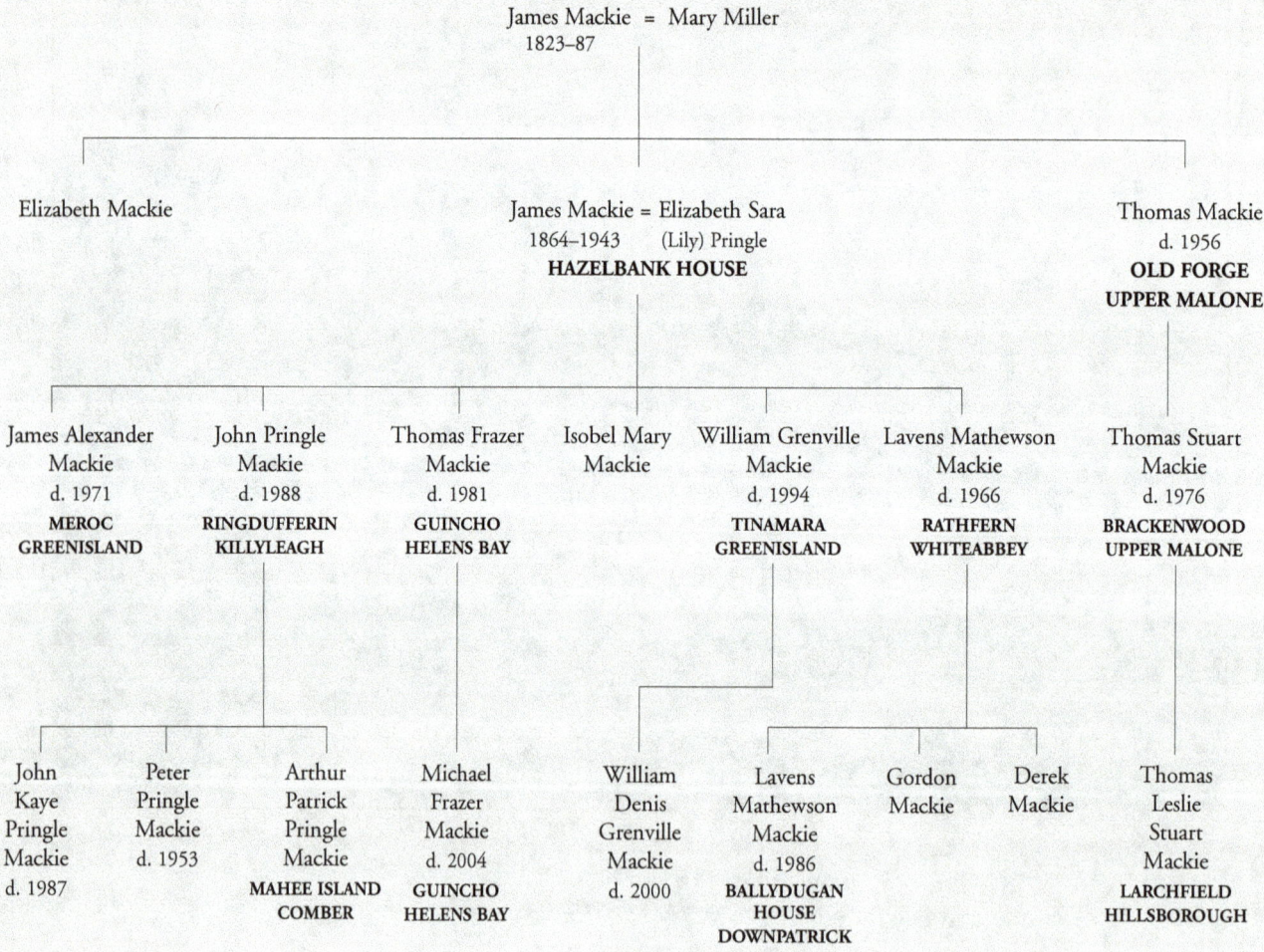

THE MACKIE FAMILY OF BELFAST

This is the remarkable story of a family business, James Mackie & Sons, which was built up virtually from nothing to become the second largest privately owned company in the British Isles. James Mackie, Senior, (1823–87), was born in Dumfries, Scotland, and served an engineering apprenticeship with a steam engine builder in Glasgow. According to Professor Sir Bernard Crossland:

> In 1843 he came to Ireland to erect a steam engine in St Mary's Flax Mill in Drogheda. Subsequently he became the mill engineer at Richardson's Linen Mill in Bessbrook.

However, at this time Belfast was becoming the centre for the spinning of flax and the weaving of linen, and James Mackie became works manager in 1845 to James Scrimegour, who owned a foundry and engineering works in Brown's Square, Belfast, before it moved to Albert Street. In 1858 James Scrimegour became bankrupt, and James Mackie bought the assets, running the Albert Street Works with four employees, repairing machinery. There was an increase in Irish linen production in the 1860s giving rise to a demand for new machines and also for servicing. The business developed with the initiative of the manufacture of 'twisting' and 'hackling' machines for the now expanding Ulster linen mills.

In addition, by 1877, his son James, Junior, then aged 14, was taking a considerable interest in his father's trade and, according to Armstrong, was reputed to have been able to repair or make any of the parts for the machines being made in the foundry. Indeed, James, Junior, even went around the various mills to repair and improve the machinery, gaining a reputation as an ingenious, yet dependable, businessman. Robert Armstrong in *Through the Ages to Newtownabbey*, states:

> If he knew that a certain machine was holding up the factory's production he worked night and day, making, adjusting, and oft times experimenting, to see that it got back to full operation as quickly as possible. It meant that he mixed with everyone – from the mill owner himself, to the ordinary worker, and therefore probably unknowingly developed what was his original gift of what he termed later as 'getting to know people'.

Unfortunately his father died in 1887, so James, on behalf of his mother, sister and brother, took control of the company now known as James Mackie & Son. This was a rapidly expanding business requiring larger premises despite competition with other established companies in the north of Ireland. Therefore, in 1893, a lease was taken on a vacant piece of ground on the Springfield Road, in west Belfast, and, with the aid of a substantial loan from the Belfast Banking Company, the Albert Foundry was built. Again, Armstrong states:

> From 1890 to 1900 James Mackie extended his business activities to the Continent, first in Germany and Austria, then to Russia, and later to a very large extent in France.

The machinery which the company was making was almost exclusively for the textile trade and by 1914 about 600 workers were employed.

In 1894 James married Elizabeth Sara (Lily) Pringle, the daughter of Alexander Pringle of Deramore House, Bessbrook. They had five sons, James, Jack, Frazer, Grenville and Lavens, and a daughter Isobel. In a Living Linen recording, LL R96/13, Michael F. Mackie, son of Frazer, tells how his grandmother used to take them all to Peebles Hydro in Scotland for their holidays. However, she was often pregnant and picked the names of her sons from gravestones in Melrose Abbey, and that is certainly where the names Frazer, Grenville and Lavens came from. Later, all five sons were employed in the business, which is well documented in the book by Eamonn Mallie and Paddy Mackie:

> When they left school, James and Lily Mackie's sons were, in turn, trained and incorporated into the company. Jim, Jack and Grenville received their technical education at the Belfast College of Technology. Frazer went to Manchester University before initially joining the company, and Lavens joined straight from school. Each brother was given the chance to make his mark and each

specialised in one or other aspect of textile machinery design and engineering. Jim, the eldest son, a keen development engineer, led the company's design and sales effort in the 1920s and 30s. Jack concentrated on machinery design and manufacturing, as did Frazer and Grenville. Lavens spent most of his time in Europe running sales and training in clients' textile mills.

Frazer ran the Strand Spinning Company, originally known as the Jaffe Spinning Company. According to Frazer it originated because, in 1909, James Mackie had very few orders for machinery and he spoke to Sir Otto Jaffe who had a large brick works on the Lagan embankment opposite the Boat Club. James asked Otto if he had any orders for bricks and he replied, 'not a one'. James Mackie had just bought a site in east Belfast and he suggested that Otto Jaffe should build a mill there keeping his works going and Mackies would make the machinery for it, keeping their works going. In time the Strand Spinning Company became important not only for the spinning of flax, but also in relation to the foundry, in that spinning machinery could be tried out and improved in the mill (LL R96/13).

Prior to the First World War James Mackie travelled widely, and according to Crossland, even journeying to Russia in 1899 in order to visit the Milehess Mill to the east of the Volga. His visits to continental countries produced orders for existing designs but also generated a demand for new machines. On his return to Belfast, James Mackie was able to explain ideas for the modification of existing machinery to the design office due to his extensive practical experience. However, business changed with the outbreak of the First World War, and in 1914 a 'Shell Shop' was opened within the foundry where shells were manufactured in gradually increasing numbers. Michael Mackie, in his Living Linen recording, stated that his grandfather was very much an entrepreneur, and did all sorts of strange things, giving this example:

James Mackie, appointed Deputy Lieutenant of Belfast 1926

MACKIE FAMILY

> And then another thing after the First War he couldn't get steel, so he went to Turkey and he bought the Turkish Fleet which we had beaten and he sailed it to Belfast and he got Harland's to take it to bits so that he could get the best steel out of these battleships that was available.

After the War business increased and this is stated by Armstrong:

> When peace reigned once more, James immediately got to work increasing the productivity by employing over 2,000 and selling their products to over 52 countries, through a sales, erection and technical staff of about 110 people.

By this time James Mackie, his five sons, his brother, and his son, were all involved in James Mackie & Sons, Ltd.

The outbreak of the Second World War brought requests from the Ministry of Supply and the Ministry of Aircraft Production for the manufacture of shells and aeroplanes. Vast quantities of munitions were manufactured at different sites by Mackies of Belfast, including armour piercing shot, gun barrels, Stirling bomber fuselages and Sunderland flying boat tail fins. Crossland states that there were altogether fourteen factories employing 12,000 people of which sixty percent were women. It was acknowledged that their contribution to the war effort was enormous.

During his lifetime James Mackie received many honours including becoming Deputy Lord Lieutenant of County Antrim, Chairman of Belfast Chamber of Commerce, and a Belfast Harbour Commissioner. He died in 1943 but under his leadership James Mackie & Sons, Ltd. had developed into a major internationally recognised company. According to Eamonn Mallie and Paddy Mackie:

> The years of the Second World War were the hardest for the company with much of the foundry and its output being switched from textile machinery manufacture to that of armaments. By then, James Mackie had stepped down due to ill health and his brother, Tom, had become Chairman, a position he would hold until the mid 1950s.

After Tom Mackie's death in 1956, Jim Mackie became Chairman, with Jack and Lavens as his joint managing directors.

Crossland has written that after the Second World War there followed fifteen immensely profitable years for the company with the design and production of new textile machines. Gordon Mackie in a recording for Living Linen LL R96/20 states that after Second World War the production of a particular design of machine for jute spinning was really the foundation of the company's fortunes. Mackies were often considered to be the largest jute machine manufacturers in the world, but the main business was not only in Europe, but also in India, in Burma, in Thailand, in Pakistan, in many countries in Africa, and Central and South America. Gradually the jute trade started to decline in Europe as it built up in the Third World countries.

At the same time Mackies did not stop making flax machinery. A new generation of wet-ring spinning frame was designed just after the War, and many were installed in Northern Ireland mills. Unfortunately, from 1960 there was a steady decline in the manufacture of linen, and the world renowned Belfast linen companies such as the York Street Flax Spinning Company and Ewarts, both of Belfast, along with many others, closed. Finally, Crossland states:

> In 1976 the Mackie family withdrew from ownership of the company having planned a tax efficient strategy and the factory complete with its lands, equipment, patents, etc, was handed over to a trust on behalf of the workforce.

Unfortunately, with the continued decline of the textile industry, the business closed in 1998.

HAZELBANK HOUSE
WHITEHOUSE, NEWTOWNABBEY

Hazelbank House was a five bay, two-storey house built, in the Italianate style, by James Gray around 1878, at Whitehouse, on the outskirts of Belfast, and set in considerable grounds. The entrance front had a large single storey Ionic portico with fluted columns, and two narrow round headed windows above on the first floor. On the ground floor there were two round headed windows on each side of the entrance, these windows being sashed and silled, surrounded by moulded architraves, and immediately above were four similar windows. The walls were quoined, and two decorative platbands continued around the house. The hipped roof, with very large chimney stacks, was concealed behind an elaborately moulded cornice and parapet.

Armstrong has written that in 1904, James Mackie, of the Mackie Engineering Works in Belfast, bought Hazelbank House and owned the house until his death in 1943. His business commitments required long periods of time away from his wife, five sons and one daughter, so that a house with a large garden, close to the shore was some compensation for his growing family. Hazelbank House was also of a suitable size for the entertainment of business guests.

The Mackie family at the front door of Hazelbank House

BACK ROW: Miss Morton; SECOND ROW: Lavens Mathewson, youngest son; James Alexander, eldest son; Isobel Marie, only daughter; William Grenville, fourth son; Ludwig Moravetz, son of our guest; FRONT ROW: Thomas Frazer, third son; Myself (James Mackie); my wife with Mrs Moravetz of Czechoslovakia. Jack Pringle, second son took the photograph.

PRONI D/3964/T/47

It has been recorded that Hazelbank House replaced an earlier house owned by Alexander George Stewart and sold to David McTear in 1796. The Ordnance Survey Memoirs for the Parish of Carnmoney, County Antrim, 1839 state:

> Hazelbank, the residence of David McTear Esquire, is agreeably situated on the shore. It is in the cottage style. The grounds include about 21 acres and are prettily planted and laid out. The house was erected originally 1800.

Thomas McTear, second son of David McTear, was born at Hazel Bank, Whitehouse, in April, 1800. He has published his 'Personal Recollections of the

Hazelbank House, 1958

The first townhall for Newtownabbey.

ARTHUR MCKEE/NEWTOWNABBEY COUNCIL

Newtownabbey Way
JFR

Beginning of the Century', written about 1882, in the *Ulster Journal of Archaeology*. In regard to Hazelbank he states:

> Some years after the death of David McTear, it was sold to James Thompson, who enlarged the house; and on taking possession of Macedon, after the death of his sister-in-law (Miss Anne Cunningham), he sold it to James Gray, who pulled down this house, and built on the same site the present mansion.

In this very interesting reminiscence Thomas McTear describes the houses and roads on the Antrim side of Belfast Lough, as it appeared to him prior to 1820. He states:

> My father used to tell us, that when he first came to live at Hazelbank in 1796, he was accustomed to ride on horseback to and from Belfast at low water along the sandy beach, which was perfectly hard, containing abundance of cockles and other shell-fish and shrimps.

More recently in the twentieth century, Hazelbank House, the former home of the Mackie family, became the first town hall for Newtownabbey in 1958. Unfortunately, it was damaged in 1972 in a terrorist attack, and subsequently was demolished. Hazelbank Park, on the shore of Belfast Lough, has been made from the surrounding gardens, and now features the Newtownabbey Way, which is a cycle path and walkway along Belfast Lough.

RINGDUFFERIN HOUSE
COUNTY DOWN

Ringdufferin House
JFR

Ringdufferin House, Killyleagh, County Down, is situated on the western shore of Strangford Lough, a few miles north of Killyleagh. This is a five bay, two-storey with basement house, built of rubble masonry, in part stucco faced and having granite quoins. The house is T-shaped in plan with the frontage of late eighteenth century date, but the long return wing may have been an earlier building. The entrance is central and is recessed within a segmental arched opening, the door having side columns, with moulded bases and capitals, supporting an entablature. A fanlight occupies the head of the doorway. The roof has a simple parapet crowned by classical statues depicting two eagles and a male figurine.

In the publication, *An Archaeological Survey of County Down*, Belfast, 1966, a description of the interior is given:

> The main E.–W. Block contains a single apartment on either side of the small central hall; the window shutters and sofits are panelled and bear gesso enrichments, the room on the W. has an enriched ceiling cornice and a good chimney piece of white marble with yellow marble slips.

Ringdufferin House has a very beautiful setting overlooking the sea, and at the end of a very long, winding driveway through undulating parkland. To the rear of the house there is a granite built stable yard, and nearby a walled garden, which is fully cultivated and maintained. Native and exotic trees are planted as specimens in mown grass to the south west of the house and along the avenue.

The publication, *An Archaeological Survey of County Down*, Belfast, 1966, states that the Ringdufferin property was acquired by the Bailie family in the seventeenth century. This book also mentions that it is thought that the present house was built by James Bailie, who succeeded to the estate in 1774, and died in 1819. Ringdufferin House has had a considerable association with the linen industry, firstly in the production of kelp, and secondly in its ownership by Jack Mackie, of James Mackie & Sons, Ltd. McErlean, McConkey, Forsythe, give a description of the production of kelp, stating that it is the commercial name for the burned ashes of seaweed which was a source of soda (sodium carbonate). They also state:

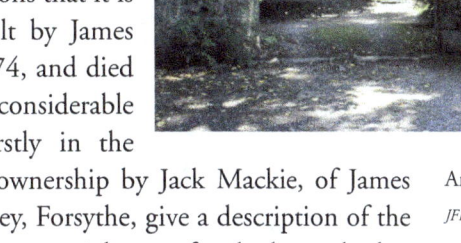

An arch to the walled garden
JFR

> Soda, as an alkali, was in great demand in the eighteenth century for a large number of industrial processes, the most important of which were in the manufacture of glass and soap and as an agent in bleaching linen.

Dr W.H. Crawford, in his publication on *The Impact of the Domestic Linen Industry in Ulster*, has written that the Irish linen industry was well established in Ulster by the end of the seventeenth century, and underwent a rapid period of development in the early eighteenth century, not least in terms of improved bleaching techniques. Therefore the demand for kelp rose steadily with Strangford Lough advantageously placed close to linen production in north Down and Antrim. McErlean, McConkey, Forsythe, record a book which has been preserved at Ringdufferin House since the eighteenth century:

> The survival of a kelp account book covering the period 1779–1807 and detailing kelp production on the Ringdufferin estate over a 30-year time span has proved an extremely valuable source of information on the local organisation of the industry.

Fortunately, the existence of this book was brought to the attention of the survey team by Paddy Mackie, son of Jack and Kathleen Mackie, who bought Ringdufferin House in 1945, giving the second link to the linen industry.

Jack Mackie and Kathleen Metcalfe married in 1926, living in Marietta, Barnetts Road, Belfast, but with the threat of bombing raids in 1939, they moved to a shooting lodge, built by Jack's uncle, Thomas Mackie, at Simmy Island, Killyleagh, County Down. The Mackie family got to know the last surviving members of the Bailie family who still lived in the Georgian Ringdufferin House, on an estate next to the island. After the death of the last Miss Bailie, Ringdufferin House came on the market and was bought by Jack and Kathleen Mackie.

The Bailie family had continued to live at Ringdufferin for generations, and the contents of the house, which remained there after the sale, were of considerable historical importance. Over a period of years, Jack and Kathleen Mackie carried out substantial repairs to the house, alongside the creation of a museum in the basement, which is described by Mallie and Mackie, 2009:

> To this day, it continues to be a constant fascination, especially for Jack and Kathleen's great grandchildren.

Jack (John Pringle) Mackie with his border terrier
Painting by Raymond Piper

MEROC
GREENISLAND, NEWTOWNABBEY

Meroc is situated on the Shore Road, Newtownabbey, at Greenisland, and was the home of James Mackie's eldest son, James Alexander Mackie, for forty years. The house lies close to the shore of Belfast Lough, and was built in 1902 by McLaughlin & Harvey in the orchard of Tinamara, a house erected in 1857 for the Belfast solicitor, Daniel O'Rorke. Both Tinamara and Meroc were occupied by Mackie brothers from the mid-nineteen thirties to the nineteen seventies, Tinamara being the home of W. Grenville Mackie.

Meroc is an Arts and Crafts house designed by the Belfast based architect William J.W. Roome for himself, and he lived there from 1902 to 1928, when he moved to Swanage, Dorset, where he died in 1937. Hugh Dixon, writing about 'Art Nouveau Decoration', states:

> Among the many Ulster architects who were influenced was W.J.W. Roome, whose design for the front of Crymble's music shop in Wellington Place, Belfast, combines a range of typically novel features with curving lines, cheerful colour and clear lettering.

Meroc is a three bay, two-storey house, having a central entrance door with canopy which supports a balcony outside the bedroom window on the first floor. The house is smooth rendered, painted white, and having a string course separating the ground and first floors. The gabled roof is slated, with ornamental barge boards, and has tall chimneys again painted white. There are bay windows on either side of the front door, and all the windows have small divided panes of glass.

Meroc doorway
JFR

James A. Mackie is shown as the owner of Meroc in the Street Directory for 1934 along with his brother Frazer in Tinamara. However, by 1935, W. Grenville Mackie is listed in Tinamara and continued to live there until 1983. James A. Mackie, (Jim), was the eldest of James Mackie's five sons, each of whom was involved in different capacities in the Mackie Engineering Works. Gordon Mackie, writing regarding 'Third Generations Mackie Textile Engineers to the World 1897–1988', in *The Lives of Great Engineers of Ulster*, Volume II, states that Jim was a keen development engineer and continues:

He led the Company's textile machinery design and sales effort in the 1920s and 30s with the help of John Gailey. Jim, whose wife Marcia was American, developed a very close friendship with Malcolm Stone of the Ludlow Corporation of Massachusetts. The Ludlow Corporation was then the biggest jute spinners in the US and later owned a mill in Calcutta.

After the Second World War, in the late 1940s and 1950s, Jim spent a considerable time in India, and in both West and East Pakistan, where there was a demand for new jute mills. India also required a massive reorganisation of its existing jute mills. According to Gordon Mackie these countries provided James Mackie & Son with a market for a very large percentage of its total production in the 1950s and 1960s. At the same time the company was supplying jute machinery to other parts of the world, and simultaneously producing a wide range of machinery for other fibres. The supply of textile machinery to the Irish linen industry was always of great importance to the Mackie Company and new machinery was often tested in the Strand Spinning Company run by Frazer Mackie.

Jim Mackie was chairman of James Mackie & Son from 1956 to 1968 and was awarded a CBE for the company's contribution to local employment and the British Export Drive.

James Alexander Mackie,
1895–1971

CAMPBELL FAMILY TREE

The Campbell Family Tree only shows male members of the family involved in Henry Campbell & Co., Ltd.

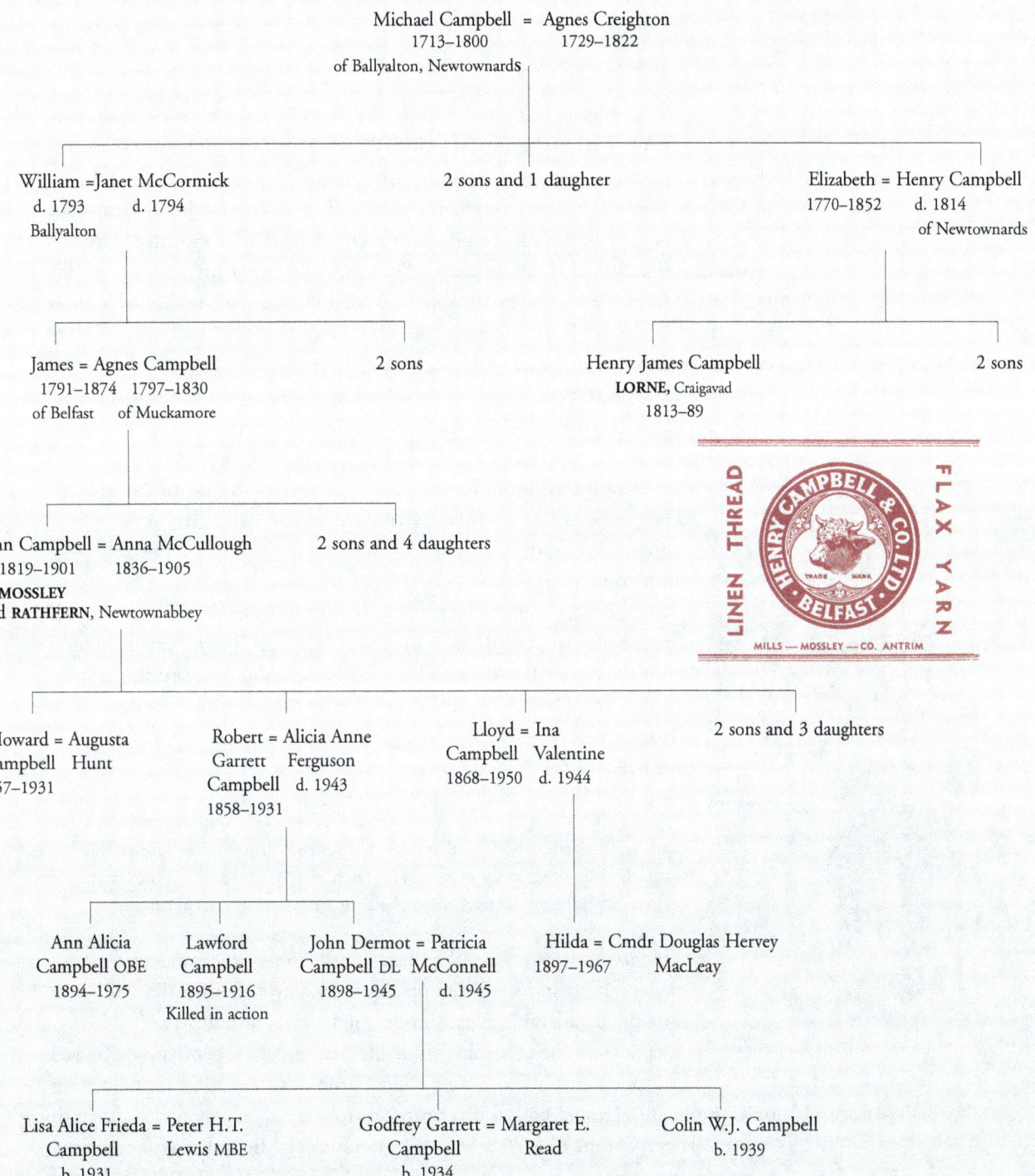

THE CAMPBELL FAMILY
OF MOSSLEY

Nicholas Grimshaw was born in Lancashire in 1743 where, as a young man, he was involved in the cotton industry. However, in 1776 he transferred to the north of Ireland, and set up works at Greencastle, three miles north of Belfast in County Antrim. He was very successful, and by 1800, Nicholas Grimshaw was ranked as one of the most important men in the cotton industry. After his death in 1805, his sons Thomas and Edmund continued his cotton printing business at Whitehouse, but they also expanded the business taking over other mills in the area, Mossley being one of them. The printing business was continued until 1834, when Edmund Grimshaw converted the works to flax spinning, which was more lucrative. New buildings were erected at Mossley Mill and a pond, which covered nearly six acres of ground, was created utilising water power to run the machinery. The Grimshaw brothers continued in business until their deaths, Edmund in 1853 and Thomas, at the age of 81, in 1855. The remaining partners struggled financially to survive the competition from other parts of the world, and creditors became very numerous.

In February 1859, Henry and John Campbell, of Gunning & Campbell, Ltd., North Howard Street, off Falls Road, Belfast, bought from the Ulster Bank the mills at Mossley, which had previously been owned by Thomas and Edmund Grimshaw, flax spinners. The Ordnance Survey Memoirs for the Parish of Carnmoney in 1839 gave this description of the property:

Two mills for the spinning of flax and tow, 22 workers' houses, manager's house and garden with a dwelling house and grounds, ornamentally planted. The machinery of the mill was run by two steam engines with boilers (25 horsepower each with shafting and gearing attached).

Henry and John Campbell had considerable experience of flax and tow spinning and were well placed to take over the Mossley Mills at a time of considerable expansion in the Irish linen industry.

The Campbell family originally came from Scotland, Michael Campbell and his wife Agnes Creighton, settling in Ulster on a farm of around 100 acres at Ballyalton, near Newtownards, in the mid-eighteenth century. James Campbell (1791–1874), a grandson of Michael, was apprenticed to James Boomer & Co., cotton spinners and manufacturers, Waring Street, Belfast. E.R.R. Green, in his book on the Lagan Valley, 1800–50, in regard to the cotton industry, states:

James Campbell
1791–1874

DONALD MACLEAY

Cheap labour prevented the introduction of power-looms, James Boomer &
Co. of Falls Road Mill are described as power-loom weavers in 1835, but they
are a solitary example.

However, by 1843 James Boomer & Co. are listed in the Street Directory as
'Flax and Tow Spinners' at their mill on the Falls Road, and James Campbell,
flax spinner, Falls Mills, residence, 5 College Square North. It appears that
Henry James Campbell, a cousin of James, also worked in James Boomer & Co.
His obituary published in the *Belfast News Letter*, 24th January, 1889, states:

> At an early age he was apprenticed to the firm of James Boomer & Co., Falls
> Road, who at that time, with the late Mr Mulholland in York Street, were the
> chief flax spinners in Ulster. After his apprenticeship he engaged for some time
> in the commission trade, and subsequently went over to Liverpool, where he
> resided for several years.

In 1843 Henry J. Campbell is listed in the Belfast Street Directory as: 'Flax
and Linen Yarn Merchant, and General Commission Agent, Office: 11 James
Street, Residence: 33 Queen Street'.

In the early 1850s the Campbell cousins, Henry and John, along with Robert
Gunning, took over an old spinning mill on the Falls Road, setting up the firm
'Gunning & Campbell' which produced fine linen yarn. This enterprise was
very successful and they later employed the architect Thomas Jackson to design
new industrial premises which were built at North Howard Street, Falls Road,
Belfast. Prior to this John Campbell had served an apprenticeship as a flax
spinner in James Boomer & Co., where his father James was now 'Managing
Partner'. James Boomer died in 1854, and a letter refers to James Campbell's
interest in James Boomer & Co., amounting to £7,107-9-4, being transferred in
1854 to Mr Charters and others. According to biographical notes in *Old Belfast
Families and the New Burying Ground*:

> John Charters, senr. of Ardmoulin House, Falls Road, was proprietor of the
> Falls Flax Spinning and Weaving Company, at that time one of the leading
> concerns of its kind in Ulster.

James Campbell therefore retained an interest in an important Belfast
spinning mill until his death in 1874.

Henry and John Campbell took over the mills at Mossley, with Henry
building up business both for Gunning & Campbell, Ltd., and Henry Campbell
& Co., Ltd., Mossley. Meanwhile John Campbell ran the Mossley Mills, moving
with his wife Anna, and two young sons from College Square North to live at
Mossley House, Whiteabbey. The Campbells were progressive, investing money
in upgrading the mill, and also building rows of houses for their workers. A
school was opened at Mossley in 1868, and its pupils were a source of supply
both for the mill and office. In addition a night school, which was very

successful, was started and was attended by the mill employees and farmers from the surrounding countryside. John Campbell was a very hard worker, and according to Armstrong;

> In 1871 the third storey was added to the Grimshaws' Mill buildings, on the north side, and eight years later, the New Mill was built, and in the same year, John Campbell took his two eldest sons, Howard and Garrett into partnership.

Henry Campbell gradually withdrew from business in the late 1860s, and built a large house at Lorne, Craigavad, County Down.

John Campbell retired in 1876, leaving Howard and Garrett as partners for the next 17 or 18 years, when Howard retired, leaving Garrett and Lloyd as the principal shareholders, running Henry Campbell & Co., Ltd., which became a Limited Company in 1897. Thread making was begun in the early 1880s, when there was a further addition to the mill buildings. Robert Garrett Campbell, CBE, chairman and managing director of the company died in November, 1931, the *Belfast Telegraph* reporting that he had been one of the cleverest men in the linen trade. During the First World War, Garrett Campbell was chairman of the Ulster Flax Spinners' Association, and for his services as a member of the Flax Advisory Board he received the CBE

Garrett had two sons, Lawford and Dermot, but Lawford was killed at the Somme in 1916, leaving Dermot, who had been too young to be in the War, but joined the company around 1918. After the First World War, it was felt necessary to strengthen the management staff, and in 1921 Colonel Louis Sydney Henshall joined the company. He, along with many others, including his sons, Herbert and James, contributed to the company's success in the ensuing years. Synthetic thread production was introduced in the 1960s, continuing in the 1970s, when the company was sold to the London based Hanson Trust. According to a publication by Newtownabbey Borough Council, *Mossley Mill, A Short History*:

> At this time it was amalgamated with Barbour Threads of Hilden, near Lisburn. The resulting company was renamed Barbour Campbell Threads Ltd. and all thread production was transferred to Hilden, while spinning remained at Mossley.

Herdmans Ltd., Sion Mills, County Tyrone, flax spinners, bought the Mossley Mills in 1993 and the business finally closed in 1995. However, Newtownabbey Borough Council were very far seeing in buying the site a year later and have converted part of the mill into the new Council Civic Centre, opened by HRH The Prince of Wales in June 2000. Mossley Mill has been retained as a significant element of the Borough's heritage.

MOSSLEY HOUSE
WHITEABBEY

John Campbell, with his wife and two infant sons, moved from College Square North in Belfast, in the early 1860s, to Mossley House, which had been extended to accommodate the Campbell family, five of whom were subsequently born at Mossley. In the summer of 1859, after Gunning & Campbell had acquired the Mossley Mills, there was a considerable amount of building, consisting of a new engine and boiler house along with some workers' houses. At a similar time, specifications for additions to Mossley House show that they were to be built with bricks from the old brickfield, which was probably in existence in the Grimshaws' time.

There had been a print works at Mossley, Carnmoney, from at least 1796, when a company known as Dalrymple Graham & Co. was formed, and it would appear a possibility that the original Mossley House was built at that time. Edmund Grimshaw, who was in partnership with his brother Thomas running a printworks at Whitehouse, purchased the printworks at Mossley from Moses

Mossley House
CROWN COPYRIGHT

John Campbell
1819–1901
DONALD MACLEAY

Anna McCullough
(Mrs Campbell)
1836–1905
DONALD MACLEAY

and Aaron Stanton in 1821. Edmund Grimshaw continued the printing business until 1833, when he built a flax mill at Mossley. His house is described in the Ordnance Survey Memoirs of 1838–9 for the parish of Carnmoney:

> Mossley, the residence of Edmund Grimshaw Esquire, is situated in the townland of Ballyhenry, near the north west corner of the parish. The house is partly 1-storey and partly 2-storeys high and is a neat looking residence.

This original house was left intact by John Campbell when a two-storey addition was made to the building, followed after some years, by a further three storey block. Mossley House, although adjacent to the mill, had a garden, which was ornamentally planted. A twentieth century description of Mossley House is given in the Ulster Architectural Heritage Society's publication for Antrim and Ballymena, 1969. Under the heading Mossley Mill it states:

> A large brick built manager's house, rambling with shallow pitched gables and bargeboards, one block of three storeys, one of two.

John Campbell eventually bought and moved to 'Rathfern', Whiteabbey, which was considered beneficial to the health of his wife who had found Mossley House damp, due to the river running through the mill site. Mossley House continued to be occupied over a period of time in the twentieth century by the various managers of Henry Campbell & Co., Ltd., until the company closed. Mossley House was demolished in the 1980s due to safety concerns and vandalism.

RATHFERN

Rathfern, Whiteabbey, was the home of John Campbell, Managing Director of Henry Campbell & Co., Ltd., Mossley, from 1880 until his death in 1901, after which the house was sold in 1906. Rathfern, which was about six miles from Belfast, was built in the early 1850s for the Mitchell family. This was a two-storey, multi-gabled house, having a slated roof with tall ornate chimneys, and decorative barge boards. Single storey bays with stone dressings projected at the sides of the building with the exception of a two-storey bay to the right of the front door. The bay windows of the lower storey were surmounted by a quatrefoil balustrade as was the portico, where there was a recessed entrance.

Rathfern
PRONI D2460/8

The family of John Campbell at Rathfern
CAMPBELL COLLEGE

> "RATHFERN", WHITEABBEY, CO. ANTRIM.
> and
> 41 ACRES OF LAND.
> SALE BY AUCTION OF
> GENTLEMAN'S RESIDENCE
>
> In the BELFAST PROPERTY MART, 37, Royal Avenue, on FRIDAY, 15th June, 1934, at 12 o'clock, Noon.
>
> The Residence has a delightful elevated situation adjacent to the junction of the Cloughfern and Doagh Roads, and contains Drawing-room, Dining-room, Smoke Room, Study, Billiard Room, Cloakroom, and ample Culinary Apartments; 8 principal Bedrooms, 2 Bathrooms and W.C's; Servants' Bedrooms, Bathroom &c., Wash-house, Coal-house, &c., with front and Back Gate Lodges. The Residence is centrally heated.
>
> There is Stabling Accomodation, including Stalls and Loose Boxes for 6 Horses, with other extensive Out-houses, including Byre, Pony Stall, Garage with capacity for 4 Motor Cars; Harness Rooms, &c. all in an enclosed and roofed-in Yard.
>
> The Grounds and Lands attached to the Residence have extensive frontages to the Cloughfern and Doagh Roads. They comprise over 41 acres, and extend up the prettily wooded slope of Carnmoney Hill, and magnificent views are obtained from the House and Grounds. The whole property is held for ever subject to Annual Rents amounting to £105. 3. 4. but with the benefit of a sub-rent of £5. per annum, leaving a net rent payable of £100. 3. 4.
>
> The Residence is conveniently situated, being about 6 miles from the City. It has been well maintained, and all Out-buildings are in godd condition.
>
> For Particulars as to Title, Conditions of Sale, &c., apply:-
>
> ROBERT WALLACE, Solicitor,
> Riddel's Buildings, Belfast.
>
> And for Cards to View:-
>
> R.J.McCONNELL & CO., Auctioneers,
> 37, Royal Avenue, Belfast.

According to an auction notice of 15th June 1934, (PRONI, D2964/CB/386), the house had an elevated situation adjacent to the junction of the Cloughfern and Doagh Roads, the grounds also having extensive frontages to both roads. The house had very ample accommodation, containing a drawing room, dining room, smoke room, study, billiard room, cloakroom and ample culinary apartments. In addition there were eight principal bedrooms and two bathrooms. The auction notice lists front and back gate lodges, although Dean only lists one gate lodge, as pre-1857, and probably for George Mitchell.

Lavens Mathewson Mackie, youngest son of James Mackie, lived in Rathfern, Whiteabbey, during the 1950s when he was joint managing director of James Mackie & Sons, Ltd., giving this house a second important link to the linen industry.

Rathfern was situated in 41 acres of land, but was demolished in 1965 to make way for a housing estate, which bears the same name.

LORNE

In 1865 Henry Campbell employed the Scottish architect John Boyd to design the house which he called Lorne, taking its name from the hereditary home of the Campbell Clan in Scotland. Lorne is of Scots baronial style, two-storey, brick built, with contrasting decorative quoins and having bay windows on the garden front. Windows in the main building are square headed with hood moulds and relieving arches. A round four-storey tower rises beside the main entrance, which has round-headed windows on the ground and first floors, and contain plain sashes. The two bay windows of the lower storey on the garden front are surmounted by a quatrefoil balustrade, while on the first storey there is a central small bay, which has an embattled parapet. The slated roof is multi-gabled with tall ornate chimneys.

The front of Lorne
JFR

One of the most striking features of Lorne is the portico, set in stone with double entrance topped in a similar way to the bay windows and having four very decorative pinnacles. Just inside the entrance are two figure heads carved in stone, which arguably could be likenesses of Henry Campbell's father and mother, Henry and Elizabeth Campbell, of Newtownards. Internally the original fireplaces have been preserved, one of which features the Campbell family crest, a 'boar's head'. Lorne is situated at Station Road, Craigavad, in considerable grounds and, since 1946, has been owned by the Ulster Guides. Their website, www.girlguiding.org.uk, states:

Two figure heads inside the entrance porch
JFR

Lorne is a 21-acre estate in Northern Ireland with a house and grounds that provide excellent facilities for all types of guiding activities.

The portico at Lorne
JFR

The boar's head motif, the Campbell family crest, on a fireplace in Lorne.
JFR

The first deed to Henry Campbell for land at Lorne is for seven acres in 1864, and this was followed by three further land deeds in his lifetime, setting Lorne in beautiful surroundings.

Henry James Campbell (1813–89) began his working life as an apprentice with the flax spinning company James Boomer & Co., on the Falls Road, Belfast. His first cousin James Campbell also became an apprentice with this company and, in time, rose to be 'Managing Partner' until it closed in 1854. Meanwhile, Henry Campbell became a flax and yarn merchant as well as a general commission agent, spending some years in Liverpool. In 1852, Robert Gunning, John Campbell (son of James), and Henry Campbell set up Gunning & Campbell, Ltd., Flax and Tow Spinners, North Howard Street, Belfast. Robert Gunning died in 1857, and the Campbell cousins, with wide experience in the industry, continued to very successfully run Gunning & Campbell, Ltd. This company bought the Mossley Mill, Whitehouse, County Antrim, in 1859, Henry Campbell providing most of the capital for the purchase, and his second cousin, John, being appointed mill manager of 'Henry Campbell & Co.'

Henry Campbell
JFR

At this period there was a large expansion in the Irish linen industry, and Henry Campbell, as a director of both Gunning & Campbell and Henry Campbell & Co., Ltd., would have had a considerable income. He planned his retirement in the early 1860s, eventually moving from 33 Queen Street, Belfast, to the house which he had built at Lorne, Craigavad, County Down, *c.* 1866. Henry James Campbell, son of Henry and Elizabeth Campbell died 23rd January 1889, aged 76 years, leaving the majority of his money, around £200,000, in trust for the founding of a school or hospital. However, the executors of his will, after very careful consideration, decided on the foundation of a school, and in 1894, Campbell College was opened at Belmont Road, in a rapidly expanding area of east Belfast.

THE HENSHALL FAMILY

After John Campbell's death in 1901, the Campbell family, notably Garrett and Howard were in partnership running the Mossley Mill for seventeen years. In terms of family succession Garrett had two sons, Lawford and Dermot, and one daughter Nan, but Lawford was killed in the First World War, leaving a prospective gap in the management structure. In a Living Linen recording LL1 R97/19 conducted by the late Denys Jemphrey, Sydney Henshall's sons, James and Herbert, told how their father came to Henry Campbell & Co., Ltd.:

> Our father, who was Sydney Henshall, was a Colonel in the Tank Corps in the First War and was out at the end of the First War 1918/19 in Germany as a policeman looking after things in Germany, and picked up an advertisement that Garrett Campbell had advertised for somebody to join the Company of officer standing with a hope of coming into the Company. So my father seized this advertisement without passing it on to anybody and came over to Belfast. Father was a Lancashire man who had trained and was a qualified architect before the First War. He was given, as I understand it, the job straight off by the Campbells, so he had then as colleagues Garrett and Lloyd still, and Dermot and Nan, and that is how the company stood after the First War.

Louis Sydney Henshall, DSO, TD, ARIBA, married Helen Flora Ewart, fifth daughter of George Herbert Ewart, on 3rd November, 1920, so bringing him into a relationship with one of the major linen families in Ulster. Mr Ian Adair, writing in *A Well-Spun Thread, Memoirs from Mossley Mill*, states that after the death of Garrett Campbell in 1931 Colonel Henshall became the prominent figure in the Mill. He continues:

> But the Colonel was the man around whom everything revolved. He had a very strong personality. He was a very good business man. Ran the Mill like a military exercise.

Colonel L.S. Henshall contributed much to the success of the Mossley Mill and by 1951 was a director and Chairman of Henry Campbell & Co., Ltd. He was also very involved in the wider Northern Ireland business community, and became President of the Belfast Chamber of Commerce in 1951/52. Dr George Chambers states:

> so he was deeply involved in the Northern Ireland contribution to the Festival of Britain, the national promotion organised to mark the centenary of the Great Exhibition of 1851 in Hyde Park … A few weeks later Colonel Henshall led the business community in tribute to the 'great and good' King George VI who died on 6 February at the age of fifty-six.

He also contributed to the wider sphere of linen manufacture in becoming 'Chairman of the Flax Spinners Association', and in the academic world he was a Member of Senate of the Queen's University of Belfast.

Colonel Henshall died in 1957, but was succeeded in the business by his sons Herbert and James, who had trained in the textile industry, and also worked in Henry Campbell & Co., Ltd. Lonsdale, their home in Newtownabbey, continued in Henshall ownership when James took the house over from his mother in 1969, and with his wife and family remained there until 1990.

Colonel L.S. Henshall
JAMES HENSHALL

LONSDALE

Lonsdale is situated on the Jordanstown Road, Newtownabbey, County Antrim on the shore side of the road. This is an elegant two-storey, three-bay house having ornamental gables with finials, on the slated roof, and tall chimney stacks. The walls of the house are smooth rendered and presently painted cream. Lonsdale was originally built for Matthew Stothard, who is recorded in the house in 1843, when it was situated in considerable grounds of twenty one acres. At the front, on the ground floor, there are two bay windows on either side of a single storey projecting entrance porch, which has side windows. On the first floor to the front there are tri-partite windows with label mouldings. Dean has recorded a gate lodge *c.* 1858, 'demolished':

> By the lough shore with its back to the road a modest single storey gabled lodge built for Matthew Stothard.

In the early twentieth century various portions of the land originally belonging to Lonsdale were sold off for other villas to be built.

Lonsdale had a considerable connection to the Mossley Mill in that it became the home of Colonel Sidney Henshall and his wife, when they bought it in 1926.

PHILIP JOHNSTON & SONS

Philip Johnston (1804–82) was the youngest son of Lieutenant William Johnston and was born in Ballinderry, near Lisburn, County Antrim. His parents died when he was very young and he was brought up by relatives who lived nearby and attended the Moravian Church. In 1827 he began work in the tea business in Rosemary Street, Belfast, and he joined the Wesleyan Methodists, remaining a member of Donegall Square Methodist Church, Belfast, for fifty-six years. Philip Johnston's business interests developed as a wholesale tobacconist and as a wholesale grocer with offices in Waring Street. In 1849 he commenced his connection with the linen business going into partnership with James Carlisle, and built a spinning mill on the Crumlin Road, Belfast, under the name of Johnston and Carlisle, Brookfield Mills. This continued until 1867 when the partnership was terminated, the mill becoming the Brookfield Linen Co., Ltd., which was a very important concern for the next one hundred years. Philip Johnston with his sons, David Woods Johnston and Samuel Alexander Johnston, went into partnership to buy and run the Jennymount Flax and Tow Spinning Mill, York Road, Belfast in 1868. Jennymount Mill was enlarged and became extremely successful in sales of linen yarn to the expanding Belfast linen industry.

Philip Johnston, Lord Mayor of Belfast, 1871

JFR

Philip Johnston was very much involved in the commercial life of the city, and having been elected as an Alderman, he was made Mayor of Belfast in 1871. During his years on the Corporation he did much to promote the interests of the Public Library. He was a prominent Methodist occupying many lay offices, and took a leading part in the formation of the Methodist College, Belfast, in 1865, where he endowed the Philip Johnston Mathematical Prizes, which are still awarded in the College. He died at his home Dalriada, Whiteabbey, on 23 September, 1882. Philip Johnston married Miss Hester Woods, and left five surviving children, two sons, David, and Samuel who married Miss Agnes Barbour, and three daughters.

Samuel A. Johnston, JP, succeeded his father as Chairman of Jennymount Mills, Belfast, which he developed, modernised, and enlarged. In 1906, in co-operation with his business colleagues, he acquired the firm of Messrs. John Barbour & Co., of Whitehouse, which came to occupy an important place in the industrial life of Ulster.

DALRIADA

Front view of Dalriada
CROWN COPYRIGHT

Dalriada is situated on the Jordanstown Road, Newtownabbey, County Antrim and is now part of the University of Ulster's campus, being used for student housing. The house was built for Philip Johnston of Brookfield Mill, Crumlin Road, Belfast, in the mid nineteenth century and appears on the 1858 map, the architect being possibly Thomas Turner. This is a three-bay, two-storey Italianate house of considerable size situated originally in thirty nine acres of land. The walls are stuccoed and quoined, and a platband separates the ground and first floor extending around a shallow bay on the side of the house. There is a single storey fine pilastered porch; the windows on the ground floor are sashed and silled being supported by console brackets. The roof, with its elaborately moulded cornice, is hidden behind a parapet with only the chimney stacks able to be seen. Dalriada also has a gate lodge recorded by Dean as *c.* 1855; architect possibly Thomas Turner.

Front and side view of Dalriada
CROWN COPYRIGHT

Armstrong states that Philip Johnston lived in Dalriada until his death in 1882, when his youngest son Samuel Alexander Johnston inherited the property to use as his residence, until he died in his 89th year on 14th March, 1931. Armstrong writes:

> In 1934 the contents of the house were sold by auction and the house closed up until the early war years when it was requisitioned by the Army to be used as a billet by British soldiers, later shared with Dutch troops, who had seen fierce action at Dunkirk …The house was de-requisitioned in 1946 and again remained empty until the early 1950s, when it was sold to the present authorities.

According to the will of Samuel A. Johnston the lands connected to Dalriada occupied seventy two acres, and the Ulster University at Jordanstown, originally the Ulster Polytechnic, was built on land which was part of the grounds of Dalriada.

Gate lodge at Dalriada
JFR

A sketch of Dalriada in the early twentieth century

THREE ACRES

Three Acres is a twentieth century house, built in 1936 for Mr Ronald Cunningham, and situated on the Upper Malone Road, Dunmurry, in County Antrim, the architects being Messrs Munce & Kennedy. This is a brick built, four-bay, two-storey L-shaped house with a hipped slated roof, and set on a height in considerable grounds, which slope down towards the River Lagan. The garden front, with two bay windows on the ground floor, has views over open countryside which include Malone Golf Course. To the front of the house the entrance is through a triangular shaped porch which has circular side windows.

Three Acres became the home of R.L.C. Cunningham, Managing Director of Jennymount Mill, in the late 1930s. Ronald Leslie Chaytor Cunningham (1899–1966) was the great-grandson of Philip Johnston, and grandson of Samuel A. Johnston, who was Chairman of the firm of Philip Johnston & Sons, Ltd., Jennymount Mills, Belfast, until his death in 1931. Ronald Cunningham was educated at Cheltenham College, and went into the army for a few years but his grandfather obtained his release in order to bring him back to work in Jennymount. The late Mrs Jill Mitchell stated in a Living Linen recording LL R98/7 that her father was aged thirty four when he was appointed managing director of the company, which was famed for the very fine yarn which it spun. Ronald Cunningham was known for his strong managerial ability, and capability in training apprentices to the spinning trade, the late Peter Larmor of Ulster

Weaving, Roland Clark of John Barbour & Co., and James Henshall of Henry Campbell & Co., Ltd., being among them. In 1959 Herdmans of Sion Mills took over Philip Johnston & Sons, Ltd., and Ronald Cunningham joined York Street Flax Spinning Company as joint managing director to assist in the closing down of this company.

Ronald L.C. Cunningham was very highly regarded in the flax spinning trade and for a time was Chairman of the Flax Spinners Association Ltd. 'An Appreciation of Ronald L.C. Cunningham', written by G.A.E. Roberts, was published in *Textiles of Ireland*, September, 1966, stating:

> A man who has made himself a master of his craft by close and continual study and practical application is bound at the same time to have developed within himself some very important moral qualities. Such a man was the late Ronald Cunningham, a leader in the flax spinning industry over the past generation. One of these qualities was enthusiasm, without which it would have been impossible to kindle in others the maximum interest in the particular project. Yes, Ronald Cunningham had enthusiasm. He also possessed the quality of self-assurance and in the industry with which he was so long and so prominently associated confidence was a very necessary quality, if the heavy responsibilities assumed by him were to be efficiently discharged.

Ronald L.C. Cunningham

VALENTINE FAMILY TREE

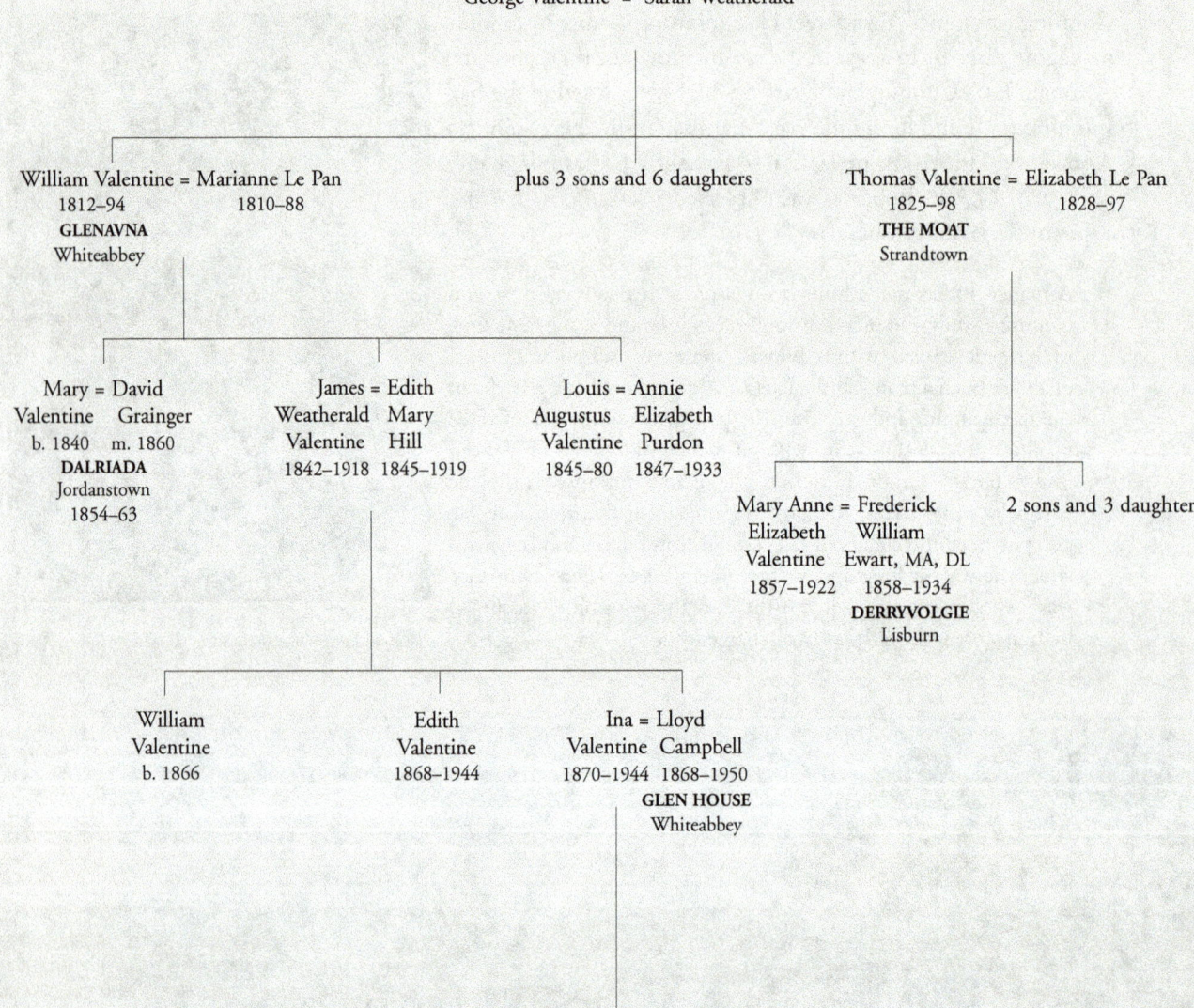

THE VALENTINE FAMILY

In the early nineteenth century George Valentine, son of George Valentine and Sarah Wetherall, married Mary Creeth, living at Richill, County Armagh. They were Quakers, and having moved to Belfast in 1824, they joined the Lisburn Meeting of the Society of Friends but later in 1832 emigrated with five children to Pickering, Toronto, Canada, where they bought a farm near Duffin's Creek and attended Quaker Meetings in Pickering. They had a family of five sons and six daughters. Two of their sons, William (1812–94) and Thomas (1825–98), rose to hold important positions in the rapidly developing linen industry in Belfast.

William Valentine was of Quaker stock and was educated at the Society of Friends' School, Lisburn, which had been established in 1774 for the education of both boys and girls of Quaker families in Ulster. This association with a number of Quaker families, established during his education, was to benefit William Valentine in his professional career throughout his life. His first employment in 1830 was as an accounts clerk with Richard & Jacob Bell & Co. who were flax spinners at Whitehouse, although William Valentine was employed in their town offices close to Waring Street, Belfast. In 1839 he was appointed to the position of accountant with the linen firm James N. Richardson, Son & Company, who had premises in York Street as General Merchants and also in Donegall Place as Linen Merchants and Commission Agents. Richardsons linen manufacture at Glenmore, Lambeg, expanded rapidly and eventually by 1841 the whole business was divided into two companies, J.N. Richardson, Sons & Owden at 14 Donegall Place, and Richardson Brothers & Co., at 10 York Street.

William Valentine

In 1838 William Valentine married Marianne Le Pan of Sligo, whose ancestry could be traced back to the nobility of France, and by 1844 he had purchased a fine Georgian terrace house at 2 Donegall Square West. His ability and knowledge of the linen industry was such that he became the managing partner of Richardson Brothers & Co., and in 1849 he was elected to serve on the council of the Belfast Chamber of Commerce. Richardson Brothers had vested interests in the export of linen goods through the port of Belfast and again in 1849 William Valentine was elected to membership of the Belfast Harbour Commissioners. In this same year he sold his house in Donegall Square West, and moved to Whiteabbey where many of Belfast's wealthy merchants owned properties.

William Valentine left Messrs Richardson in 1857 when he was appointed a director of the Northern Banking Company on the death of Mr John McNeill of Whiteabbey, and in 1877 on the death of Mr J.T. Bristow he became chairman of the directors. His business interests were extremely wide in that he became a director of various railway companies such as the Belfast and Northern Counties line, while as Chairman of the Belfast Steamship Company he contributed to the increase in facilities of cross channel traffic. In 1862 William Valentine bought the ground in north Belfast which is now known as Fortwilliam Park, and which owes its development to his enterprise. William Valentine had a continuing interest in the linen industry throughout his business career, being a member of the committee for 'The Society for the Promotion and Improvement of the Growth of Flax in Ireland'. Both of his sons, James W. Valentine and Louis Augustus Valentine, were partners in different linen companies at various times in their lives. Lastly, his grand daughter, Ina Valentine married Lloyd Campbell, who was a director of Henry Campbell & Co., Ltd., Mossley, Co. Antrim, one of the major linen yarn spinners in Ireland.

In his early career Thomas Valentine was a partner with John Craig and Baldwin Mulligan in ownership of flax spinning mills on the Falls Road. In 1866 various mills came together to become the Northern Spinning and Weaving Company, and by 1868 Thomas Valentine was the managing director. However, around 1881 this company went into liquidation, and the business was subsequently incorporated in the New Northern Spinning and Weaving Company, Limited, of which Sir William Ewart was first chairman and Thomas Valentine was managing director. In 1880 he was a member of the Council of the Flax Supply Association, which had been established for the improvement of the culture of flax in Ireland.

At the same point in time Thomas Valentine sold The Moat and moved to Sandhurst, Knock. Thomas Valentine was widely known in commercial circles in Belfast, being a member of the Belfast Chamber of Commerce, a director of the Belfast Steamship Company, Ltd., and of the Sydenham District Tramway Company. He was especially well known as a Mason, being a prominent and highly esteemed member of the Craft.

Ina Valentine

Lloyd Campbell

Glenavna front, 1939
RICHARD GRAHAM

GLENAVNA HOUSE

The land on which Glenavna House was built was originally known as Harmony Hill, an estate which had belonged to William Cowan of Cowan & Co., who were in business as flax spinners at Whiteabbey. There had been a small Georgian house on the site, which dated back to the late eighteenth century, but in the 1840s a newly built extension of considerable size was added to the original house leaving it as the rear wing to the new house. William Valentine acquired the Glenavna Estate from William Cowan in 1849, and in 1853 he commenced a major planting of the grounds of the estate surrounding the house and along the banks of the Three Mile Water, which was a river running through the grounds. This area eventually became known as Valentine's Glen, and in 1858 the house was re-named Glenavna.

William Valentine died at Glenavna on 24th January 1894, and his executors put the estate up for sale by R.J. McConnell & Co., on 25th May 1894. An interesting description of the property at Whiteabbey is given in the sale advertisement (PRONI: D2964/CB/26).

> The residence is approached from the Shore Road by two carriage drives, the principal one having a good gate lodge at the entrance.
> The accommodation comprises three large Reception-rooms, Library, six Bedrooms, and six Servants' Apartments, Dressing-rooms, Linen and China Closets, Hot Presses, Baths (h. and c.) and Lavatories, Butter, Mistress's and Servants' Pantries, Wine Cellar, &c., and every requisite for the convenience of a gentleman's family.

Sale of Glenavna, 1894

The Pleasure Grounds are extensive, and laid out with great taste, comprising terraces, lawns, shady wood and walks, summer house, and orchard, well timbered with fruit trees, walled-in kitchen garden of about 1 acre, vineries, greenhouses, peach house, and forcing beds; also beautiful fernery, with ornamental waterfall. The remainder of the ground is laid down in grass and is well watered by a stream running through the Property.

Glenavna was a two-storey, three-bay house to the front, having a tripartite window to one side of the front door and a bay window to the other side. There was a hipped and slated roof with moulded eaves and cornice, and the walls were quoined. However, to the rear of the Victorian building it became three storey with a shallow roof, this part designed to house the servants' quarters, and leading on to the much smaller original Georgian house at the back of Glenavna. There was considerable architectural detailing around the windows and the doorway of the Victorian building, with the bottom storey windows reaching almost to the ground.

In 1860 Glen House was built in the grounds of the Valentine estate at Glenavna on the opposite bank of the Three Mile Water. This house had a shared driveway and gate lodge with Glenavna, which is recorded by Dean as pre-1857. A second gate lodge on Old Manse Road is again recorded by Dean as c. 1900. Glenavna had many owners after William Valentine's death and eventually became Glenavna House Hotel in 1963, opening with ten bedrooms. There was considerable enlargement of the hotel in 1984 with 32 luxury ensuite bedrooms and an executive suite on the second floor. Six conference and banqueting suites were also added which occupied much of the area formerly taken up by the private apartments of the original house. Unfortunately the whole property was destroyed by fire in 2004.

The Gate Lodge, 1939

RICHARD GRAHAM

THE MOAT
STRANDTOWN

In 1863 Thomas Valentine, younger brother of William who lived at Glenavna, purchased a very old house belonging to John L. Bell in the parish of Dundela, which was situated in 87 acres of ground, with frontages to both the Belfast–Bangor Road and Old Holywood Road. This had previously been an ancient ecclesiastical site where the parish church of Ballymeaghan had stood, belonging to the famous abbey of Bangor, although nothing of that period then remained. Thomas Valentine replaced the old house, building commencing in 1863 and finishing in the autumn of 1864, the architect being William J. Barre. The Moat is a large mansion built in the Italianate style of brick, which is relieved by the introduction of stone bands. Dunlop gives the following description:

> The open porch is an arcade of three semicircular arches, with moulded edges, carried on piers with carved capitals, and is surmounted by an open pierced parapet. The effect altogether is very fine.

Thomas Valentine
JFR

The accommodation comprised a large entrance hall, drawing room, dining room, morning room, library, billiard room, cloakroom, kitchen and other culinary apartments. On the first floor there were six bedrooms, two dressing rooms and three bathrooms, with additionally three servants' bedrooms and bathroom. In 1937 the estate of thirty acres contained six cottages, a walled-in-garden, glass houses, garage and stabling accommodation, along with gardens and lawns. At this point the property was put up for sale and in 1938 The Moat was converted into apartments, with the land sold off for building. Dean states that the 1863 house belonging to John L. Bell had a gate lodge and this old lodge continued to serve until its demolition in the twentieth century.

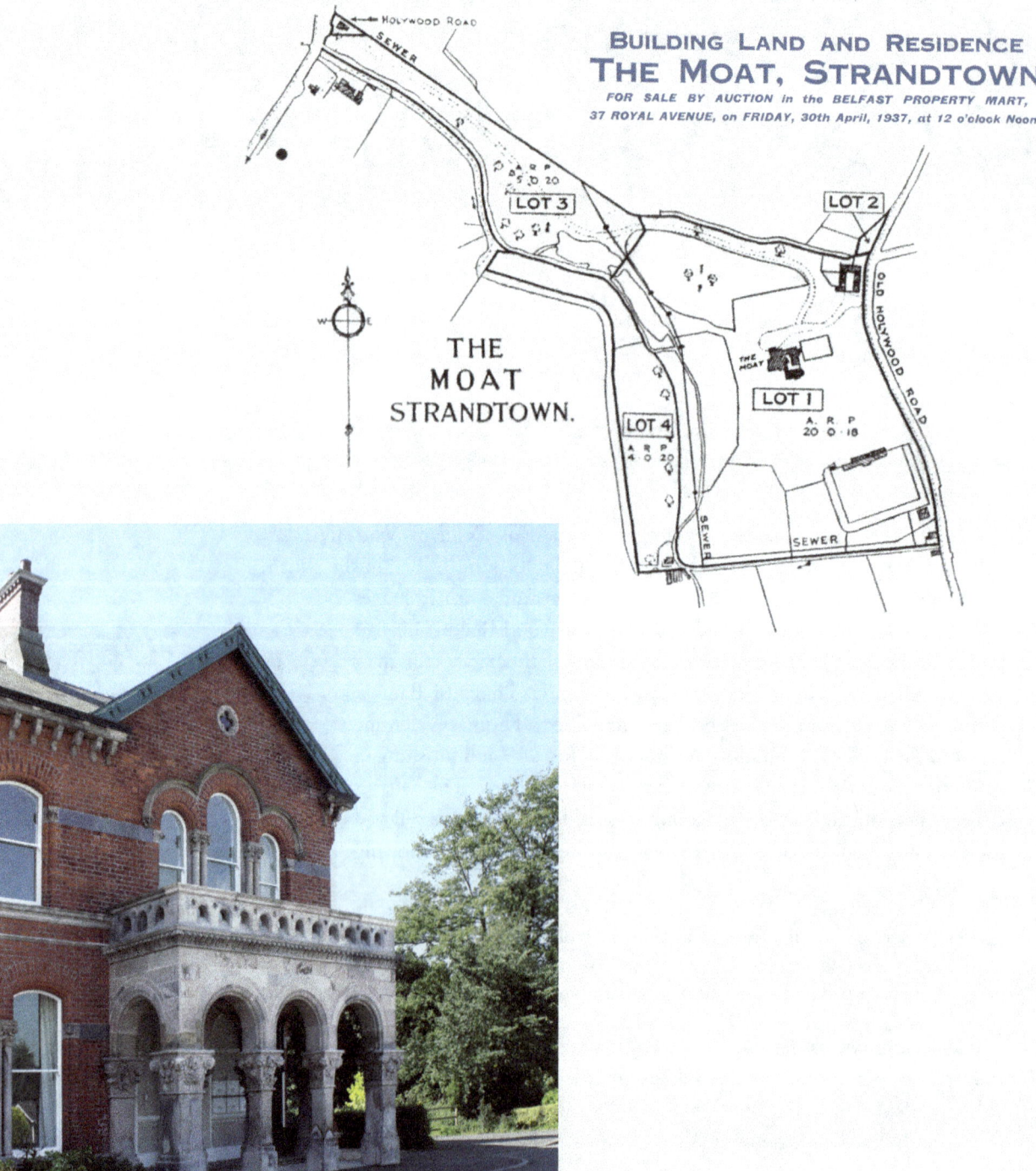

The Moat, 2012
JFR

ABBEYDENE
formerly LISMARA

Abbeydene is situated at 385 Shore Road, Newtownabbey, and was built c. 1855, first appearing on the Ordnance Survey map for 1858, when the owner was John Finlay, a flax and tow merchant with offices in Donegall Square East, Belfast. Brett, in *Buildings of County Antrim* states:

> A large, handsome, foursquare merchant prince's mansion of about 1850, of fairly unusual golden sandstone, on the high bank east of Macedon Point, looking south over Belfast Lough.

Lismara, as the house was originally named, was built by Sir Charles Lanyon in 1850 for John Finlay, who was a flax merchant. This is a two-storey, three-bay house of considerable size, built in Italianate style, which originally was set in nineteen acres, and had grounds planted out with a range of trees and shrubs from around the world. The entrance front has a large enclosed portico with four Tuscan columns and round headed windows, which are below the segmental pediment. The ground floor has two single sash windows to either side of the entrance, immediately above on the first floor are two similar windows, all with moulded architraves, and there is a central triple window. The walls are quoined and two decorative platbands continue around the house. The roof is hipped with deep, bracketed eaves, and a dentil course. Photographs of Lismara some years ago show tall ornamented chimney stacks but these appear now to have been reduced in size. Dean lists a gate lodge to Lismara c. 1855, architects probably Lanyon and Lynn, but now demolished. He states:

> Another Italianate lodge almost identical to that at Cromore, County Londonderry, but slightly more elaborate. For the Finlay family it was in buff coloured sandstone ashlar like the house. Symmetrical, three bay with a hipped roof carried on eaves brackets.

Lismara had a number of owners with connections to the linen industry. In the 1870s the house was the seat of James Hind, son of John Hind, whose company, John Hind and Sons were the proprietors of the Durham Street flax spinning mill, until their failure in the depression of the linen industry of 1884. James Hind died 6 December 1885 and the house lay unoccupied until it was purchased in 1891 by Edward Robinson for £6,250, a sum which included all the furniture.

Edward Robinson (1849–1906) was a major Irish linen retailer in the domestic market who set up business with John Cleaver (1842–1926) in the firm Messrs Robinson & Cleaver Ltd., once one of the major retailing stores in Belfast. Edward Robinson began his career by serving an apprenticeship with James Lindsay & Co., Ltd., general drapers, silk mercers, and linen merchants, Ulster Arcade, Donegall Place, Belfast. While working with this firm Edward Robinson met John Cleaver, who had come from London to manage one of the departments in Lindsay & Co. In 1870 they went into business together at 30

Edward Robinson

Robinson & Cleaver Building, Donegall Square North c. 1900

PRONI D/3598/1

Castle Place, selling linens which were made locally, for which there was a considerable demand, and by 1879 they had moved to larger premises in High Street, Belfast. However, for some years the business continued to grow, and a site was acquired at the corner of Donegall Place and Donegall Square North for the building of a new department store, which was designed by the Belfast architects, Young and Mackenzie. Robinson & Cleaver's Irish Linen Warehouse opened in 1888, and by the early twentieth century had become Belfast's most popular department store. They supplied Queen Victoria with linens for the Royal households, and in 1902 were awarded a Royal Warrant.

After the death of Edward Robinson in 1906, Lismara continued to be occupied by his widow until 1915, when the house was bought by Crawford McCullagh, who had been elected Lord Mayor of Belfast in 1914. He was knighted in 1915, and was elected on seventeen subsequent occasions as Lord Mayor, being promoted to baronet in 1935. It was in his role as Lord Mayor, in 1946, that it fell to him to entertain General Eisenhower at Lismara. After his death in 1948, his son, the second Sir Crawford McCullagh, renamed the house 'Abbeydene', and called a new house, built for himself in the grounds, 'Lismara'. Subsequently Abbeydene became an old people's home, but latterly in 2002, now called Abbeydene House, it was restored as a spacious private period residence with south facing gardens. At present it is listed as a Northern Ireland guest house.

Supreme Allied Commander and future President of the United States, Dwight D. Eisenhower poses for a photograph with Sir Crawford McCullagh, Lord Mayor of Belfast, and members of his family on the steps of Lismara House, 24 August 1945.

NORTHERN WHIG

Robinson & Cleaver Building, 2012

JFR

SEAPARK HOUSE
CARRICKFERGUS

Seapark, sometimes named Seapark House, is situated at 109, Shore Road, Carrickfergus, and is close to the shore of Belfast Lough, just south of Carrickfergus. The Ordnance Survey Memoirs of 1839–40 for Carrickfergus state:

> Sea Park is the residence of the Very Rev. John Chaine, Dean of Connor. The house is 2-storey high, slated, situated about 1 and a half miles west of Carrickfergus, on the shore and near the mail coach road from Belfast. It was built by Thomas Stuart Esquire, Belfast, about the year 1804. His son, William Stuart Esquire, occupied it. Dean Chaine is only 4 years in it. He rents it from William Stuart Esquire. It contains 16 acres of ornamental grounds and planting.

Dean Chaine (1802–62) was the son of William Chaine of Ballycraigy, Muckamore, County Antrim, who was a wealthy linen bleacher and merchant. John Chaine was Dean of Connor and rector of Carrickfergus from 1839 to 1855, but, according to Brett, 'was much beset by creditors, with whom he compounded twice'. Atkinson also mentions Seapark in 1817:

> the seat of Thomas Ludford Stewart comprises a handsome new-built house, and 30 acres of demesne, ornamented with young plantations.

SEAPARK HOUSE, CARRICKFERGUS

Seapark was bought in 1852 by John Owden, who promptly commissioned the architect Thomas Jackson to double the size of the house. John Owden was an Englishman of Huguenot descent who came to Ireland as a young man, going into partnership with James Nicholson Richardson (1782–1847) of Glenmore in 1825. The new partnership was known as J.N. Richardson, Sons & Owden, and was based in Belfast, although the company had extensive linen business interests throughout north east Ireland. In 1841 he married Jane Greeves (1803–71), who was a Quaker, and youngest daughter of John Greeves, linen bleacher and merchant of Bernagh House, The Grange, County Tyrone. They had one daughter, Margaret, who in 1864, married Thomas Greer (1837–1905) of Tullylagan, County Tyrone, and in time was a director of J.N. Richardson, Sons & Owden. Their son, Thomas MacGregor Greer (1869–1941), inherited Seapark from his father but chose to live at the family seat, Tullylagan in County Tyrone. He sold Seapark in 1927 to Sir George Clark, DL, formerly of Workman Clark & Co., Ltd., shipbuilders in Belfast, who lived there until 1947.

Later Seapark became an old people's home but has latterly been restored to private ownership.

Seapark is an exceptionally attractive and well proportioned detached four bay, two-storey, stucco house in Italianate style. This is an ornately detailed building with a four-stage tower to west, and further interest is provided by the broken asymmetrical layout. The entrance has a canted bay with a portico of coupled Ionic columns, and the surviving windows of the original house remain Georgian-glazed. Seapark has a gate lodge, which is listed by Dean as *c.* 1865, architect Thomas Jackson. This is a detached three bay, single storey, Italianate building, having a hipped roof with panelled soffits to eaves, and moulded window surrounds.

Seapark gate lodge
© *CROWN COPYRIGHT HMSO*

There is no doubt that John Owden was a partner in a highly successful linen manufacturing company. Bassett in his *Book of Antrim*, published in 1888, states:

> Messrs J.N. Richardson, Sons & Owden, Ltd., have been famous as manufacturers of linen goods of every description for more than a century. The wholesale warehouse at Belfast occupies an entire block facing the White Linen Hall, in Donegall Square. It is six storeys high, was built in 1867 of Scotch red sand stone, and is beautifully and expensively fitted all through. The weaving factories are in Down and Armagh. In the vicinity of Lisburn, at Glenmore, the bleach works are situated. They were started 130 years ago, and are said to be the most extensive in the world, turning out 10,000 miles of linen textile every year.

John Owden was the son of John Owden of Talbot House, Cuckfield, Sussex, born *c.* 1804, but was made an orphan when young. After coming to Ireland and joining J.N. Richardson in the linen business John Owden lived in Belfast at Brooklands, a large neo-classical villa which he had built in 1840 on the site of an old farm at Malone. Owden continued to use Brooklands as his town residence for some years following his move to Seapark. His brother was Sir Thomas Scrambler Owden (1809–89), who became Lord Mayor of London in 1877. John Owden died in 1870, and Seapark was left to Margaret, who continued to live there with her husband Thomas Greer, MP for Carrickfergus 1880–85.

Richardson's Warehouse, now Marks & Spencers

JFR

3
SOUTH COUNTRY ANTRIM

MOYLENA BRIDGE AND WEIR, MUCKAMORE, ANTRIM
Postcard

CUNNINGHAM FAMILY TREE

The Cunningham Family Tree principally shows male members of the family associated with the linen industry

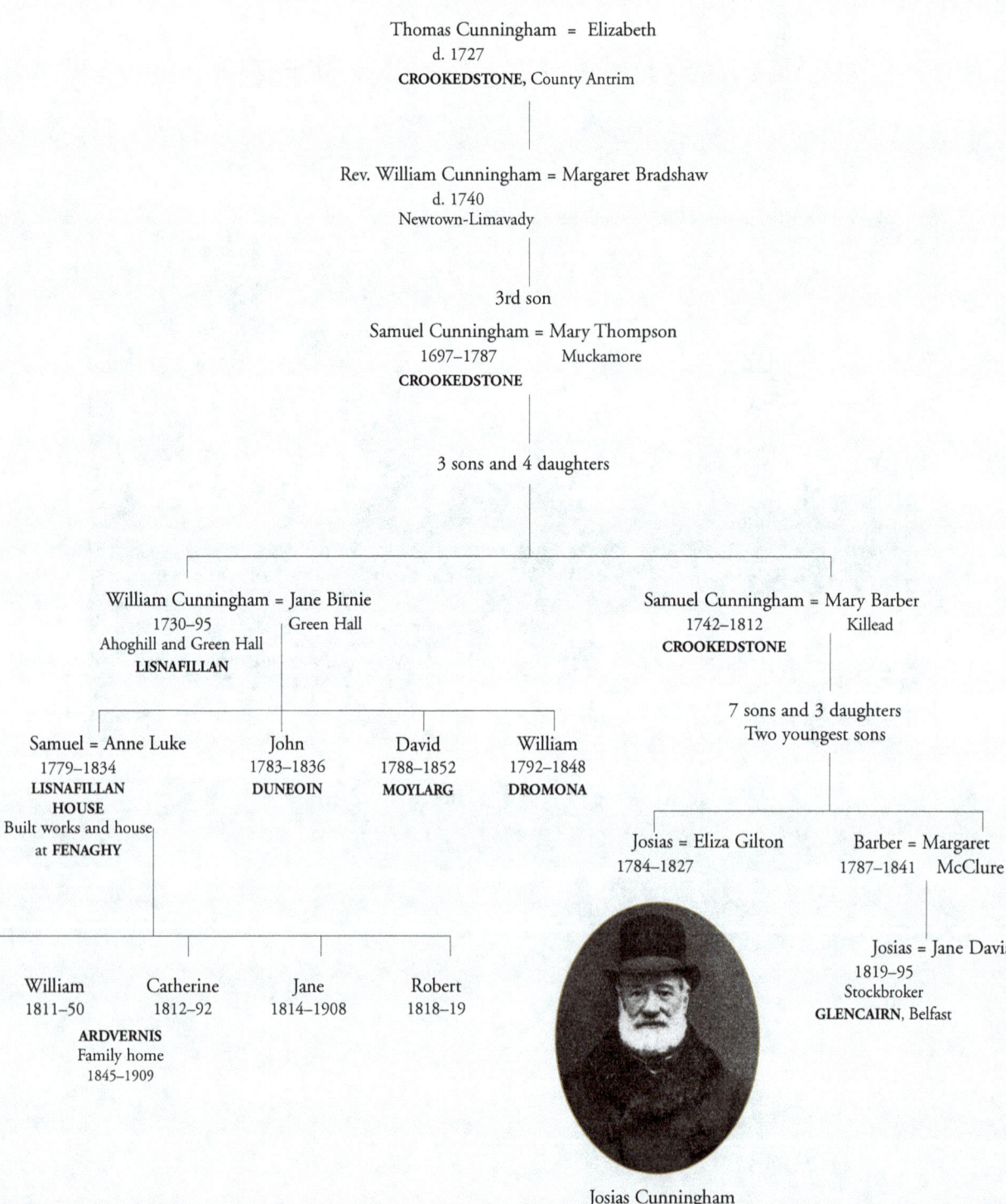

Josias Cunningham

CROOKEDSTONE
ALDERGROVE

Crookedstone is remarkable in being an extremely old house built in 1699 by Patrick Cunningham, and having the date inscribed above the front porch. The house is situated down a very long lane at 1 Ballyarnott Road, and overlooks flat farmland running down to Lough Neagh. This is a five-bay, two-storey, thatched whitewashed farmhouse, which is still owned and occupied by the Cunningham family, although, as is shown by the advertisement, it passed out of their possession for a short period in the early nineteenth century. The interior of the house has original oak beams and planks, and a kitchen which probably is much as it must have been when built. A modern extension at right angles to the original house and accessible from it was built in 1966.

In the eighteenth and early nineteenth centuries one branch of the Cunningham family had considerable interests in the linen industry as is shown by this history by Lawlor.

The fireplace and original beams, Crookedstone, 2011

JFR

The Cunninghams were settled at Crooked Stone near Antrim in the middle of the seventeenth century, Thomas Cunningham (will dated 1727) had a son [should be grandson as shown on family tree] Samuel who succeeded him, and by his wife Mary Thompson of Muckamore had at least two sons. The eldest, William, inherited Lisnafillan from his wife's family, and of his four sons, Samuel Cunningham succeeded his father there, and built the works and the original house at Fenaghy; John built the bleach works at Duneoin; David ran the bleach works at Glarryford, and was also a partner with William in the Dromona bleach green.

Over a period of time the Cunningham family owned nearly all the bleach works on the river Main from Glarryford to Galgorm.

Although the family interest in the linen industry has died out there remains a considerable farming interest at Crookedstone. The eldest son of Samuel Cunningham (1742–1812), also named Samuel, died on a voyage home from the West Indies in 1796, and is recorded in the Ordnance Survey Memoirs for the Parish of Killead, 1838, concerning the Presbyterian Meeting House:

In the burial ground a handsome monument consisting of a square column of cut stone, surmounted by something resembling a grenade, was erected by his friends, at a cost of 100 pounds, to the memory of Mr Samuel Cunningham, formerly of this parish, who died abroad in 1796.

The doorway with the date 1699 above
JFR

A younger brother of Samuel, Josias, (1784–1827), was a partner with his brother Barber in the firm of Josias & Barber Cunningham, Wholesale (Importing) Tobacco Merchants, Rosemary Street, Belfast. His other brothers were also in business, and in 1822, he put the farm at Crookedstone along with 38 acres of land up for auction. Later, when the property again came on the market, it was bought back by the Cunningham family, and remains in their possession in the twenty first century.

ISLANDREAGH HOUSE
DUNADRY

This house is situated adjacent to a very old bleaching site on the Six Mile Water near Muckamore, which on Lendrick's map of 1780 is shown as Islandreagh Bleach Works, 'Mr Luke'. Unfortunately, at present there are two houses both known as Islandreagh House, one at Islandreagh Road and this one at Islandreagh Drive, which is approached over a narrow bridge spanning the railway line. Islandreagh House is said to be in part late seventeenth century, and probably built by the owners of the mill on the Six Mile Water. This is a four bay, two-storey house with slated roof, which externally does not betray its age. There are new windows, chimneys, and a porch combined with pebble dashed, quoined walls which all combine to give a nineteenth century appearance to the outside. According to family memoirs Samuel MacClure bought Islandreagh House and the bleach works in 1874, subsequently building beetling mills and a warehouse in 1882. Around 1888 a return wing was added to the house, using bricks salvaged from the demolition of the former owners' home in Donegall Square, Belfast, to make way for Robinson & Cleaver's Irish Linen Warehouse.

Samuel MacClure was succeeded in the Islandreagh Dyeing and Finishing

> BLEACH-GREEN & FARM TO BE SOLD,
> At WM. JAMISON'S, Innkeeper in Belfast, on FRIDAY the 12th of June next, at the Hour of TWELVE o'Clock.
> THE PREMISES are situated in Islandreagh, two miles distant from Antrim, and ten from Belfast, on the Six-mile River, adjoining the Village of Dunadry — The Farm contains 20 Irish Acres, tithe free, in very high condition. The BLEACH-HOUSE is 144 feet in length, three Stories high, 94 feet of which are 22 feet in width, and 50 feet 17 feet in width, in which are two Double Beetling Engines, 10 feet 10 inches in the beams, Water-Wheel 4 feet in the fall; on another Wheel are Wash Mills, and one Engine 8 feet in the Beams. The BOILING HOUSE contains two Furnaces, and Rub Boards. The supply of Water is abundant and regular. There is an extensive Dwelling-house and Offices, all held under the Marquis of Donegall, for the Remainder of 61 Years from May, 1802, at the Yearly Rent of £11, 19s.
> The situation would be eligible for the Spinning of Cotton or Linen Yarn. Terms of Payment at Sale.
> For further particulars apply to Mr. Hugh Johnson, in Belfast; or to James Swan, on the Premises.
> April 14, 1812.

Samuel MacClure
JFR

Company by his son Robert, and, eventually in the twentieth century, by his son Samuel Arthur MacClure, who died in 2004. The earliest reference to the site is given by James Beck regarding an advertisement in the *Belfast News Letter*, October 1768, which concerns a robbery at the bleach yard of James and John Luke, near Antrim. H.C. Lawlor has written that the house and mill were owned by James Luke from 1778 to his death in 1808. In an advertisement of 1 May 1812 the premises were offered for sale by James Swan, and Atkinson states that in 1817 it was the seat of James Swan, Esq. The references to Beck of Islandreagh are numerous in the early part of the nineteenth century where he is mentioned as a Draper, and also as a Bleacher Merchant. In 1843–4 Henderson's Directory under Antrim gives J. Beck & Sons, Linen Manufacturer, Bleacher, Islandreagh. Latterly the site appears to have been let to various bleachers until it was eventually bought by Samuel MacClure.

CLADY HOUSE
DUNADRY

Clady House is situated at Shanoguestown Road, Dunadry, on a picturesque site beside the Clady Water, amidst magnificent mature trees. This is a large eighteenth century house shown on Lendrick's map of 1780, and is thought to have been built by Hugh Swann, who was a linen bleacher and merchant. The house is three bay, two-storey with attics and basement, and is stuccoed with quoined walls, and slated roof. A considerable feature of the front of the house is the Georgian glazing with three triple windows on the first floor, and two on the ground floor, on either side of a fine doorcase with fanlight and side lights. Clady House was considerably restored in the 1960s and the front facade has pediments on the ground floor windows, along with dripstones, and a dentil cornice beneath the eaves. A return wing which had been added to the original building was removed, and an attractive courtyard with handsome outbuildings was created. There is a plain pitched roof, an attic window in each gable, and at the rear, a very tall round-headed window lighting the staircase. In the interior, one room has a delicate plaster cornice with a centre medallion on the ceiling, and there is reeding in the doorcases and in the dividers of the three-light windows. C.E.B. Brett writing about Clady House states that:

Clady House

JFR

John R. Cowdy and his family occupied Clady House in the 1960s. He was formerly of the bleachers Anthony Cowdy & Sons.

After the death of Hugh Swan's widow, the property was bought by William Cinnamond, and remained in the family until 1900, when the family fell upon hard times — Since then, it has had a number of more fortunate owners, and retains the feeling of an uncommonly light, airy and pleasant house.

Lawlor, in 1942, gave a description of the considerable number of bleach greens associated with the Six Mile Water and associated rivers. He states:

> The Six Mile Water and its tributaries the Clady, Four Mile Burn and Doagh Stream, have always been remarkable for the number of mills on their banks, driven, before the introduction of the steam engine, entirely by water-wheels. For the most part they were originally bleach greens, but there were at least four paper mills, a cotton mill and one considerable flour mill.

There were many bleach works on the upper reaches of the streams in the Six Mile Water valley. Lawlor states that it is exactly three miles from Dunadry to Antrim, and in 1783 there were eleven mills in this short stretch, besides about as many on the Clady River which joins the Six Mile Water. The Ordnance Survey Memoirs of 1838 have recorded a Mr Swann possessing two bleach mills in the townland of Straidballymorris. A second reference states:

> The beetling engine in Straidballymorris townland, Mr Hugh Swann proprietor, on Clady Water.

A reference to Hugh Swann, Clady, is also given in Pigot's Directory of 1824 where he is described as a Linen Bleacher and Merchant. Hugh Swann died in 1848 aged 95, but his son Hugh Swan Junior is recorded in the Henderson Directory 1843–44 as a Linen Merchant, Bleacher, Dyer and Finisher, Clady, Antrim.

Clady House doorway
JFR

CLADY COTTAGE
DUNADRY

Clady Cottage is situated on Clady Road, Muckamore, and is set in an attractive garden with fine mature trees, adjacent to the Clady River. This is a beautifully situated, two-bay, originally single storey thatched house with attic, built about 1780 and renovated in 1958. Clady Cottage has been enlarged by successive owners, who raised the roof by half a storey with windows in the gable ends, and removed the chimneys to their present position. The walls are of rubble blackstone with brick dressings, the wide windows have unrecessed Georgian-glazed sashes, and the panelled entrance door, with decorative sidelights and fanlight, is set in an elliptically arched opening.

Clady Cottage is situated in the townland of Straidballymorris, where, in 1835, the Ordnance Survey Memoirs record a bleaching establishment, along with a beetling mill having a fall of water of twenty feet. Some years later the house and grounds were bought by John Cowan, who set up works for the bleaching, dyeing and finishing of linen. He spent a considerable sum of money on new buildings and new machinery, enabling him to turn out goods dyed and well finished, and, as a result, established a large connection, especially in Manchester.

John Cowan's son, W.T. Cowan succeeded his father in Clady Cottage and continued the business, which was listed as Clady Bleach Works, Dunadry, in Smith's *Linen Trade Directory* of 1876, and again in Carter's *Linen Directory* of 1909. In 1958 the Cowan family sold the property to the Webb family of the Old Bleach Linen Company, Randalstown, continuing the linen connection to Clady Cottage.

The Six-Mile-Water at Muckamore

CHAINE FAMILY TREE

The Chaine Family Tree only shows male members of the family involved in the linen business

William Chaine = Jane Whittle
1778–1862   1764–1839
BALLYCRAIGY HOUSE
Muckamore

- John Chaine
  1802–62
  Dean of Connor
  Seapark
  Carrickfergus

- William Chaine
  Moylena Cottage
  Muckamore

- James Chaine = Maria Whittle
  1805–42   1804–82
  BALLYCRAIGY HOUSE   Castle Upton
  Muckamore   Templepatrick

- Stafford Chaine
  Spring Farm
  Muckamore

James Chaine, MP, DL = Henrietta de Salis Creery
1841–85   Newcastle, County Down
BALLYCRAIGY HOUSE
CAIRNCASTLE LODGE
Larne

- William Chaine, DL
  1864–1937
  CAIRNCASTLE LODGE
  Director of York Street
  Flax Spinning Co., Ltd.

- James Chaine = Christine McCollum
  1867–1910
  Larne

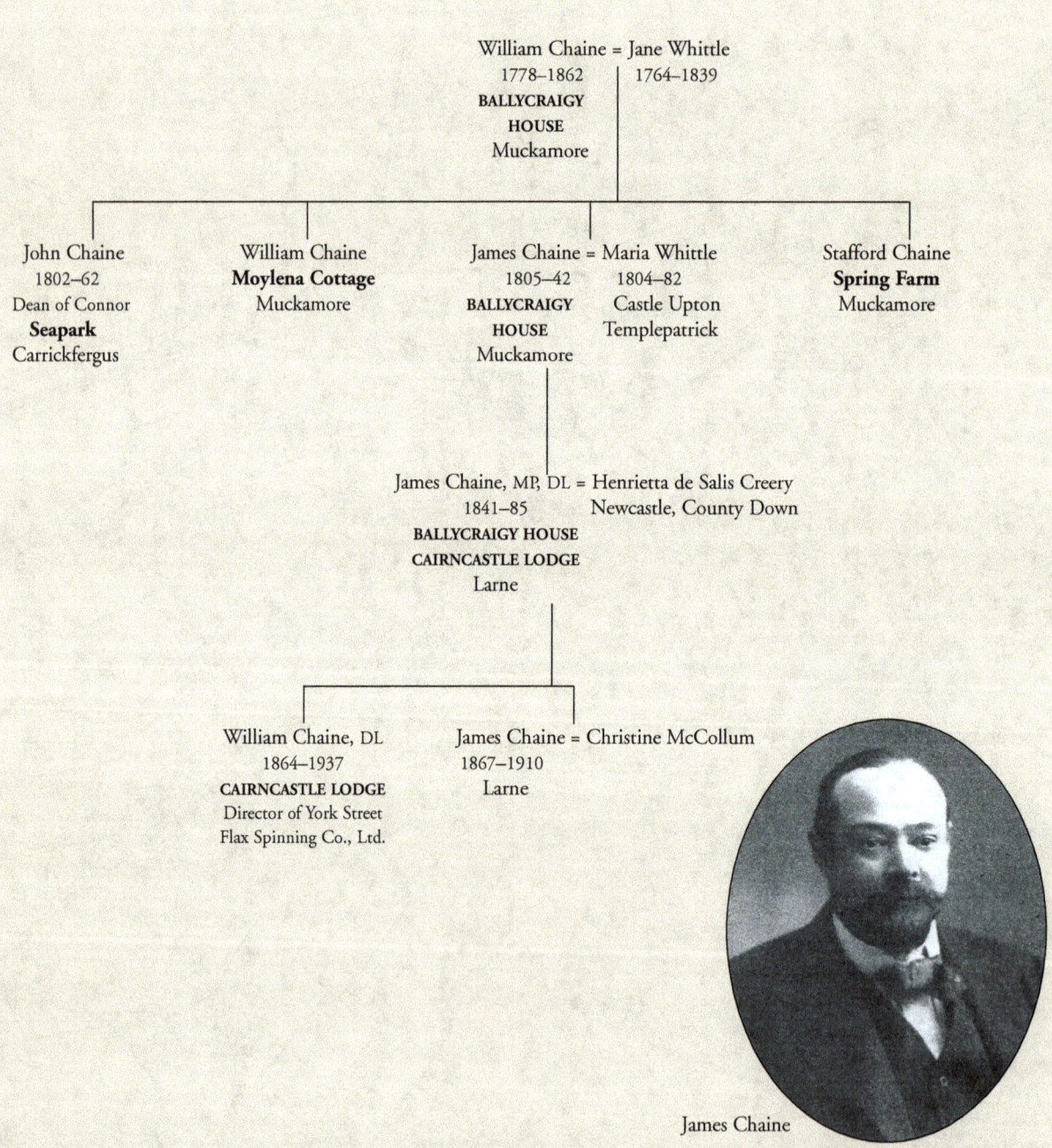

James Chaine

THE CHAINE FAMILY
OF SOUTH ANTRIM

In the late eighteenth and early nineteenth centuries the Six Mile Water, and its tributaries the Clady, Four Mile Burn and Doagh Stream, had a considerable number of mills on their banks, driven, before the introduction of the steam engine, entirely by water wheels. Three families, the Thompsons, Chaines and Refords, appear to have dominated the linen and bleaching trade at Muckamore near Antrim town. William Chaine, the son of John Chaine of Portglenone, came to Muckamore in 1797, having married Miss Jane Whittle of Thistleborough, Glenavy. According to Heather Thompson this marriage appears to have given William the opportunity to purchase his first bleachworks, those of Wallace & Whittle at Muckamore. She also states:

Chaine Tower at Larne Harbour
JFR

> The connection with the Whittles was also important for William when he came to building up trading markets for his linen. The Whittles owned property in Jamaica, including a quinine plantation, and William was able to use their links in the Caribbean to expand his commercial interests in Jamaica, Cuba and South America. The Chaines and the Whittles remained closely knit in succeeding generations, the Whittles owning a considerable flour mill at Muckamore.

William Chaine gradually built up his linen business and property interests in the Antrim area, buying the bleach greens owned by the Refords, Swans, Gillmers, McConchys and Thompsons, and making the mills and bleach greens into a very well run business which employed between 300 and 500 people at any one time. He died in 1862, aged 84, having been assisted in the business by his son James, but who predeceased him in 1842. His second son William took no interest in the business, and William Chaine, Senior, in his will, left Muckamore Bleaching and Linen Business to his grandson James Chaine (1841–85).

This James Chaine made a considerable contribution to life in County Antrim by purchasing Larne Harbour and 203 acres of land, in 1865. He improved Larne Harbour and re-started a ferry service between Larne and Stranraer, setting up a company known as the Larne and Stranraer Steamboat Company. However, it was also essential to improve the flow of passengers and of goods such as linen to Larne, and in 1874 James Chaine succeeded in having a Bill passed through Parliament for the construction of a Ballymena–Ballyclare–Larne railway, which was completed in 1878. James Chaine, DL was elected to Westminster as MP for County Antrim in 1874, having been appointed Sheriff for the County in 1873.

Previously, in February 1864, he had married Henrietta de Salis Creery of Newcastle, County Down, and they had two sons, William (1864–1937) and James (1867–1910). Unfortunately, James Chaine died on 4th May 1885, at the early age of 44, having contracted a chill which developed into pneumonia, at Larne Harbour while seeing off their Royal Highnesses the Prince and Princess of Wales in April 1885, after their visit to the seaport. According to the *Belfast Telegraph* in an obituary:

> … he took a leading part in the ceremonies which were enacted at the farewell on that occasion, as, indeed, he had done in the preparations for the reception of the Royal visitors in the seaport for the prosperity of which he laboured so much …

In his will James Chaine left his eldest son William (1864–1937) his business interests, but he requested that he completed his degree course at Magdalene College, Cambridge. The Chaine Memorial Tower was erected at Larne Harbour in 1887 in memory of James Chaine and all he had accomplished for the port of Larne.

James Chaine, MP, DL, had retired from his linen interests in 1883, selling the majority of his bleach greens and properties to the York Street Flax Spinning Co., Ltd., so enabling them to finish considerable quantities of brown linen at Muckamore. Some years later, his son William Chaine, DL, became a director of the York Street Flax Spinning Company. William and his mother chose to live at Cairncastle Lodge, Larne, where he managed the family estate, and they left Ballycraigy House.

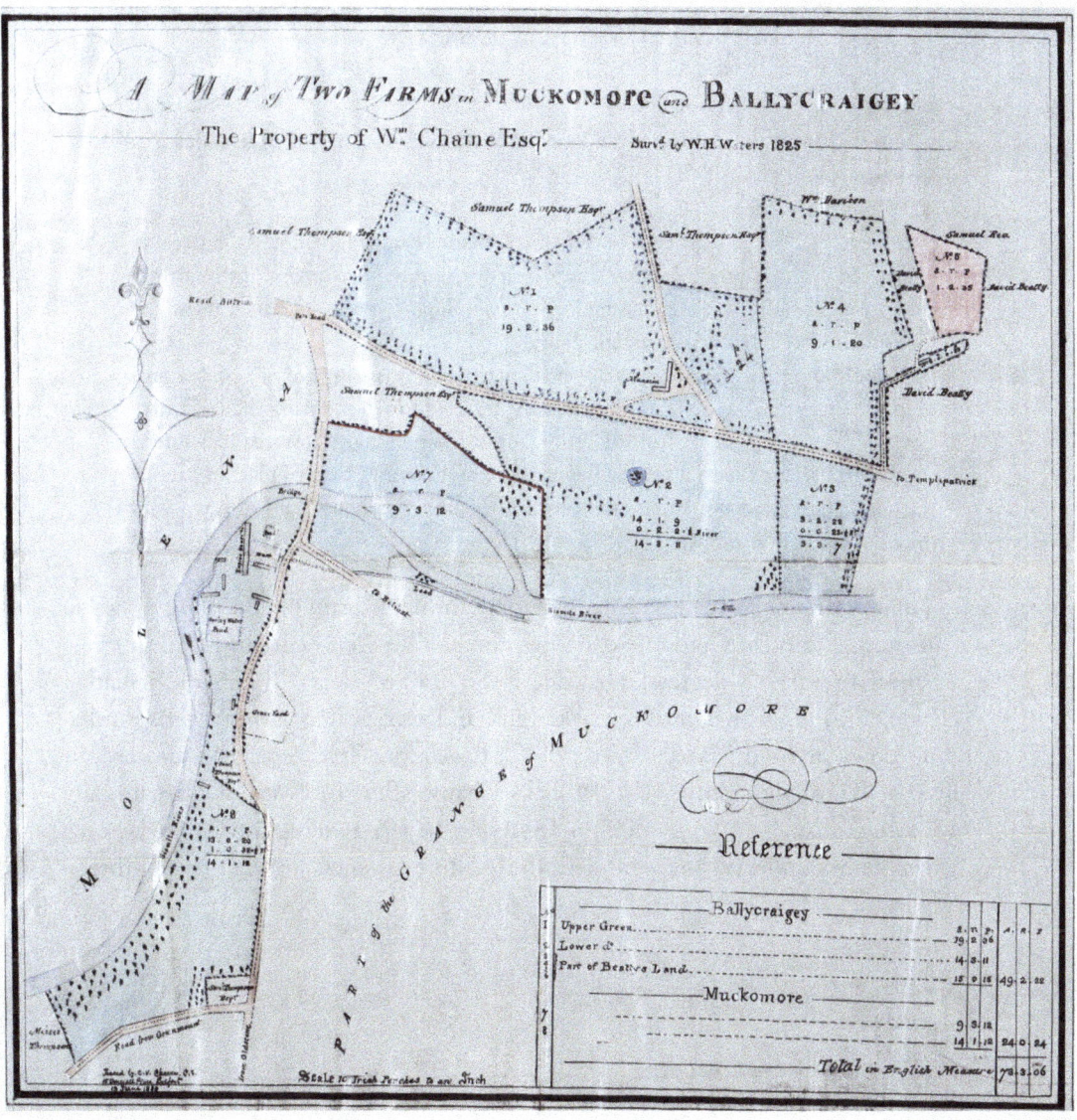

Map of Ballycraigy House and Muckamore
PRONI

BALLYCRAIGY HOUSE
MUCKAMORE

At different times this house had a variety of titles, starting in the eighteenth century simply with the name Ballycraigy, followed in the mid nineteenth century by Ballycraigy Manor, and ending in the twentieth century with Ballycraigy House. Lawlor states that in 1798 Ballycraigy House was abandoned as a rectory and was purchased by Mr Whittle of the flour mill at Muckamore. William Chaine married Jane Whittle around 1800, and Lawlor suggests that a short time later she inherited Ballycraigy House from her father, although the Whittle family retained their ownership of the flour mill at Muckamore. The

LINEN HOUSES OF COUNTY ANTRIM AND NORTH COUNTY DOWN

Ordnance Survey Memoirs of 1838 for the Parish of Antrim give a description of this house:

> Ballycraigy, the residence of William Chaine Esquire Senior, is agreeably situated 1 and a quarter miles south east of the town of Antrim and within a few yards of the road from that town to Belfast. It takes its name from the townland in which it is situated.
>
> The house is 2-storey and very spacious, consisting of 12 successive apartments which have from time to time been added to it during the last thirty years. The lawn is rather confined in front of the house and towards its western side it is used as a bleach field. There are several rows and belts of planting about it, and the view from some of the windows embraces the beautifully wooded bank on the opposite side of Moylinny glen.

William Chaine lived at Ballycraigy House until his death in 1862. His family consisted of four sons and one daughter, three of his sons being involved in the business to varying degrees. His eldest son trained as a Church of Ireland clergyman, and was rector of Carrickfergus, and also Dean of Connor. His third son, James married Maria Whittle of Castle Upton, Templepatrick, and they lived at Ballycraigy House with William Chaine after the death of his wife in 1839. Unfortunately, James died in 1842, but he left a young son James, who, when he was twenty one, was left the Chaine business by his grandfather William.

Illustration of Ballycraigy House from the *Irish Builder*, 15 October 1869

BALLYCRAIGY HOUSE

James Chaine married Henrietta de Salis Creery in 1863, taking up residence in Ballycraigy House. They had two sons, William (1864–1937) and James (1867–1910), and they decided to enlarge their house, with a report being published in the *Irish Builder* of 15th October 1869.

BALLYCRAIGY MANOR, ANTRIM

This week we give an illustration of Ballycraigy Manor, near Antrim, the residence of James Chaine, Esq, JP, which is at present undergoing extensive alterations and enlargements. The front of the old structure, now forming the left wing of the new building, and which was originally of Italian design of the plainest character, is being recast, as shown in the view.

The right wing, which is entirely new, covers an area of about thirty-six squares, and provides the following accommodation:
A principal staircase, 30 ft. by 27 ft., with wine cellars underneath; dining room, 30 ft. by 24 ft., with serving room, 13 ft. by 13 ft., adjoining; billiard room, 30 ft. by 20 ft.; smoking room, 19 ft. by 16 ft.; fire-proof plate closet in tower, and three large bedrooms on ground floor, and on first floor seven large bedrooms, &c.

The style of the building is Castellated Tudor, and the materials used in the building are local. The contract for the works has been taken by Messrs. Thomas Dixon and Co., builders; and the architect is Mr W. Redfern Kelly, C.E., Belfast.

Unfortunately, Ballycraigy House was demolished in the 1950s and a housing estate was built on the site. The illustration taken from the *Irish Builder* is the only indication of the appearance of the house.

James Chaine had extensive interests in Larne where he owned Cairncastle Lodge, and he divided his time between Muckamore and Larne.

GLENHURST
MUCKAMORE

Glenhurst is situated at 20 Oldstone Road, Muckamore, and is close to the Muckamore Bridge over the Six Mile Water. This house was built by William Chaine for his mill manager, possibly around 1830, when he owned two beetling mills and several bleach greens at Muckamore. The Ordnance Survey Memoirs record in 1833 improvements in the area:

> the very extensive beetling and bleaching establishment of the Messrs Chaine and Son (one of the most extensive in Ireland) which may be said to have been originated by Mr Chaine about the year 1797, as it then consisted of a single engine.

Pierce and Coey describe Glenhurst as an attractive Regency Gothic house with a five-bay, two-storey, main building, and a two-bay, single-storey wing. The very attractive windows have decorative margined sashes set in Gothic pointed openings, and there are Tudor drip mouldings on the ground floor windows. Glenhurst has a half glazed panelled entrance door, with decorative fanlight, which is flanked by plain pilasters supporting a broken pediment.

In 1883 the York Street Flax Spinning Company bought the Muckamore Bleach Green, with houses, mills, land, and watercourses from James Chaine, and had continued ownership until 1958 when the company went into liquidation. Glenhurst was then purchased by the present owners as sitting tenants from the liquidator.

MOYLENA
MUCKAMORE

Moylena is situated at 81 Belfast Road, Muckamore, with an entrance just past the junction of the Oldstone and Belfast Roads, and on a sloping site which lies between the Belfast Road and the railway line. The Six Mile Water is nearby, just beyond the railway line, and this made the site valuable, in terms of the bleaching of linen, for over two hundred years. Three families, the Thompsons, Chaines, and Refords, at various points in time, appear to have dominated the linen and bleaching trade in Antrim. The first reference to this property, known then as Moylinny, is in 1733, when it was leased by the Massereene estate to Lewis Reford, linen draper. Heather Thompson states:

> The Refords erected and ran three mills, two beetling mills, and a bleachworks – The Green at Muckamore. All of these used the water from the Six Mile Water River.

Moylena Bridge over the Six Mile Water

JFR

Lewis Reford died in 1760 leaving a very comprehensive handwritten will, which gave precise details of all his properties, and to whom they were left.

> MOYLENA HOUSE & FARM,
> BY AUCTION.
>
> TO BE SOLD BY AUCTION, without reserve, at the COMMERCIAL BUILDINGS, Belfast, on the 2d December next, at ONE o'clock,
>
> THE beautiful and well-known FARM of MOYLENA, containing 116 Acres, held by Lease under the MASSEREENE FAMILY, for Lives renewable for ever, and subject to the small Chief Rent of £24, 11s. 4d. per annum.
>
> This Farm is of superior quality, and in excellent condition, situated within half a mile of Antrim, and 1½ of Belfast, on the Coach Road, and particularly valuable for Town Park. There are Two excellent DWELLING-HOUSES, with suitable Office-Houses, and a walled-in Garden; two Springs, one of which supplies the extensive Bleach-Green of Mr. CHAIN, at Muckamore, the other supplies the Paper Manufactory of Boghead, and could be rented to the present occupier at any time for a valuable consideration.
>
> There is a good Water-fall, on which originally extensive Machinery was placed, and well worth the attention of the Linen Trade.
>
> There is also a large quantity of valuable and ornamental Timber on this Property, and a great expense has been gone to, in improving the prospect and appearance of the House and Demesne, and altogether would be a desirable Concern for a Gentleman and Family.
>
> The Proprietor, Mr. J. REFORD, will shew the Premises, and give any further particulars required.
>
> GEO. C. HYNDMAN, Auctioneer.
>
> 21st Oct, 1822.

To Joseph lands situate near Muckamore Bridge in the Parish of Antrim adjoining the river containing about 84 acres, formerly called Wilsons or Wilkinson's farm and lately known by the name Moylinny Farm.

Atkinson, visiting in the area in 1817, comments:

This snug lodge and tolerably extensive farm is held under the Massereene family, by Mr Joseph Reford, of the firm of Steen and Reford, proprietors of a bleach yard on the river Clady.

Unfortunately, by October 1822, Joseph Reford appears to have been in considerable financial difficulties and Moylena House and Farm were advertised to be sold by auction in Belfast on the 2nd of December. PRONI D/1216/1 All the Reford bleach greens and mills were acquired by William Chaine Esq. Senior in 1823, and James Boyle writing in the Ordnance Survey Memoirs of 1838 reports:

Moylinny Cottage, the residence of William Chaine Esquire Junior, is beautifully situated 1 mile south east of Antrim, near the road from that town to Belfast, in the townland of Moylinny and on the bank overhanging the romantic glen of that name.

Moylena is a very interesting property in that the rear part of the house, to the left of the photograph, appears to be the oldest, and this part is three-bay, two-storey, with a hipped roof. However, parts of Moylena are one-storey, two-storey, and three storey. Various owners added to the house over the years, and as Brett states, the entrance, with nice fanlight and geometrical side lights, is tucked

Rear of Moylena House
JFR

Postcard of Moylena House *c.* 1920

under over-sailing eaves between two broad canted bays. He also states that it is a complicated house, with many stairs, and some of the grandest rooms at the top of them. The windows are Georgian glazed with the exception of the nineteenth century dormer windows at the front.

The Chaine family must have significantly improved Moylinny Cottage in that a Draft Memoir written in 1835 by J.F. Tait for the Ordnance Survey Memoirs states:

> Moylinny Cottage, the residence of William Chain Esq. Junior, is situated on the northern bank of the Six Mile Water, about a mile from the town of Antrim. It was built in the year 1832. There is a good deal of wood about it, principally fir.

An old photograph of Moylena, on a postcard *c.* 1920, shows a green house attached to the house and a later addition of a sun room, both of these on the garden side. These have now been removed to the great improvement of the house.

FIRGROVE HOUSE
MUCKAMORE

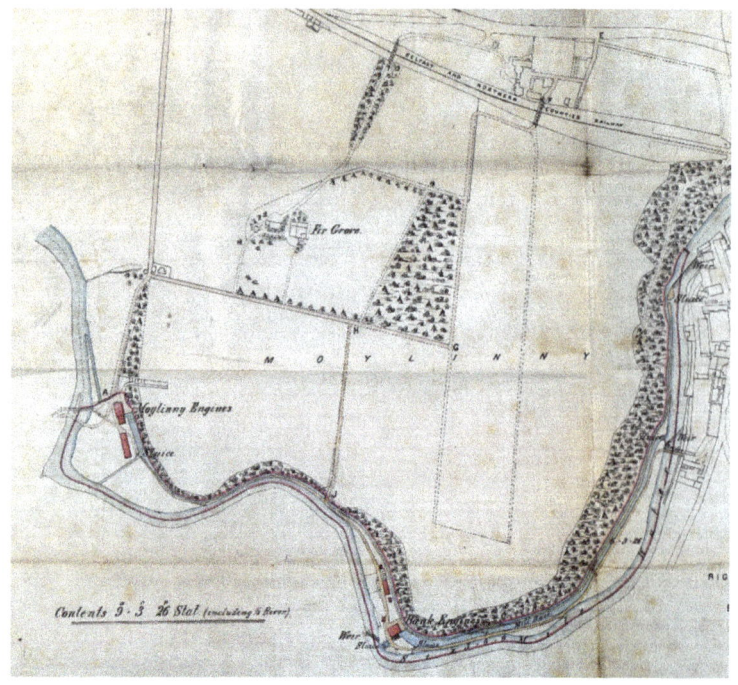

Bob Hanna, Manager of Muckamore Bleach Works (York Street) lived at Firgrove House
THE LATE ROBERT MARTIN

Detail of Firgrove, Moylinny & Bank Engines map
PRONI D/1326/33/20

Firgrove House, in the townland of Moylinny, was situated off the Belfast to Antrim Road about half a mile from Antrim. This was a late eighteenth century eight-bay, two-storey with attics house, all on a small scale, and was owned in the early nineteenth century by the Thompson family. However, in 1851 an agreement between John Thompson of Greenmount and William Chaine transferred ownership of the following:

> Muckamore Bleach Green with houses, mills, machinery, land, watercourses, weirs, dams, rights … situate on the west side of the road from Muckamore Bridge to the upper end of the Bleach Green.

The Chaine family carried out extensive renovations to the interior of Firgrove House in the 1850s, adding at the east end a large bow-fronted drawing room, which contained a rich modillion cornice. Dean has recorded a gate lodge built *c.* 1850 at Firgrove, which was probably built by the Chaines. In 1883 all of the Chaine bleach greens and associated properties were sold to the York Street Flax Spinning Company, and Firgrove was used as the residence for

Regd. Trade Marks: 'TOWER DYE' · 'MEADOW BLEACH' · Phones: BELFAST 20631 · ANTRIM 2138 · Grams: Yorkshire, Muckomore

York Street
FLAX SPINNING CO. LTD.
MUCKOMORE
Co. Antrim N. Ireland

Specialities
'SANFORIZED' REGD. TRADE MARK
SHRUNK FINISH
Processors for
TEBILIZED BRAND TESTED
CREASE-RESISTING FABRICS

BLEACHERS, DYERS & FINISHERS of LINEN, COTTON & RAYON GOODS · YARN & THREAD BLEACHERS & DYERS · HYDRAULIC MANGLERS

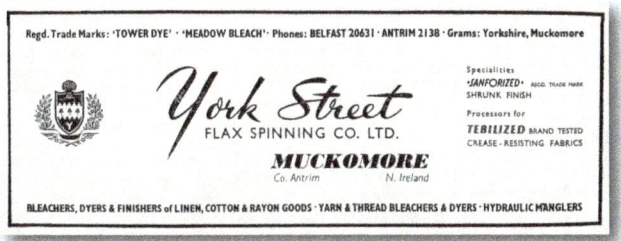

their director of the bleach and dye works, Mr George Sturrock Reade, from 1901. He married in 1912, continuing in residence at Firgrove, but added to the house in 1915 a single storey extension, incorporating a library and a porch. A further extension was added to the west end of the house for staff bedrooms on the ground floor, and a bedroom and nursery for the children above on the first floor. Mrs Reade was a keen gardener making a lovely garden, containing borders with herbaceous plants and a central feature of a sun dial, at the south end of the house.

The Reade family left Firgrove House in 1943 to live at Carncairn Lodge, Broughshane, and they were followed by Mr and Mrs Robert Hanna, Mr Hanna being the general manager of the Muckamore Bleach and Dye Works. A long tradition of bleaching at Muckamore ended in 1961 when the York Street Flax Spinning Company went into voluntary liquidation. Firgrove House and grounds were bought by the Ministry of Agriculture's Forestry Department who planted trees, but the house became the club house for Muckamore Cricket and Lawn Tennis Club in 1983. However, the whole area ultimately became part of the Industrial Development Board's Science and Technology Park at Antrim in 1990, and in April 1994 Firgrove House and the gate lodge were demolished.

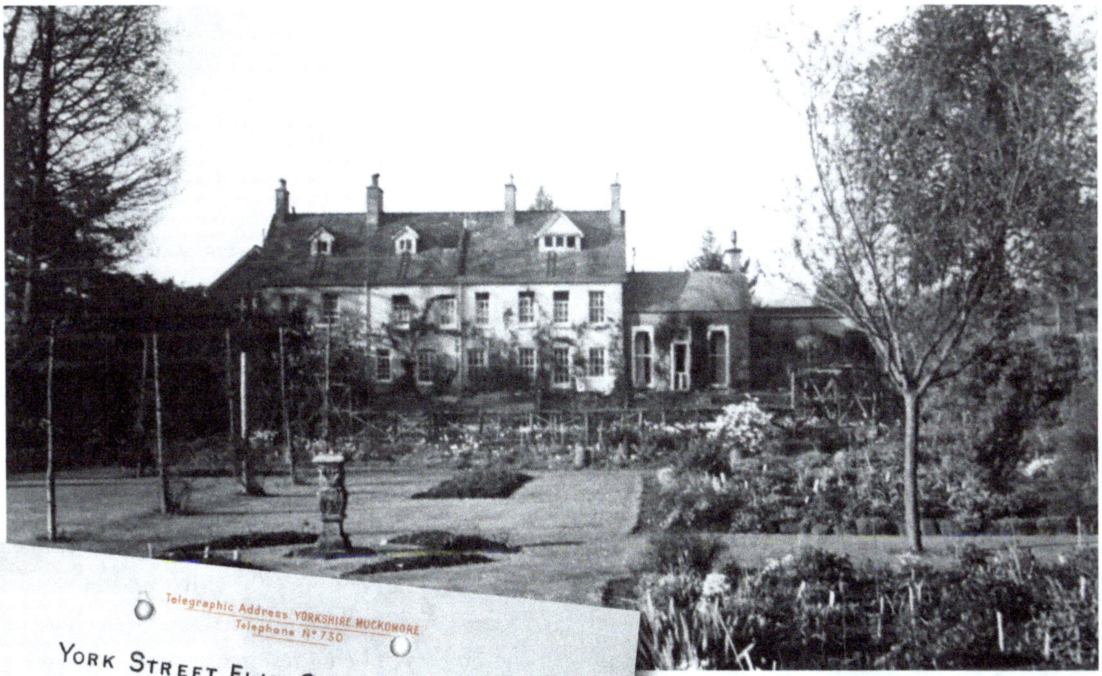
Firgrove House
READE FAMILY ALBUM

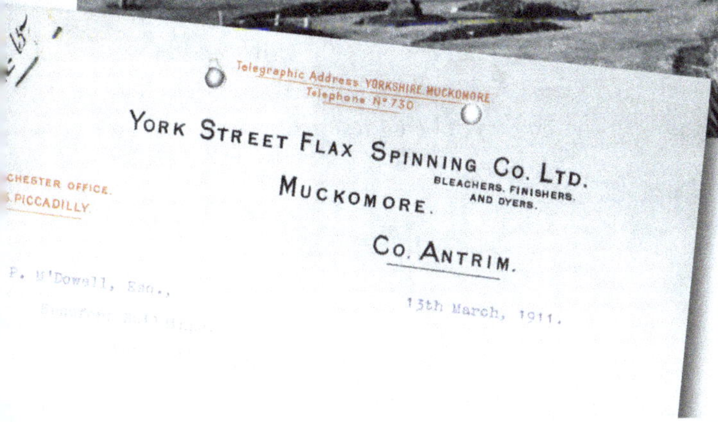
Telegraphic Address YORKSHIRE MUCKOMORE
Telephone No 730
YORK STREET FLAX SPINNING CO. LTD.
BLEACHERS, FINISHERS AND DYERS.
MUCKOMORE.
CO. ANTRIM.
...CHESTER OFFICE
...PICCADILLY.
P. M'Dowell, Esq.,
13th March, 1911.

INVERMUIR HOUSE
DOAGH

Invermuir House is situated in the grounds of the old Cogry Flax Spinning Company, Doagh, near Ballyclare in the valley of the Six Mile Water, and in south east County Antrim. This house was built in the early twentieth century immediately in front of the original Cogry House, which was the residence of Mr William McMeekin from 1879, when he bought the mill and the entire site. The new building was renamed after the three McMeekin children, Ivan, Vera and Muriel.

Invermuir is a five bay, two-storey house, having a central entrance door with glass canopy which stretches across the whole front, and supports a decorative balcony on the first floor. Internally, glass doors decorated with the McMeekin coat of arms lead out to this balcony which has a ten paned window. Across the front there is a wrought iron railing which encloses the glass canopy, and has a tiled floor. The house is brick built but smooth rendered with a ground floor return wing, and a string course separating the ground and first floors. The gabled roof is slated, having a snow board, and tall chimneys at either end of the roof. Unfortunately the house became unoccupied and fell into disrepair, but it is now in the process of being restored.

The McMeekin coat of arms decorate the glass doors

JFR

According to Bassett:

> Flax spinning, as an industry, was begun at Cogry in a small way about the year 1845. The late Mr William Moon, of Liverpool, ultimately purchased the interest, and expended over £50,000 upon buildings and machinery. Mr Samuel E. Broadbent, who had been associated in the management for 20 years, acquired full ownership in 1870. Nine years later he sold to Mr William McMeekin, J.P., the present owner, who carries on the concern under the style of the Cogry Flax Spinning Company.

About 400 people were employed at the Cogry Mills, the greater number living in houses belonging to the concern. Yarns from the Cogry Mills which were described as belonging to the heavy end of the trade, were purchased by linen manufacturers throughout the United Kingdom. Various members of the McMeekin family kept the mill operating in the twentieth century but it finally closed in 1958.

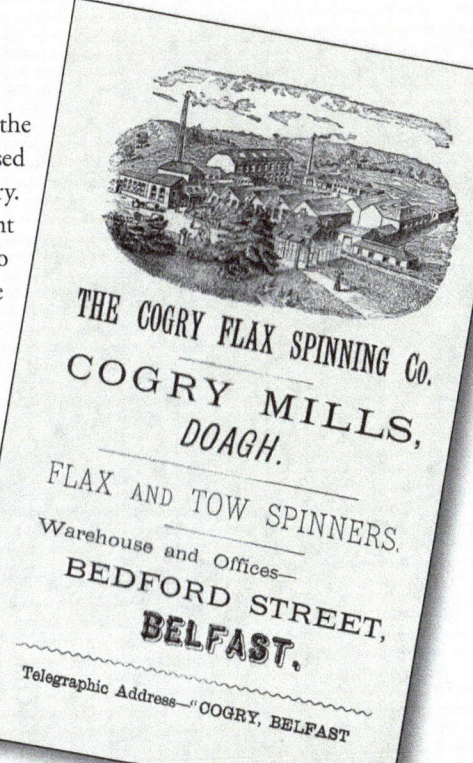

Billiard room fireplace
JFR

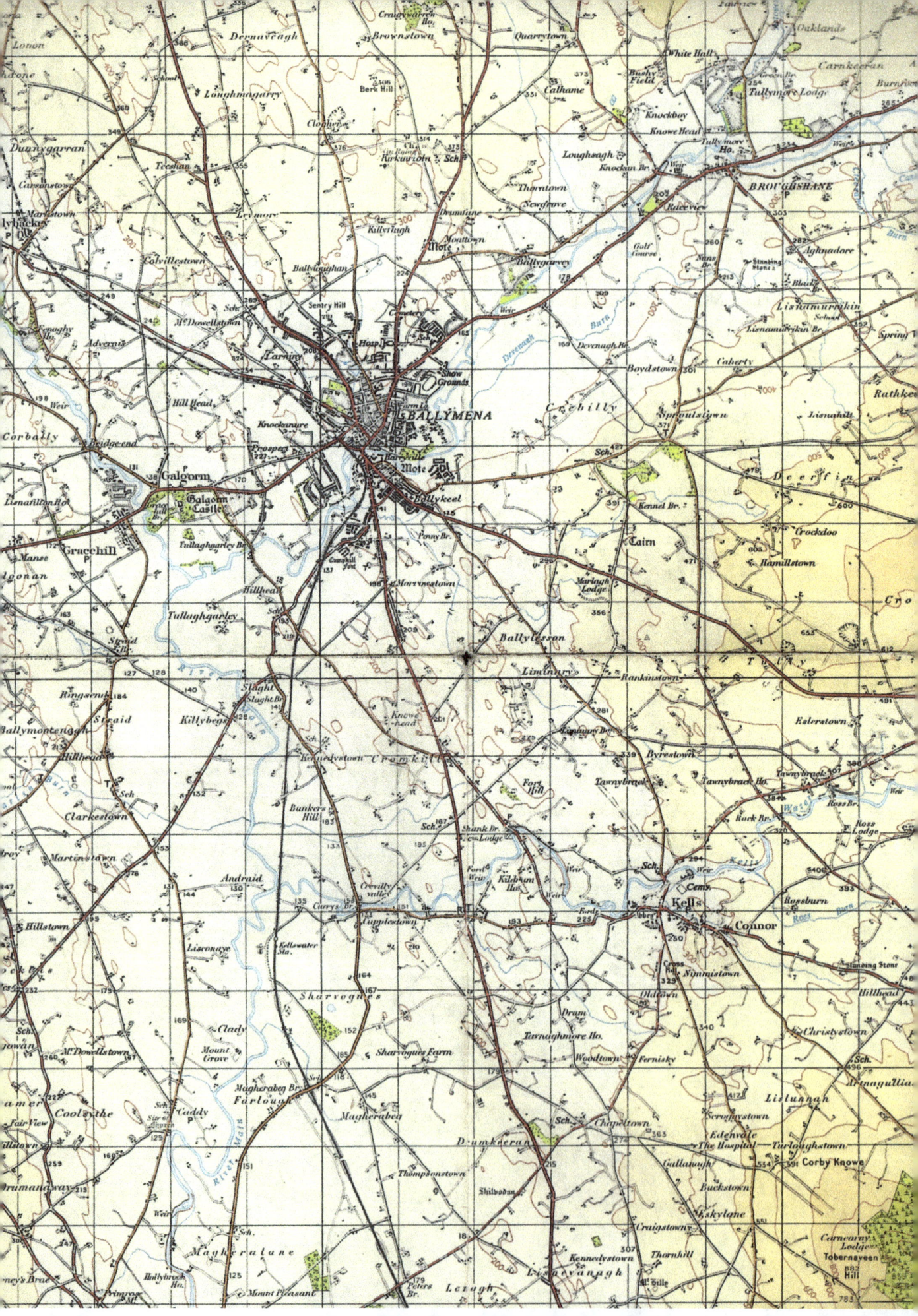

4
MID-COUNTY ANTRIM

THE RIVER MAIN AT FENAGHY

WEBB FAMILY TREE

This is an abbreviated Family Tree referring to houses lived in by male family members who were involved in the Old Bleach Linen Company.

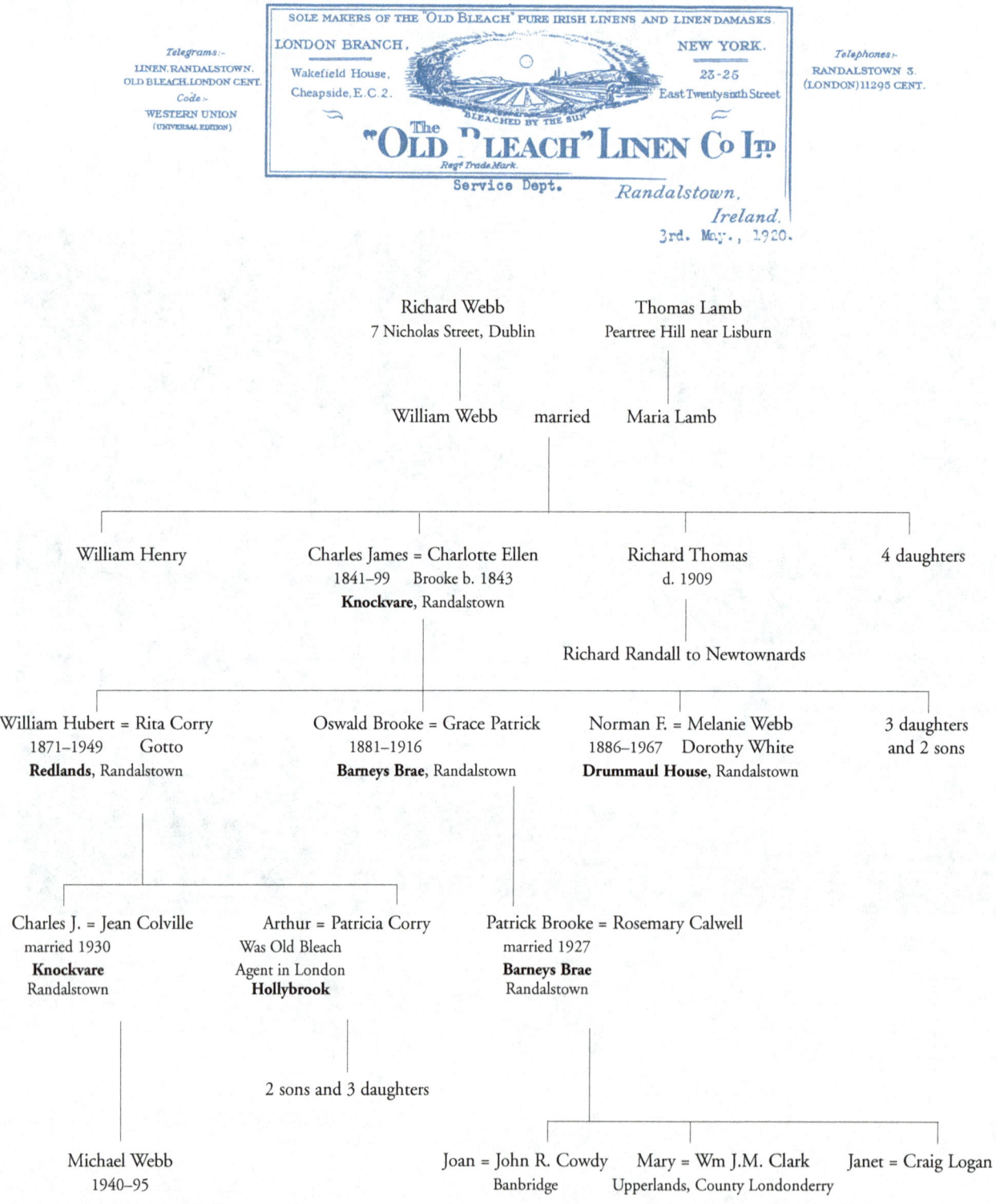

THE WEBB FAMILY
OF RANDALSTOWN

William Webb, son of Richard Webb of Nicholas Street, Dublin, married Maria Lamb of Lisburn, living firstly off the Antrim Road in Belfast, but then they transferred to Dublin in 1846. They had seven children and two of their sons, Charles James and Richard Thomas, returned to Ulster and, in 1864, set up the manufacture of linen in Randalstown, County Antrim. Records for Randalstown in 1861 show that on the banks of the River Main, adjoining the town, stood corn, flax, beetling and linen yarn spinning mills. Bassett writing in 1888 states that Messrs. C.J. and R.T. Webb, for twenty five years have been manufacturing linen, and bleaching linen and linen yarn, under the style of the Old Bleach Linen Company. The bleach works and weaving factory are beautifully situated in the valley of the Main. Bassett also gives a description of the works:

> The buildings at present used are one, two, and three storeys in height, and cover a considerable amount of ground. Half the covered space is occupied by power looms, and the bleaching machinery combines the best improvements. Driving power is supplied by water and steam. Messrs. Webb bleach only for themselves. Their goods are celebrated for high quality, and are known throughout the linen trade as 'the old bleach linens.' The chief markets for the sale of the linens are England and the United States.

Old Bleach linen manufacture was always at the top end of the trade, and the quality of their product was of prime importance to the firm.

C.J. Webb married in 1869 Charlotte Ellen Brooke, a Quaker from Dublin, and they had nine children. After his death in 1899, three of his sons were involved in the company, the eldest, W. Hubert Webb managing sales. He expanded the business in America, where he travelled for thirty one years, crossing the Atlantic on the White Star Shipping Line. Hubert Webb married Rita Corry Gotto, and about 1902 he asked his brother-in-law, James P.C. Gotto, to come into Old Bleach and set up damask weaving, which he agreed to, and German damask looms of the very best quality were installed around 1905. At this point James P.C. Gotto contributed £15,000 to the Old Bleach Linen Company, where the company shares were divided in three between Hubert Webb, Oswald Webb, and James Gotto.

Hubert's brother Oswald was involved with the linen manufacture in Randalstown, but became a soldier in the First World War, unfortunately being killed at the Somme in 1916, but leaving a young son Patrick, who in time joined the Old Bleach Company. A third brother, Norman F. Webb, known as

Roy, was on the artistic side of the business, and became responsible in the 1930s for the hand painting of linens, which came into the damask range, encompassing tray cloths, tablecloths, and huckaback towels. James P. Gotto became managing director of the weaving factory, keeping the company on a very stable footing with linen of the highest quality, until his retirement in 1944. His son Chris joined the company in 1931 becoming assistant manager on the weaving end at the factory. After the Second World War a carpet factory was set up by Old Bleach with Chris Gotto in charge, but he left after six years to pursue his interest in farming.

A third generation of the Webb family joined the company in the 1920s, Charles and Arthur, being the sons of W. Hubert Webb, and Patrick the son of the late Oswald Webb. Old Bleach linens were always of the highest quality and were exported all over the world but, unfortunately, the financial side of the business was not well managed and this increased after the Second World War. Financial problems increased in the 1950s, and, in 1959, Old Bleach was sold to Carrington-Viyella.

HRH Princess Alexandra visited the Old Bleach Company, Randalstown, on Friday, 19 February, 1965, and was shown round the factory by Mr J. Moore, the General Manager.

The sale of linen goods continued to decrease in the 1970s, and Carrington-Viyella eventually closed the factory down in the early 1980s. The production of textiles continued for a short period at the Dorma Old Bleach Works, in the former Old Bleach Carpet Factory.

Ivor Reynolds explains the colour fixation technique to Princess Alexandra at Randalstown.

KNOCKVARE
RANDALSTOWN

Charles J. Webb

Knockvare is situated at Old Staffordstown Road, south of Randalstown, with the house first recorded in 1870 as Knockvarre, the residence of Charles J. Webb and Richard T. Webb, linen manufacturers. This is a three bay, two-storey, early nineteenth century house, having bay windows on the ground floor, which may have been a later addition to the house. The roof is slated and gabled, with relatively tall chimneys, and the walls are quoined. The windows are sashed and silled on the ground floor, with a platband forming the first floor sills. Above the recessed front door is a moulded architrave.

According to Bassett in 1888:

> Mr C.J. Webb, JP, Knockvarre, Randalstown, is the head of the firm. Mr R.T. Webb resides at Landscape, Greenisland, near Belfast, but is in Randalstown every day.

The name Knockvare has altered over the years and is now spelt with only one 'r'. After the death of her husband Mrs Webb continued to live at the house, and, some years after her death, her grandson Charles J. Webb made it his family home. At present Knockvare remains in the ownership of descendants of the Webb family.

REDLANDS
RANDALSTOWN

W. Hubert Webb

Redlands, which is situated at Old Staffordstown Road, Randalstown, was built adjacent to Knockvare in 1908 for W. Hubert Webb, whose mother remained living in Knockvare. This is an Edwardian, red brick villa built in a similar style to those designed by the Dromore architect Henry Hobart. Redlands is a five bay, two plus attic storey house, with an entrance sheltered by a conservatory style porch surmounted by a tiled roof. The windows are slightly round headed, sashed and silled by a platband, which separates the ground floor from the first floor. There are bay windows on the garden side of the house.

Redlands was the home of W. Hubert Webb, his wife Rita Corry Gotto, and their family of three sons and two daughters. After the death of her parents, Heather Webb their younger daughter, who was unmarried, continued to live in Redlands. W. Hubert Webb, DL, was the senior director of the Old Bleach Linen Company, Randalstown, and President of the Belfast Chamber of Commerce in 1922, but he also became the foundation President of the Association of Northern Ireland Chambers of Commerce in 1923.

BRIARFIELD
RANDALSTOWN

Briarfield is situated along a cul-de-sac off New Street, Randalstown, and is not far from the Old Bleach Linen factory. This is a red brick Edwardian villa of considerable size, which may have had an extension built to the rear of an earlier house as it has a double roof. The house is two-storey, three-bay to the front, with an entrance porch surmounted by a tiled roof. To the side there is an attractive bay window with slated roof rising to the level of the first floor windows, which are recessed and silled. Briarfield is a combination of two-storey and to the rear three storey buildings, having slated roofs through which rise brick chimneys.

Briarfield was the home of James Porter Corry Gotto, brother-in-law of W. Hubert Webb, on whose invitation he joined the Old Bleach Linen Company, setting up their damask weaving section. He became the managing director of the weaving factory and in time was joined by two of his sons, Christopher, who assisted his father in the factory, and Felix who worked with Roy Webb in the hand painting of the damask range of linens. James Gotto made a very significant contribution to the work in the Old Bleach Linen factory.

James Porter Corry Gotto

BARNEY'S BRAE
RANDALSTOWN

Barney's Brae is situated north west of Randalstown, one and a half miles out of the town on the Portglenone Road. This is a three bay, two plus attic storey house with shallow eaves, and ornamental gables. The walls are quoined and there is a slated roof with decorated chimney stacks. It would appear that the original windows, which were recessed, sashed and silled have been replaced. On the ground floor there are bay windows on either side of the front door, which has a porch lit by tall thin windows on each side. To the left of the house is a small two-storey building which may have been the original house on the site. Barney's Brae has the appearance of having been built in the 1840s or 1850s.

This house is listed as belonging to Oswald Brooke Webb *c.* 1903, perhaps bought at the time of his marriage to Grace Patrick. He was involved in running the engineering at the Old Bleach factory at Randalstown, before joining up in

Captain Oswald Brooke Webb

1914, to fight in the First World War. Unfortunately he was killed in 1916 leaving a son Patrick Brooke Webb, who was only twelve years old when his father was killed.

Patrick Webb followed his father into Old Bleach, looking after the laundry, bleaching and dyeing. He married Rosemary Calwell in 1927, and lived in Barney's Brae, bringing up a family of three daughters.

Patrick Webb and his wife Rosemary

Sketch of Barney's Brae by Bob Ross

DRUMMAUL HOUSE
RANDALSTOWN

Drummaul House is situated centrally in Randalstown at 41 New Street, and was built in 1853 as the vicarage for the parish church of Drummaul, which is situated in a commanding position close to Randalstown. This house has been described by the Ulster Architectural Heritage Society, on buildings in Antrim and Ballymena, including Randalstown.

> A square stone block of coursed rubble basalt; a three-bay, two-storey facade, (two-bay sides with a bow window) with freestone surrounds to the windows, a projecting porch with a good fanlight; outhouses to one side. The house is in its own grounds, set well back from the road, behind trees and a hedged wall.

The roof of Drummaul House is hipped and slated, while the windows are sashed and silled.

Norman F. Webb (Roy) and his wife Dorothy moved from Hollybrook to live at Drummaul House around 1943. He took overall responsibility in the Old Bleach Linen Company for the hand painting designs, which came into the damask range of tablecloths, tray cloths, etc., in the 1930s. This was a very successful new range, and he worked with a Miss Bradshaw who was in charge of the girls employed in the hand painting of fabrics. The hand painting process was initially developed by the head chemist, Mr McCall, at the Old Bleach Works, and after his retirement by Mr Ivor Reynolds.

Drummaul House is now a nursing home.

HOLLYBROOK HOUSE
RANDALSTOWN

This house was built in 1776 probably by Adam Dickey, who according to Lawlor, in *Fibres and Fabrics Journal*, was actively engaged in the linen trade. Hollybrook House is situated about a mile north of Randalstown on the Magheralane Road, in the Parish of Drummaul, and adjacent to the River Main. Brett gives the following description of the house in his *Buildings of County Antrim*:

> A fine five-bay two-storey house, with three round-headed dormers, apparently original; roughcast, Georgian-glazed; the porch possibly later, with Greek key pattern ornament on the lintel.

Brett also suggests that the two-storey return, which is slightly lower, may have been the earlier house on the site. It is thought there was a bleaching mill on the River Main which belonged to Adam Dickey, and this borne out by an auction of the contents of Hollybrook, shown in an advertisement in the *Belfast News Letter*, 19 March 1861, which includes linen manufacturing utensils and warping mills.

Hollybrook doorcase
JFR

Latterly, for a number of years in the twentieth century Hollybrook became the home of Norman F. Webb (Roy) of the Old Bleach Linen Company. However, his nephew Arthur, who was the Old Bleach agent in London, returned to Randalstown after the outbreak of the Second World War, and in 1943 he moved to Hollybrook, while Roy moved to Drummaul House in Randalstown. Arthur Webb became a general manager in the Old Bleach factory and a director of the company.

Since then, Hollybrook House has had a number of owners.

```
SALE TO-MORROW.
HOLLYBROOK, RANDALSTOWN.
SALE OF
FURNITURE, PRINTS, HORSES, TAX-CART,
COWS, CALVES, FARMING IMPLEMENTS,
THRESHING-MACHINE, LINEN SCREW-
PRESS, WARPING-MILLS, &c.
```
To be Sold by AUCTION, at HOLLYBROOK HOUSE, near Randalstown, on WEDNESDAY, 20th March, at Eleven o'clock,

THE HOUSEHOLD FURNITURE, COMPRISING Mahogany Pedestal Sideboard; Pillar Dining-Table, Centre and Two Ends; Mahogany Couch and Chairs in Hair-Web; Rosewood Pillar Loo Table, Rosewood Victoria Chairs, Sweep-back Chairs, and Cabriole Seat, in Crimson Damask; Mahogany Couch, covered in same Damask; Mahogany Cabinet and What-not; Polished Metal Fenders and Fire-Irons; Japanned Coal Vase; Tapestry and other Carpets; Hearth Rugs; a number of Framed Engravings, including "Horse Shoeing," "Dignity and Impudence," and "Death of the Stag," by Landseer, with others; French Table Lamp; Hall Lamp; Mahogany Four-post and Albert Bedsteads and Hangings; Birch French Bedsteads; Feather Beds; Hair Mattresses and Bedding; Mahogany Dressing Tables and Glasses, Wash Stands, Bedsteps; Bedroom Chairs, Window Curtains, Carpets, &c.; Dinner Service of Stoneware, Tin Dish Covers, Evening China, Cut Glass Decanters, &c.; Kitchen Tables and Cooking Utensils; a large LINEN SCREW PRESS, with Brass Box; Office Desks, Deal Yarn Press; Measuring Machines and other Manufacturing Utensils, Yarn Poles, &c.

HARNESS and FARM HORSES; TAX-CART and Harness, Saddles, Bridles, Side-Saddle; MILCH COWS; CALVES; a new Two-Horse THRESHING MACHINE, by Abercrombie and Craig, of Paisley, with Churning Gearing attached; Carts and Harness; Metal Pig Trough; Farming Implements, &c.

Terms—CASH. Purchasers to pay the Auction Fees.

The Stock, Farm Implements, &c., will be sold at Two o'clock.

GEO. C. HYNDMAN, Auctioneer.
1043   7, Castle Place, Belfast.

YOUNG FAMILY TREE

This is an abbreviated Family Tree referring only to male family members involved in the linen industry.

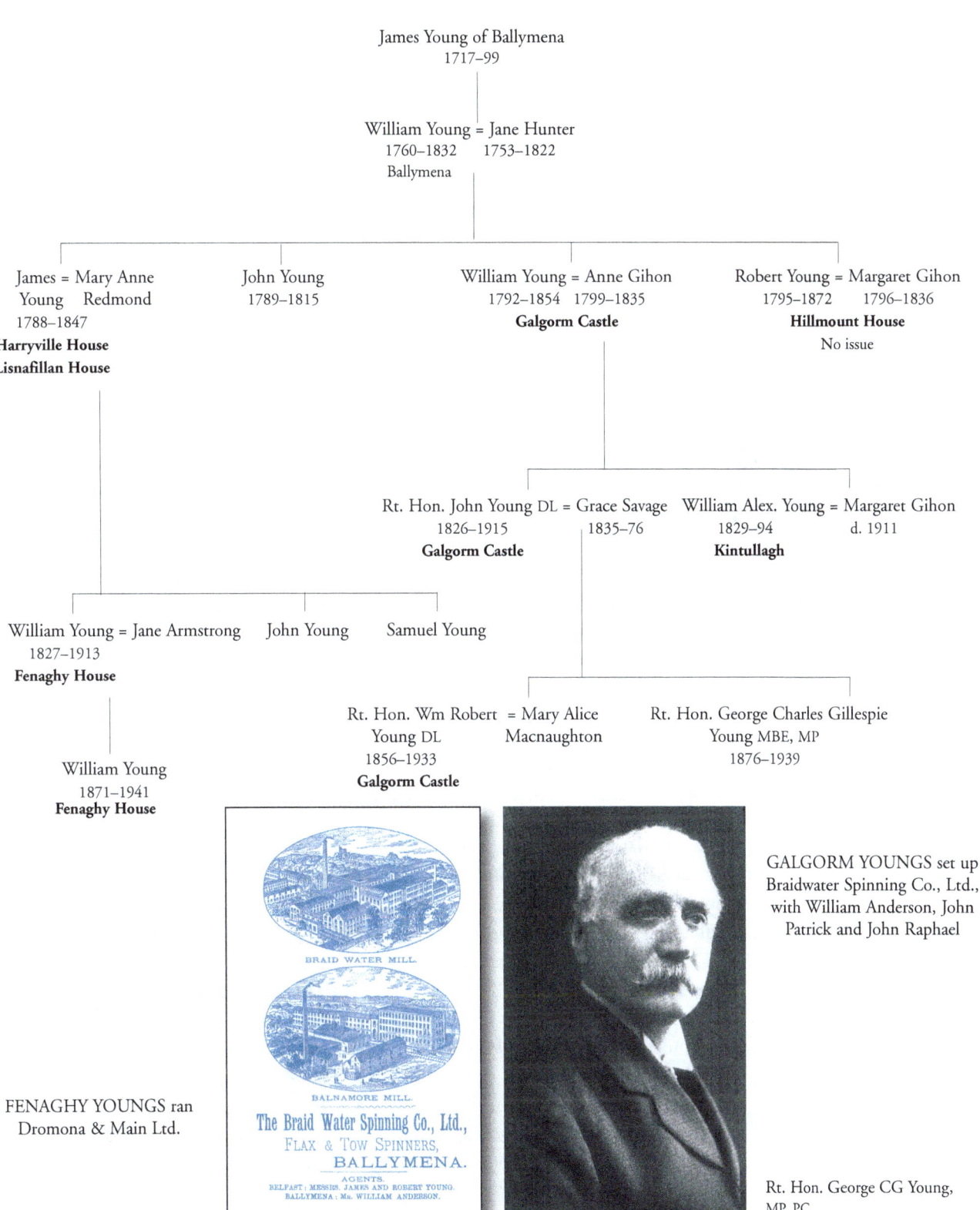

James Young of Ballymena
1717–99

William Young = Jane Hunter
1760–1832   1753–1822
Ballymena

James = Mary Anne   John Young   William Young = Anne Gihon   Robert Young = Margaret Gihon
Young   Redmond   1789–1815   1792–1854   1799–1835   1795–1872   1796–1836
1788–1847   **Galgorm Castle**   **Hillmount House**
Harryville House   No issue
Lisnafillan House

Rt. Hon. John Young DL = Grace Savage   William Alex. Young = Margaret Gihon
1826–1915   1835–76   1829–94   d. 1911
Galgorm Castle   **Kintullagh**

William Young = Jane Armstrong   John Young   Samuel Young
1827–1913
Fenaghy House

William Young
1871–1941
Fenaghy House

Rt. Hon. Wm Robert = Mary Alice   Rt. Hon. George Charles Gillespie
Young DL   Macnaughton   Young MBE, MP
1856–1933   1876–1939
Galgorm Castle

FENAGHY YOUNGS ran
Dromona & Main Ltd.

GALGORM YOUNGS set up
Braidwater Spinning Co., Ltd.,
with William Anderson, John
Patrick and John Raphael

Rt. Hon. George CG Young,
MP, PC

THE YOUNG FAMILY
OF BALLYMENA

Rt Hon John Young, PC, DL

Lawlor in *Fibres and Fabrics Journal*, August 1942, states that the founder of this family was a James Young (1717–99), who was a general merchant in Ballymena. His son William (1760–1832) succeeded to his father's business, but also, in 1800, took over the linen business of the Browns of Broughshane. This occurred when the last of the Brown family of Glencairn migrated to join their relatives already established in Baltimore, Philadelphia, and New York, now the world-wide international banking house of Brown Shipley & Co. The Browns had not only been linen drapers, buying hand spun yarn, but also had owned an extensive bleach works near Broughshane. William Young & Sons acquired the Lisnafillan Bleach Works about 1820, and in 1825 also bought the Hillmount works, James, the eldest son, moving to Lisnafillan House, having lived at Harryville House. At this time the Hillmount bleaching works were owned by Mr John Hill, but he became bankrupt, and Hillmount House, the bleach green and mill, were sold to the Young family. Brett states that Hillmount House was occupied by Robert Young (1795–1872), the buying partner in the family firm.

William Young died in 1832, and his sons James and Robert ran the firm as 'James and Robert Young', with considerable assistance from the third son William, who was an eminent and skilled physician. According to Lawlor:

> It prospered exceedingly, and with Brown, Shipley & Co., as its agents in America the business spread extensively in North and South America and the Spanish Pacific Colonies.

In 1845 James Young purchased the bleaching works, surrounding demesne, and Fenaghy House, from the representatives of Samuel Cunningham. James Young died in 1847 leaving three sons, William, John, and Samuel, but only William continued in the business, living in Fenaghy House. The firm of James and Robert Young progressed in the bleaching and finishing business under William Young (1827–1913), and his son William (1871–1941), adding to the works at Fenaghy those at Cullybackey and Dromona, all, eventually, being combined in the company, Dromona & Main Limited.

Meanwhile, Dr William Young (1792–1854) of Ballymena, third son of William, founded the firm of William Young & Sons, which flourished, and, in 1850, he purchased the Castle and estate of Galgorm from Stephen, third Earl of Mount Cashel. He died in 1854, leaving two sons, the Rt. Hon. John Young,

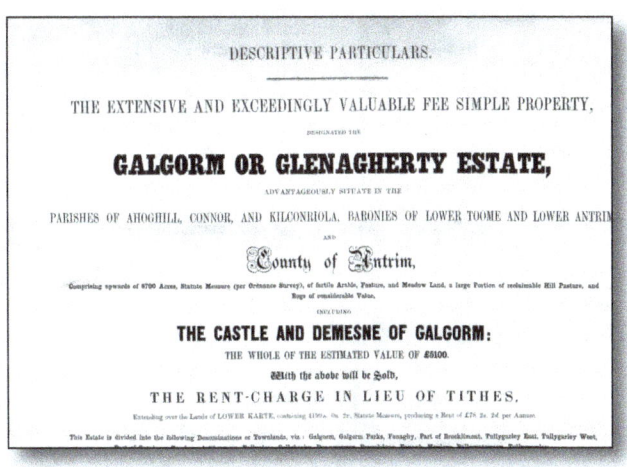

Sale of Galgorm Castle
PRONI D/3027/3/9

DL (1826–1915) of Galgorm Castle, and William Alexander Young, (1829–94) of Kintullagh, Ballymena. In 1865 the Galgorm Youngs, joined by William Anderson, John Patrick, and John Raphael, founded the Braid Water Spinning Company, Ltd. in Ballymena, which was highly successful in the boom in the linen trade caused by the American Civil War. The Ballymena mill was built on the west bank of the Braid, opening in 1866, and, over a period of years, various extensions were made to the buildings. The Balnamore Spinning Mill, Ballymoney, was bought by the Braid Water Spinning Company in 1886, substantially adding to the spinning capacity of the company.

The Rt. Hon. John Young, PC, DL, LLD, of Galgorm Castle, was for many years Chairman of the Board of Directors of the Braid Water Spinning Company. Mr Young was prominent in the administration of the local affairs of County Antrim, and was a member of the old Grand Jury. He was elected President of the Belfast and Northern Ireland Chambers of Commerce in 1879, and also became President of the Linen Merchants' Association. He had a long connection with the Northern Counties Railway Company, and his public services were recognised by a Privy Councillorship, and other honours.

Rt. Hon. John Young, DL

The Rt. Hon. William R. Young, PC, DL, was the eldest of the twelve children of the Rt. Hon. John Young, and succeeded his father in Galgorm Castle. He was largely identified with the linen industry in Northern Ireland, and was Managing Director of W.R. Young & Co., Bedford Street, Belfast, linen merchants. He was an active member of the Ulster Unionist Council, in 1919 being made a Privy Councillor for Ireland, and in 1920 was appointed High Sheriff for County Antrim.

The Board of the Braid Water Spinning Company consisted of: Messrs George C.G. Young, Malcolm Patrick of Dunminning, Samuel Anderson of Balee, Frank Cooke of John Preston & Sons, and Samuel J. McConnell, Managing Director. The Rt. Hon. George C.G. Young represented the predominant Young interests in the company accounts, but left the running of the Mill to S.G. McConnell. In politics he was the Member of Parliament for Bann Side being a strong supporter of Lord Craigavon, and was appointed a Privy Councillor in 1936. Following in his fathers' interests he was a director of the Northern Counties Railway Company, but died in August, 1939.

GALGORM CASTLE
BALLYMENA

This is a double-pile house built between 1627 and 1645 by Rev. Dr Alexander Colville for his own use, and situated on the Galgorm Road a short distance west of Ballymena. In effect the house is a combination of two gabled houses built side by side with a thick central wall, seven feet wide, carrying the chimney stacks, and dividing two sets of rooms. At the front Galgorm Castle is a five-bay, three-storey high building with a central convex then concave Dutch gable; the sides of the house are two-bay, four-storey high with attics. The Ulster Architectural Heritage Society in its publication on historic buildings in Antrim and Ballymena, 1969, regarding Galgorm Castle states:

The rooms were still panelled in oak when Mrs Delaney visited the house (then called Mount Colville) in 1758. Only the oak stair with turned balusters and large round heads to the newels remains of this work.

About 1830, when owned by the Rt. Hon. Stephen, Earl of Mount Cashel, Galgorm Castle was modernised with regular

William Robert Young, DL
Photograph taken *c.* 1910

Doorcase
JFR

Galgorm Castle
DR WILLIAM ROULSTON

GALGORM CASTLE

Side view of Galgorm Castle and above the gate lodge
JFR

bays of sash windows in brick surrounds being inserted, and twenty years later Flemish curves were added to the gables, and the front doorcase.

Galgorm Castle was sold up by the Encumbered Estates Court in November, 1850, the earl of Mount Cashel having become bankrupt, and it was bought by Dr William Young, MD, who had previously lived in the town of Ballymena, beside the offices of James and Robert Young, Linen Merchants & Bleachers. Galgorm Castle has a gate lodge, which, according to Dean, was built by Dr William Young *c.* 1852. He states:

> A lodge, compared to the big house, plain. In basalt, solid three bay below a hipped roof. It replaced an earlier pre 1832 building.

After the death of Dr William Young in 1854 Galgorm Castle was occupied by his elder son, the Rt. Hon. John Young, DL, who was involved with others in the setting up of the Braid Water Spinning Mill in Ballymena. The building, although unoccupied, remains owned by his descendants.

Galgorm Castle from the *Dublin Penny Journal*, 1834

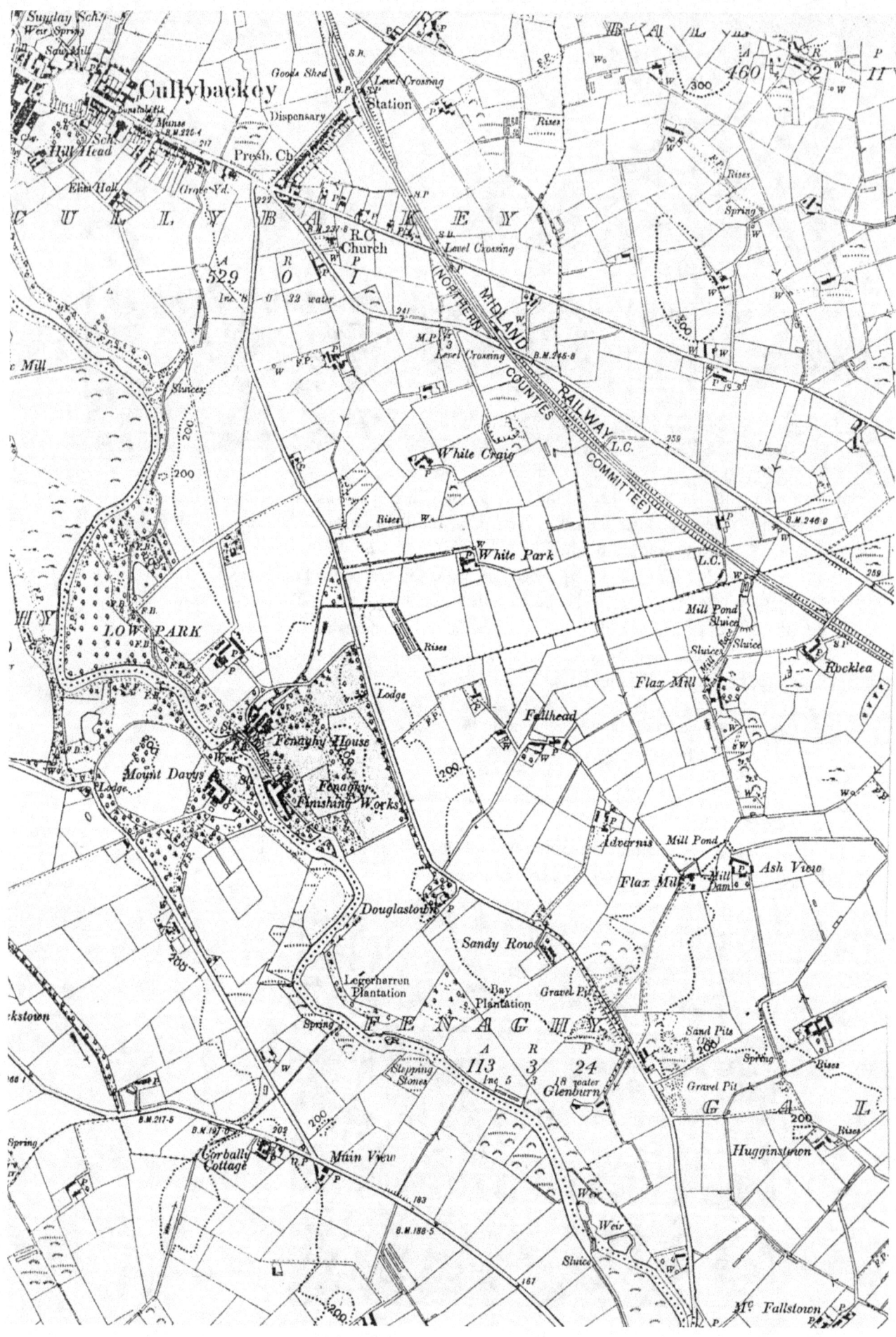

FENAGHY HOUSE
CULLYBACKEY

William L.R. Young

The wooded demesne and residence of Fenaghy belonged to the Young family from 1845, when it was purchased by Mr James Young (1788–1847) from the Cunningham family. In the Ordnance Survey Memoirs of 1833, for the Parish of Ahoghill, Fenaghy is described as 'a neat 2-storey house, the residence of Mrs McMannus', who was renting it for three years from Mr Samuel Cunningham. The original house on the site is thought to have been pre-1780, but this was demolished, and Mr William Young (1827–1913) had a new house erected on the same site *c.* 1857, along with two gate lodges. Dean gives the following description:

> Delightfully situated on the bank of the River Main, the house and each of its gate lodges all contemporary in vastly differing styles. The house is extravagant Italianate looking very like the work of Thomas Jackson who is known to have worked for a Mr Young in the Ballymena area.

The gate lodge at the main entrance, which is particularly attractive, is Tudor in style with Dutch gables, and lattice panes in the windows; accepted as being by Charles Lanyon.

Fenaghy House doorcase
JFR

Fenaghy House is a five-bay, two-storey stucco villa with a projecting two-storey porch, which is quoined and has Doric columns. On the ground floor the windows are of greater height than those on the first floor, and are heavily articulated with architraves, console brackets, and moulded surrounds. The slated roof, with its elaborately moulded cornice, is partially hidden behind a parapet, with the chimneys rising at either end of the building. At the south west side of the house there were two conservatories, and outside the large walled garden there was a range of lean-to glasshouses growing peaches, nectarines, and vines. These have all now gone as Fenaghy House was converted to a hotel in 1992. The attractive elevated site of the house was described by Craig Wallace, in *Gardens in Mid-Antrim*, 1960.

The tall windows of Fenaghy, home of Mr and Mrs W.L. Young and of the Young family, for over a century, look out upon a long vista of sloping lawns merging into fields, which, framed by trees to right and left, rise gradually to the skyline beyond.

On the eighty acre site the Young family had their mill and bleach green, being adjacent to the River Main.

River Main at Fenaghy
JFR

Ardvernis House
JFR

ARDVERNIS HOUSE
GALGORM

Ardvernis, situated on the Fenaghy Road at Galgorm, near Ballymena, is approached up a long curving avenue, lined with mature beech trees, and was formerly a part of the Fenaghy property. With regard to Advernis, Brett states:

> A nineteenth century stucco gentleman's cottage, said to date from 1839, just too late for inclusion in the first Ordnance Survey maps or memoirs, and to have been built by the then owners of Fenaghy.

However, Lawlor, in writing about the Dickey family, indicates that around 1800 Adam and John Dickey ran the Lowtown linen bleaching works between Cullybackey and Fenaghy on the left bank of the Main River. Lawlor writes:

> Adam Dickey lived in the old Georgian House, Ardvernis, near the works.

Lawlor also states that Samuel Cunningham, who succeeded his father in Lisnafillan, built the works and the original house at Fenaghy, a mile or so up the Main River on the opposite side. Samuel Cunningham died in 1834, and Ardvernis House became the Cunningham home from 1845 to 1909. William, the only son, died unmarried in 1850, leaving his mother, and sisters, Catherine and Jane, at Ardvernis. They worshipped at the old Presbyterian Meeting House,

CUNNINGHAM FAMILY TREE

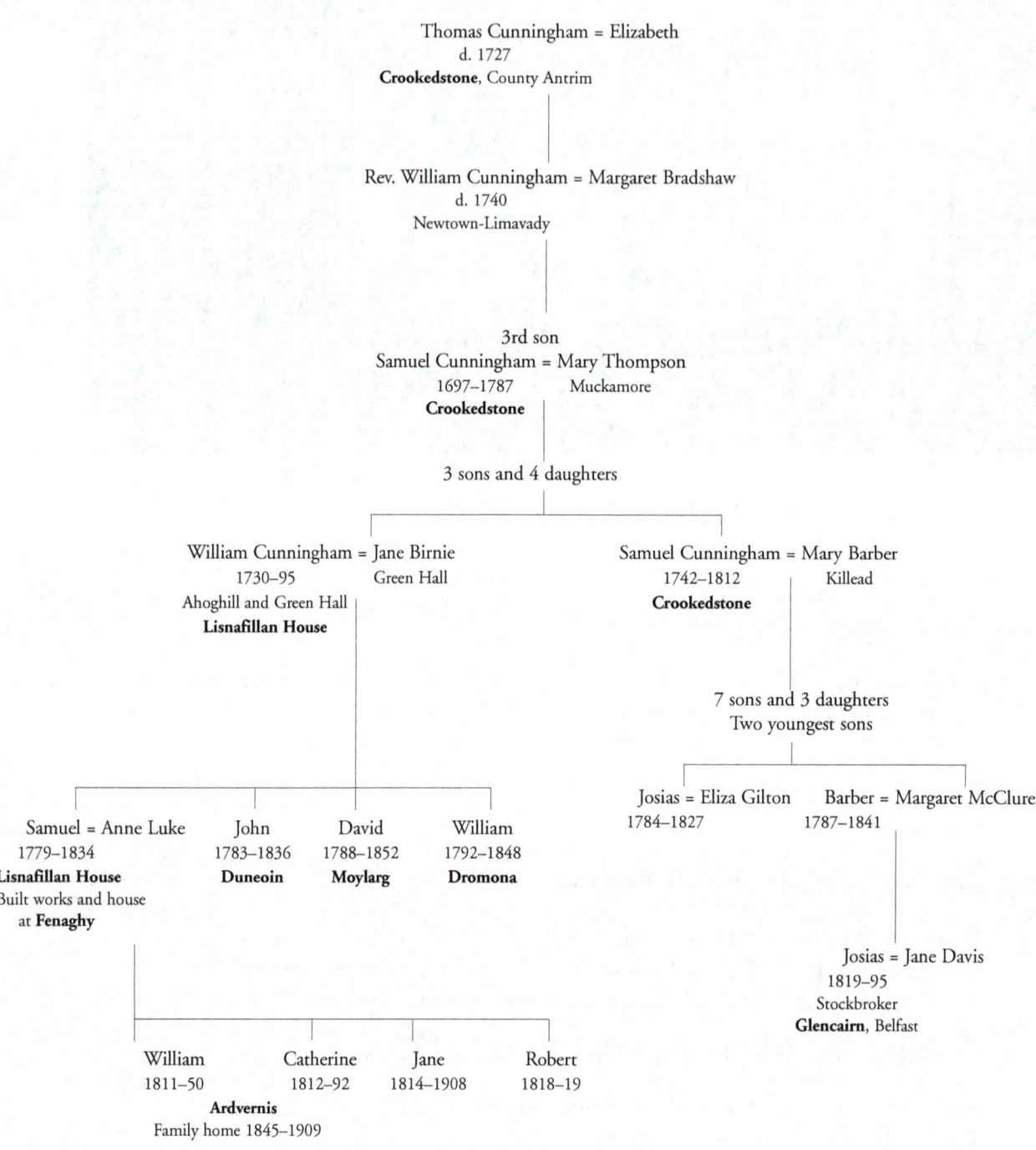

established in 1727 in Cullybackey, and, in 1880, the Misses Catherine and Jane Cunningham expressed a wish to erect a new building in memory of their mother. The Cunningham Memorial Church, Cullybackey, opened in September 1881, and remains a very impressive building at the end of the main street in the village.

Advernis House is a three-bay, one storey with attics house, which has a slated roof with a chimney stack at each end of the roof ridge. The central doorcase is recessed, having a fanlight and side lights. Originally the large windows at the front had sixteen panes but Ardvernis has recently been modernised and the windows are now twelve paned, set in a formal architrave with simple hood moulding above. There are attic windows in the gables, and a later two-storey extension at the rear, which may have been built by the Cunningham family in 1845. Ardvernis House now contains three reception rooms on the ground floor with a capacious entrance hall and modern kitchen. The first floor has five bedrooms including a master bedroom with ensuite facilities.

Anne Cunningham
CONGRGATIONAL ARCHIVE CULLYBACKEY

Catherine and Jane Cunningham
CONGRGATIONAL ARCHIVE CULLYBACKEY

The avenue leading to Ardvernis House

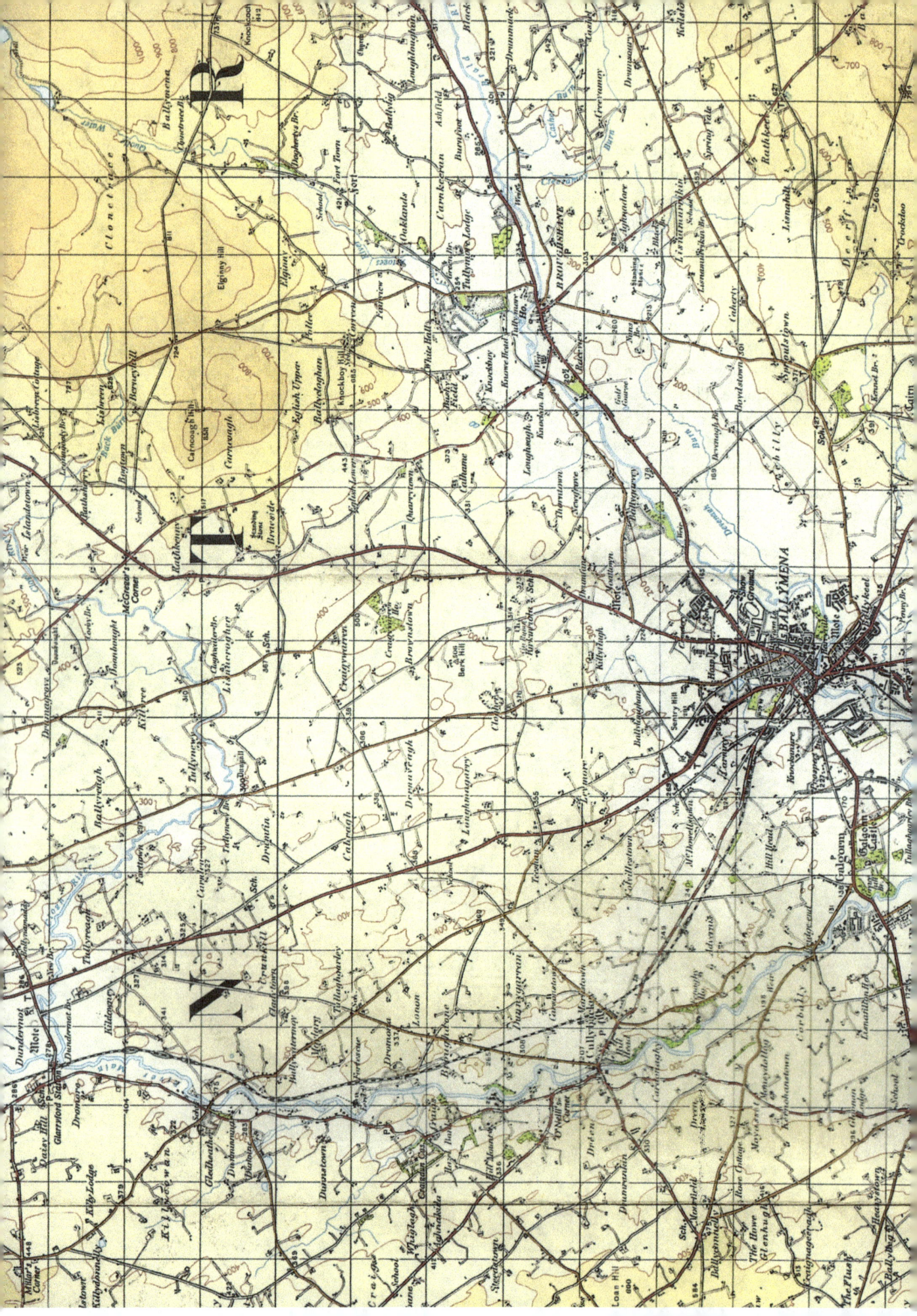

5
MAIN VALLEY
WEST COUNTY ANTRIM

OLD CULLYBACKEY

PATRICK FAMILY TREE

The Patrick Family Tree shows family members involved in the linen trade.

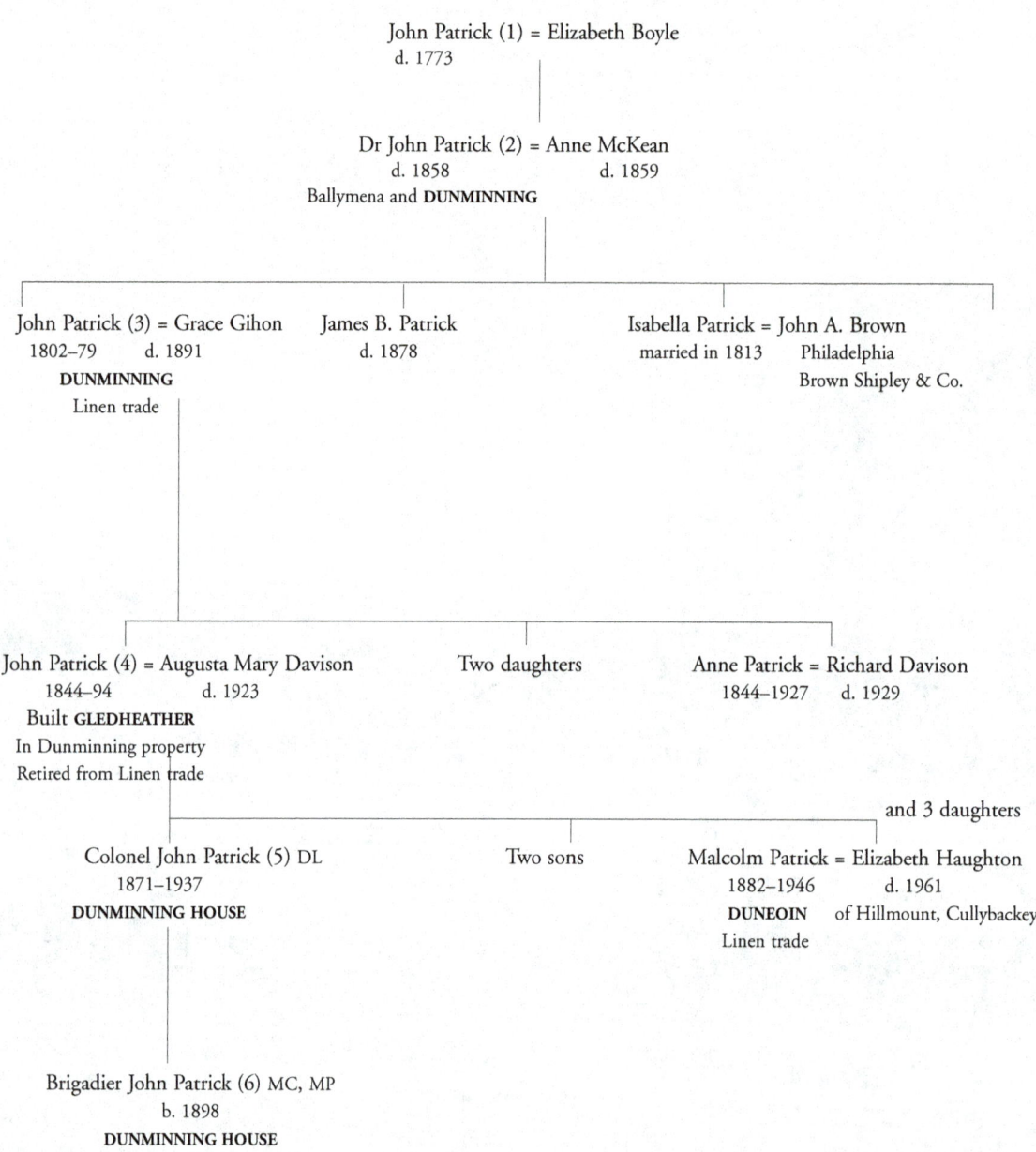

THE PATRICK FAMILY
OF DUNMINNING AND BALLYMENA

In the early years of the nineteenth century Dr John Patrick was an eminent medical practitioner in Ballymena, but he also was engaged in the linen trade, living in Bridge Street over his warehouse and consulting room. However, around 1840, he purchased from the Birneys, who emigrated to America, their bleach works, with the early Georgian house adjoining at Dunminning, Glarryford, on the Main River. Dr Patrick died in 1858, and was succeeded at Dunminning by his son John (3) who carried on the linen business for many years, living in Dunminning House. Dr Patrick also left a daughter Isabella, who had married in 1813 John A. Brown of Philadelphia, formerly of Broughshane, of the firm Brown Shipley & Co. John Patrick (3) married Grace, daughter of William Gihon, further enhancing the relationship with other linen families. He was very successful in the linen business, and with the wide business connection of the Browns in America, extended it profitably.

John Patrick (4), having inherited a considerable fortune from his father, retired from the linen trade and built the house Gledheather on the Dunminning estate. He married Augusta Mary Davison, daughter of John Davison of Raceview, another linen family, and left four sons, the eldest being Colonel John Patrick (5), DL. The youngest son, Malcolm, continued the family linen tradition by owning the old bleach works at Duneoin, at one time owned by John and William Cunningham, sons of William Cunningham of Lisnafillan, but running it as a flax processing mill. Malcolm Patrick married Elizabeth F. Haughton, only daughter of Thomas Wilfred Haughton, of Hillmount, Cullybackey, linking the Patricks to another well known linen family. Malcolm's youngest sister, Grace Patrick, married Oswald Brook Webb of the Old Bleach Linen Company, Randalstown.

Captain John Patrick, JP

DUNMINNING HOUSE
GLARRYFORD

Front door of Dunminning House
JFR

Dunminning House is situated on the Dunminning Road, Glarryford, and is a late Georgian mill owner's house. This is a five-bay, two-storey house over a basement, which to the front has been filled in. The walls are roughcast painted white, and the steep slated roof has large chimney stacks at either end. There is an elegant front door, which has a broad fanlight with side lights and reeded pilasters.

The Ordnance Survey Memoirs of 1833 for the Parish of Rasharkin record this house:

> Dunminning, the residence of Thomas Birnie Esquire, is a neat, modern and commodious dwelling, prettily situated in the townland of the same name and near the Main river, the banks of which for more than a mile are beautifully varied and clothed with a thriving plantation of fir, larch and some ash and beech, the property of Mr Birnie. There is a handsome lawn and numerous and extensive walks in the plantings.

However, prior to this Atkinson, in about 1817, describes Dunminning showing its importance to the linen trade:

DUNMINNING HOUSE

It is the seat of Thomas M Birnie, Esq. and comprehends a handsome modern edifice, on a lawn pleasingly elevated and imbosomed in hills; 10 acres of demesne and farm lands, and a valuable establishment in the bleaching department, in which 15,000 pieces of linens are annually finished, besides double that number in a brown state, under the firm of Birnie and Conyngham.

At some point in time between 1836 and 1840 Thomas Birnie, who had become a very wealthy man, emigrated to America, and the Dunminning bleachworks were purchased by Dr Patrick of Ballymena. His son John Patrick continued, very successfully, bleaching linen but later generations of the family, although living in Dunminning House, did not continue in the linen trade.

DUNMINNING COTTAGE
GLARRYFORD

Dunminning Cottage, Glarryford, apparently built about 1810 to house the toll keeper for Dunminning Bridge over the River Main. This is a charming example of the use of traditional materials made 'Gothic' simply by the pointed shape of its doors and windows. The cottage was bought by the Patricks of Dunminning House as a residence for their gardener, and a matching pointed doorway was opened in the demesne wall immediately opposite. This is a delightful rendered thatched cottage with an arched door and small sash windows.

River Main at Dunminning

DUNEOIN
CULLYBACKEY

Duneoin is situated on the Duneoin Road, Cullybackey, and is about five miles from Ballymena. According to Bassett, writing in 1888, Duneoin Green was established around the beginning of the nineteenth century by Mr John Cunningham, and in 1837 he was reported to be bleaching about 34,000 webs annually. Bassett also states that he built a comfortable private residence, which had a handsomely planted lawn and pretty gardens. Duneoin is a three-bay, two-storey house with attic windows in the gables, having white painted walls and a slated roof. The front door, which is approached by eight steps, has a radial fanlight, sidelights and reeding.

The Ordnance Survey Memoirs of 1835 for the Parish of Rasharkin mention this house but spell the name differently:

> Dunoyne, the residence of John Cunningham Esquire, is a pretty cottage situated in the townland of Dunminning.

John Cunningham (1779–1836), second son of William Cunningham of Lisnafillan, and a descendent of Thomas Cunningham of Crookedstone, is mentioned as being in the linen trade by Lawlor in September 1941:

> [He] built or purchased the bleach works at Duneoin on the Main river near

Glarryford: in this he was succeeded by his son William who apparently died without issue. Duneoin then passed through the hands successively of Thomas Giffen, John Woods and John McIlroy. In recent years it has been converted into a flax processing works by Mr Malcolm Patrick, MP, of the Dunminning family, its present owner.

However, Malcolm Patrick's heirs sold the house in 1962.

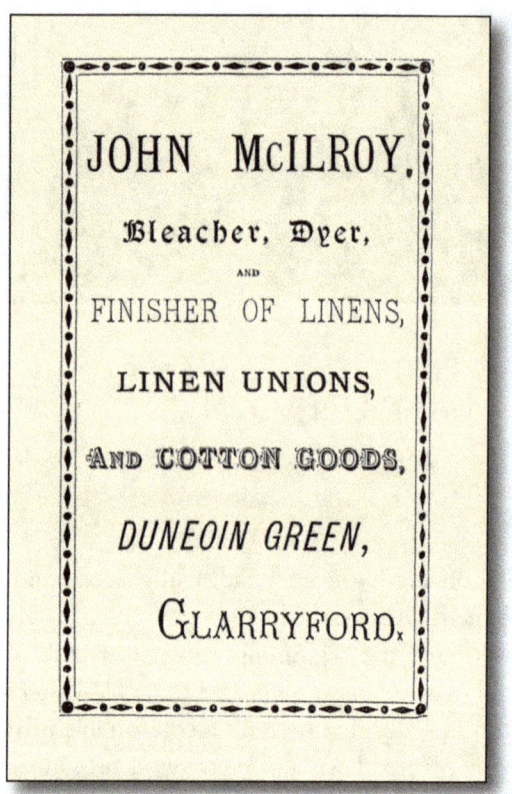

HILLMOUNT HOUSE
CULLYBACKEY

Hillmount House is situated in a wooded valley about one and a quarter miles from Cullybackey on the Hillmount Road, and is approached by a lime avenue which sweeps past fields to the entrance. Lawlor has recorded that the bleach works erected by the Hills of Hillmount, was amongst the earliest in Ulster, and indicates that their bleach works probably date from about 1710. Over one hundred years later the Ordnance Survey Memoirs of 1833 record Hillmount in the Parish of Ahoghill:

> Hillmount, the residence of Robert Young Esquire, is seated on the banks of the Main, in the townland of Craigs.

Hillmount has been described by Brett as a fine three-storey Georgian mill owners' house, which could have been built by a member of the Hill family around 1720, probably around 1760, but certainly prior to 1778. The house is shown as the seat of Mr John Hill on Lendrick's map of 1780, and on Williamson's revision map of 1808. The main central building of Hillmount House is five bays wide, with triple windows in the middle above the doorway, which is particularly fine, having reeded engaged columns, geometrical glazing bars in the side lights, and a shallow fanlight. The roof is slated with the chimneys at the gable ends, and as the gables are topped by crow-stepped upstands, Brett has suggested that there may have been an earlier thatched roof. During the Napoleonic wars the Hill family prospered and added the single storey bow fronted bays at either side of Hillmount House, as well as excavating a lake in front of the house.

Hillmount is a house of unusually high quality, and this is borne out in Brett's detailed description:

Hillmount House doorway
JFR

There are many elegant details inside and out: the keystones have pretty little balls atop; the quoins are nicely reversed where the side bows overlap the main facade; the stone window sills are supported on pairs of neat little consoles; there are no downspouts on the front, the rainwater is carried away round the sides. Inside, there is restrained reeding in the woodwork of window and door cases, and even in the unusual projecting chair-rails.

Unfortunately, by 1825 the Hills had fallen on bad times, and Mr Hill was imprisoned for debt in Carrickfergus Gaol. Later, as is shown in the auction advertisement, it was there that Dr William Young, of Ballymena, negotiated the purchase of Hillmount House, the bleach green, and mill, on behalf of his sons Messrs James and Robert Young. Writing in the *Fibres & Fabrics Journal*, of March 1942, Lawlor comments:

The Youngs, who were running Lisnafillan works at this time, continued as owners of Hillmount for many years, Robert Young living in Hillmount House. In 1881, Robert Young having died without issue, Hillmount was sold to Messrs. Frazer & Haughton, Ltd., in whose hands it has developed and prospered to the present time.

> **AUCTIONS.**
>
> **COUNTY OF ANTRIM.**
> TO BE SOLD BY AUCTION,
> At Messrs. HYNDMAN'S AUCTION MART, in CASTLE-PLACE, Belfast, on MONDAY, the 29th October next, at TWO o'Clock in the Afternoon,
> THE BLEACH-MILLS, HOUSE, and LANDS, of HILLMOUNT, situate about three Miles from Ballymena, three from Portglenone, and 20 from Belfast. On these premises are situated one of the most extensive and best circumstanced LINEN BLEACH-GREENS in the North of Ireland, with a superabundant and never-failing supply of Head and Spring Water, having a good fall, and the entire command of the River Main; most conveniently situated, being contiguous to some of the best Linen Markets in Ulster; the MACHINERY is in complete order. The DWELLING-HOUSE is one of the most commodious in the County, containing every requisite convenience for an extensive establishment, with suitable Offices, all in perfect repair. On the Land, which is held for Lives Renewable for Ever, at a low Rent, a considerable sum has been expended in useful and ornamental Plantings and Improvements. The Gardens are large and well stocked, and the entire concern, for beauty and convenience, can scarcely be excelled. For many years no Concern has been offered for sale in the North of Ireland, so well meriting the attention of Linen Merchants. There is Turbary and also Coal Mine in the neighbourhood.
> For particulars, apply to Messrs. ALEX. and JOHN MONTGOMERY, 25, Arthur-street, Belfast. No other person is authorized or can give any information.
> Belfast, 25th Sept., 1832. (98

During the 1880s Messrs Frazer & Haughton spent a considerable sum of money on remodelling the buildings and machinery for bleaching and finishing linens, sheetings, and damasks of every description. Both Mr J.W. Frazer, JP, and Mr T.W. Haughton, with their respective families, lived in Hillmount House until 1921, when the Haughtons moved to Harperstown House, which they had built on the Hillmount Road, Cullybackey.

The following excerpt from a brief history of the company (T2062/3) is of interest:

> The firm of Frazer & Haughton Ltd. was established in the year 1883, the original Partners being Mr J.W. Frazer and Mr T.W. Haughton, both of whom had been engaged in the Linen trade in the firm of Thomas Haughton & Co., Banford, Co. Down owned by Mr T.W. Haughton's uncle.
>
> The new firm set up a merchanting business in Belfast supplying various types of Linen goods both in the Home, Continental and American Markets.
>
> In the course of their activities they acquired from Mr William Young the Hillmount Bleach Works situated at Cullybackey, Co. Antrim. These works had a high reputation and were chiefly engaged in bleaching and finishing Plain Linen Goods for the Belfast merchants.

Hillmount House remains owned by descendants of Mr John W. Frazer.

HARPERSTOWN HOUSE
CULLYBACKEY

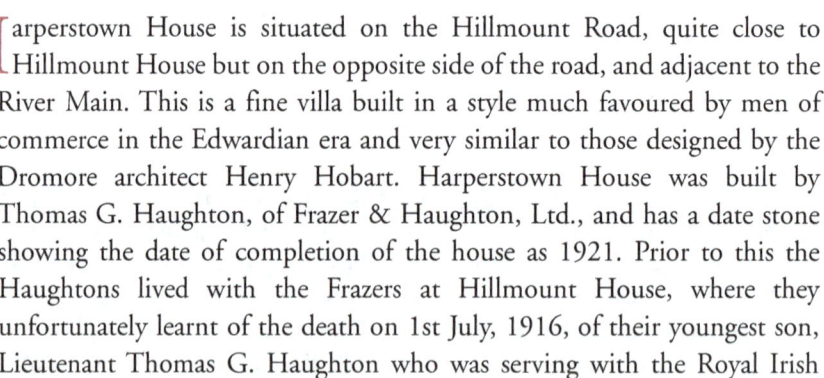

Date stone
JFR

Harperstown House is situated on the Hillmount Road, quite close to Hillmount House but on the opposite side of the road, and adjacent to the River Main. This is a fine villa built in a style much favoured by men of commerce in the Edwardian era and very similar to those designed by the Dromore architect Henry Hobart. Harperstown House was built by Thomas G. Haughton, of Frazer & Haughton, Ltd., and has a date stone showing the date of completion of the house as 1921. Prior to this the Haughtons lived with the Frazers at Hillmount House, where they unfortunately learnt of the death on 1st July, 1916, of their youngest son, Lieutenant Thomas G. Haughton who was serving with the Royal Irish Rifles in France.

Harperstown House is a three bay, two-storey plus attic house, where the outside is stuccoed, hiding the brick work. The entrance is sheltered by a loggia style porch surmounted by a tiled roof, and the windows are mostly tripartite and silled. The slated roof is hipped with the roof ridges tiled, and tall chimneys rise through and above the height of the roof. Set in a very attractive wooded site, the house has two bay windows on the garden front, one bay rising to the first floor, and a large attic tripartite window overlooking the garden.

T Wilfred Haughton

Mr T.W. Haughton JP, became chairman of the company in the early 1900s, and was also elected as President of the Linen Merchants' Association in 1912. Thomas Wilfred Haughton (1855–1936) was followed in Harperstown House, Cullybackey, by his eldest son, John Wilfred Haughton, CBE, (1886–1961), who served in the First World War, and later worked in Frazer & Haughton, Ltd. Additionally, J.W. Haughton was President of the Ulster Tourist Board 1952–61, and also President of the Ulster Automobile Club 1953–61.

Rear of Harperstown House
JFR

RED COTTAGE
CULLYBACKEY

Situated on the same side of the road as Hillmount House, but closer to Cullybackey, Red Cottage is very different to other houses in the neighbourhood. This is a two-storey multi-gabled house which shows the influence of the Arts and Crafts movement started by William Morris in the mid-nineteenth century, although Red Cottage appears to have been built in 1920–21. The feature of the red tiled roof is echoed in the tiling of the loggia style porch which extends across a major portion of the front of the house.

Red Cottage was the home of Samuel Gillmor Haughton (1889–1959), second son of Thomas Wilfred Haughton, and Dorothy Lyall Wilson, who married in September 1912. S.G. Haughton served in the Second World War, was MP for County Antrim 1945–50, High Sheriff 1955, and for a period became Managing Director of Frazer & Haughton, Ltd., linen bleachers.

KILCONWAY
CULLYBACKEY

This house was possibly built in the latter half of the nineteenth century for the manager of the bleach green at Hillmount, as it is adjacent to the bleach green and the River Main, being on the Hillmount Road. Kilconway House is a three-bay, two-storey substantial stone house, which has a conservatory to one side. The main windows, which are sashed and silled, have brick surrounds, and there are triple windows on either side of the front door, which has a fanlight and side lights; attic windows can be seen at the sides of the house. The roof is slated with a red tiled ridge, and has brick chimneys rising at either end.

Kilconway House was the home of Wilfred James Haughton (1921–99), eldest son of John Wilfred Haughton CBE, of Harperstown House. His principal work was as an artist but he had an additional interest in Frazer & Haughton, Ltd., at Hillmount. Wilfred J. Haughton married, in 1944, Priscilla Elizabeth McLaughlin, who was a daughter of E.F. McLaughlin, Director of McLaughlin & Harvey, and they had three sons and one daughter.

Wilfred J. Haughton (Junior)
UAHS

ROBINSON FAMILY TREE

S. J. ROBINSON,
Yarn Boiling
AND
Bleaching Works,
KILLYLODGE MILLS,
GLARRYFORD.

Hugh Robinson = Susannah McKay
1760–1836   died aged 99
KILLYLODGE
Glarryford
Linen manufacturer

Hugh Robinson = Jane Tomb   plus four sons   plus three daughters
1816–56   d. 1890
KILLYLODGE
Glarryford
Linen manufacturer
Drowned at sea on voyage
to America

Alexander Gaston Robinson = Mary R. Harkness   Stewart John Robinson = Alicia A. Motherwell
1844–1925   d. 1918   1847–1921   1852–1940
KILLYLODGE   **DROMONA**
Glarryford   Craigs, Cullybackey
Linen manufacturer   Dromona Dyeing & Finishing Works

Robinson family

DROMONA
CULLYBACKEY

Dromona House, which was close to the River Main, at Craigs, Cullybackey, was built in the early years of the nineteenth century, but, unfortunately, has been demolished. The property is mentioned in the Ordnance Survey Memoirs for the Parish of Ahoghill, 1833.

> Dromona, the residence of William Cunningham, is situated on the River Main, in the townland of Moylarg.

This was a substantial five bay, two-storey house, which had bay windows at either end of the front of the house. There was a hipped, slated roof with a moulded cornice, and solid chimneys stacks rising above it. The windows were sashed and silled, but had not retained their Georgian glazing. One of the very interesting aspects of Dromona House was the entrance, set within an arch with decorative roof supported on two Tuscan pilasters.

According to William Shaw, writing about Cullybackey in 1912, a Mr Batts erected mills for the finishing of linen goods at Dromona about the year 1800. The business was then carried on by William Cunningham, youngest son of William Cunningham of Lisnafillan. After his death in 1848 John McVickar continued the linen business, and in the 1860s Griffith's Valuation records him in Dromona House with 86 acres of land and beetling mills. Stewart John Robinson became the owner of the property in 1889, and made great improvements in the buildings and machinery, even having a private line of

1914 Darracq car at Dromona House

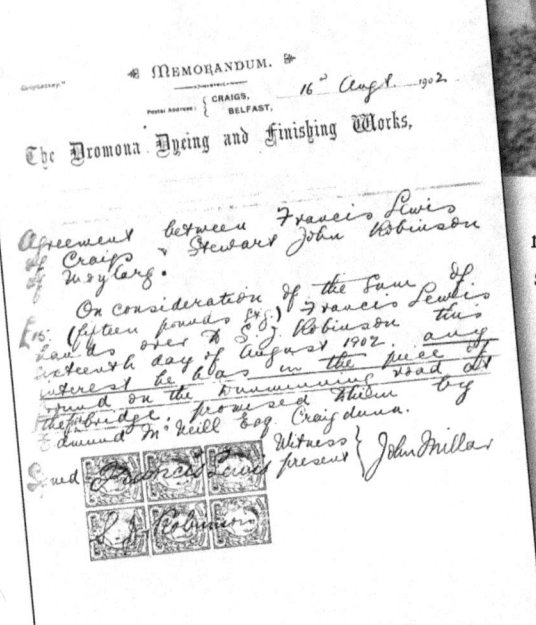

railway laid down connecting the works with the Midland system. With regard to Stewart J. Robinson, Shaw writes:

His grandfather, Mr Hugh Robinson, who built the Beetling Mills at Killydonnelly in 1802, was agent for the estate of Sir Thomas Staples and Colonel Caulfield, which comprised thirteen townlands. He was also Seneschal of the Court, High Constable and Captain of the Rasharkin and Finvoy Yeomen. The property at Killylodge is now owned by his grandson, Mr Alexander Robinson, J.P. The Dromona Works were purchased some time ago by Mr Young of Fenaghy, but the residence and demesne lands remain the property of Mr Robinson.

At the Dromona Works, Stewart J. Robinson did a large trade with Manchester and district in bleaching, dyeing, and finishing. Some years prior to his retirement the Dromona Works and the Main Works, Cullybackey, owned by William Young of Fenaghy, were amalgamated under the title Dromona & Main Ltd.

1921

ROBINSON—November 10, at Dromona, Craigs, Co. Antrim, Stewart John Robinson.

Death of Mr. Stewart J. Robinson.
DROMONA, CRAIGS.

The death of Mr. Stewart John Robinson, which took place rather unexpectedly at his residence, Dromona, Craigs, County Antrim, on Thursday, 10th inst., came as a shock to his relatives and hosts of friends. The deceased gentleman lost his sight some five years ago and had been in failing health for some time, but the end came with a suddenness that was not expected. He was a son of the late Mr. Hugh Robinson, of Killylodge, County Antrim, and a grandson of the late Mr. Hugh Robinson, also of Killylodge, who was such a prominent figure in the district during the rebellion of 1798, when he commanded the Yeomanry, and was also High Seneschal of the court, etc. The late Mr. S. J. Robinson was engaged in the boiling and manufacturing of linen yarns, a business which he carried on at Killylodge Mills. He attended the Ballymena Linen Hall up till almost 32 years ago, when he bought the Dromona Works which he built up to their present dimensions from only one or two houses, and carried on bleaching, dyeing, and finishing, doing a large trade with Manchester and District. Some years before, the late Mr. Robinson retired from business, the Dromona Works and Maine Works, Cullybackey, owned by Mr. William Young, at Fenaghy, were amalgamated under the title of Dromona and Maine Works, Ltd., Mr. Robinson and Mr. Young being the first directors. The deceased is survived by his widow, three daughters and one son, Mr. Hugh Allen Robinson, with whom there is much sympathy in their bereavement. The funeral was private, only relatives, intimate friends, and some of his former employees being present.

READE FAMILY TREE

The Reade Family Tree only shows male members of the family involved in the York Street Flax Spinning Co., Ltd.

Thomas Reade, MD = Helena Harriet Sturrock
Belfast   daughter of Rev James Traill Sturrock
Rector of Seapatrick, County Down

Robert Henry Sturrock Reade, DL = Dorothea Emily Florence Robbins
1837–1913   d. 1883
Chairman York Street Flax Spinning Co., Ltd.
WILMONT
Dunmurry, County Antrim

George Sturrock Reade, DL = Elise Allen Tregellas
1877–1950   d. 1951
Director York Street Flax Spinning Co., Ltd.
FIRGROVE, Muckamore, County Antrim
CARNCAIRN LODGE, Broughshane, County Antrim

Major Robert Henry Reade, MC, DL = Kathleen Grace Casement
Director York Street Flax Spinning Co., Ltd.
CARNCAIRN LODGE, Broughshane, County Antrim

George S Reade, DL
COURTESY RICHARD READE, DL

CARNCAIRN LODGE
BROUGHSHANE

Carncairn Lodge, is situated on the Carnlough Road, Broughshane, being formerly known as Glencairn House, and is referred to by Lawlor writing in September, 1941, concerning the Brown family of Broughshane, Ballymena.

> This family was seated in the mid 17th century at Kenbally, a mile or so north west of Broughshane … the family later built the fine old Georgian house of Glencairn lying east of Broughshane. Here in 1715, was born William Brown.

Lawlor continues:

> William Brown apparently developed the [linen] business left him by his father, and sometime after the death of John White of Whitehall in 1760, leased the White's bleach works there.

William Brown's second son Alexander emigrated to America in 1800, having transferred his linen business and his lease of the bleach works to William Young of Ballymena, who traded first as William Young & Sons of Ballymena and Broughshane.

Brett, in *Buildings of County Antrim*, states that the house in its present form was built by the Rev. William Crawford, rector of Skerry from 1825 until 1869. The Ordnance Survey Memoirs for the Parish of Skerry, written in 1835 by James Boyle in relation to 'Gentlemens' Seats' states:

CARNCAIRN LODGE, BROUGHSHANE

Glencairn, in the townland of Carnkeeran, the residence of the Rev W. Crawford, rector of the parish, three-quarters of a mile east of Broughshane.

It appears possible that the house was built around 1830. Carncairn Lodge is a large Georgian style house, two-storeys high, five-bays wide and two-bays deep, with a wing at the back, all the walls being cream painted roughcast. It is thought that some parts of the original Glencairn House may be incorporated in the rear wing. There is a hipped slated roof, which has wide eaves, and there are two modern chimney stacks. The windows are Georgian glazed, 3-over-3 pane sashes on the first floor, and 6-over-6 pane sashes on the ground floor. The house has a recessed fanlighted doorway which is harled.

George Sturrock Reade and his family left Firgrove House in 1943 to live at Carncairn Lodge, Broughshane, possibly on his retirement as Director of York Street Flax Spinning Co., Ltd., Belfast.

VALLEY COTTAGE
CREVILLY VALLEY

Valley Cottage, Crevilly Valley, is adjacent to the Kells Water close to the point where it joins the River Main, south of Ballymena town. This is a modest house, roughcast with stucco trim, set amidst magnificent trees, and was originally built by a mill owner, Jesse Millar, probably in the 1840s, as both the house and a rear building appear on the 1852 map. The main house is one and a half storey, three bays wide, having a tall Georgian glazed window on either side of the porch, and a single Gothic style window in a peak above the porch. There is a two-storey return to the left of the front with windows upstairs and down Georgian glazed, and this leads to a two-storey building at the rear, which may have been used to store linen. According to Brett 'the fine single storey canted bay to the right, with three Georgian glazed windows, containing dining room and drawing room, were added by the present owner in 1982'.

The Ordnance Survey Memoirs for the Parish of Connor in 1833 lists a bleach green at Crevillyvalley along with beetling and wash mills. The Memoir, under the heading of 'Gentlemen's Seats', records:

> Kildrum, in the townland of the same name, the residence of Jesse Millar Esquire.

VALLEY COTTAGE, CREVILLY VALLEY

It would appear that Jesse Millar built Valley Cottage, a rear two-storey building, and a gate lodge, close to his bleach green moving there from Kildrum in the 1840s. The bleach green and mills were on the opposite side of Kells Water from Valley Cottage, and bleaching continued at the site until the 1920s.

Valley Cottage storage for linen

JFR

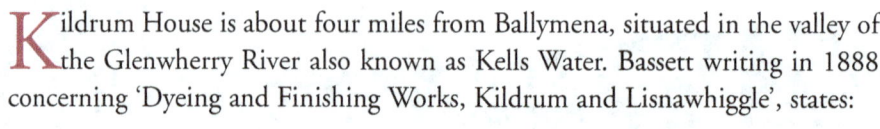

KILDRUM HOUSE
KELLS

Kildrum House is about four miles from Ballymena, situated in the valley of the Glenwherry River also known as Kells Water. Bassett writing in 1888 concerning 'Dyeing and Finishing Works, Kildrum and Lisnawhiggle', states:

> Mr John Hanna's dye works at Kildrum, and finishing works at Lisnawhiggle, Ballymena, date from the last century.

This John Hanna was the third generation of the family to bleach at Kildrum, as is shown again by Bassett:

> Mr John Hanna, the first of the name here, established a bleach green at Kildrum in 1798. Mr William Hanna, after the death of his father, carried on the bleaching industry.

Although Lendrick, in his map of 1780, shows a house named Kildrum, and a 'Bleach Yard', Brett has written that the present Kildrum House dates from the age of elegance between 1790 and 1810, which points to the house being built by the first John Hanna. However, by 1833 the Ordnance Survey Memoirs record that Kildrum was the residence of Jesse Millar Esquire. In 1888, although the Kildrum works were owned by the third generation John Hanna, he lived at Crevilly Valley, Ballymena.

Kildrum House is a two-storey, five-bay Georgian house with slated roof. There are very tall 12-pane windows on the ground and first floors, and round headed windows in the gables lighting the attics. A notable feature is the segmental-headed door case with cobweb fanlight, Greek key pattern architrave, and Tuscan columns. Brett admires the elegance of the house:

> the glazing bars are the slimmest I have ever seen (most of the panes are the original glass), and the cross grained mahogany banister rail and its terminal curlique are equally elegant. There is delicate plasterwork in the central hall and stairwell.

Brett also comments on Kildrum House nestling between a wide lawn with ancient yew tree, and, at the rear, the stone buildings of the farmyard. The house has been restored and is occupied.

Kildrum retains its importance in the twenty first century as one of the few remaining linen bleaching, dyeing and finishing works in the north of Ireland.

GREENFIELD HOUSE
KELLS

Greenfield House is situated close to the village of Kells, and was originally the property of the Arthur family of the nearby linen mill. According to the Ulster Architectural Heritage Society listing for Antrim and Ballymena, although, as stated by Brett, mistakenly entered as Templmoyle House, Greenfield House is described as:

ARTHUR & CO.,
BLEACHERS, DYERS AND FINISHERS
OF LINENS, UNIONS AND
COTTON GOODS IN ALL SHADES,
GREENFIELD,
KELLS.

> A substantial two-storey, five-bay house of *c.* 1780, cement rendered with moulded window surrounds and cement quoins; a good late eighteenth century door in a segment-headed central arch. Inside, two long deep rooms on either side of the hall/staircase; the old kitchen and office wing behind. Originally the property of the Arthur family of the nearby linen mill; restored in 1914 by the Dinsmore family.

This is a double-pile house which has attics, and a slated roof. The front windows have had plate glass inserted but the side windows retain their Georgian glazing.

The site of the linen mill at Greenfield is one of the oldest bleach greens on the Glenwherry River, but it has had many owners. Atkinson, visiting in 1817, records Greenfield as the seat of Mr William Johnston, a respectable bleacher on

GREENFIELD HOUSE, KELLS

the Mount Cashel estate, and by 1835 the Ordnance Survey Memoirs, describing it as a 'modern and comfortable 2-storey residence', states that this was then occupied by — Maxwell. During the next fifty years there were four further owners and Brett then states:

> In 1888, Arthur & Co. bleachers, dyers and finishers, occupied Greenfield Mill, but possibly not Greenfield House, which at some time passed into the ownership of the branch of the Dinsmore family, which ran the 'Old Green Woollen Mills'. The last of this branch sold the house in 1954.

John Dinsmore, JP

Curry's Bridge over Kells Water

JFR

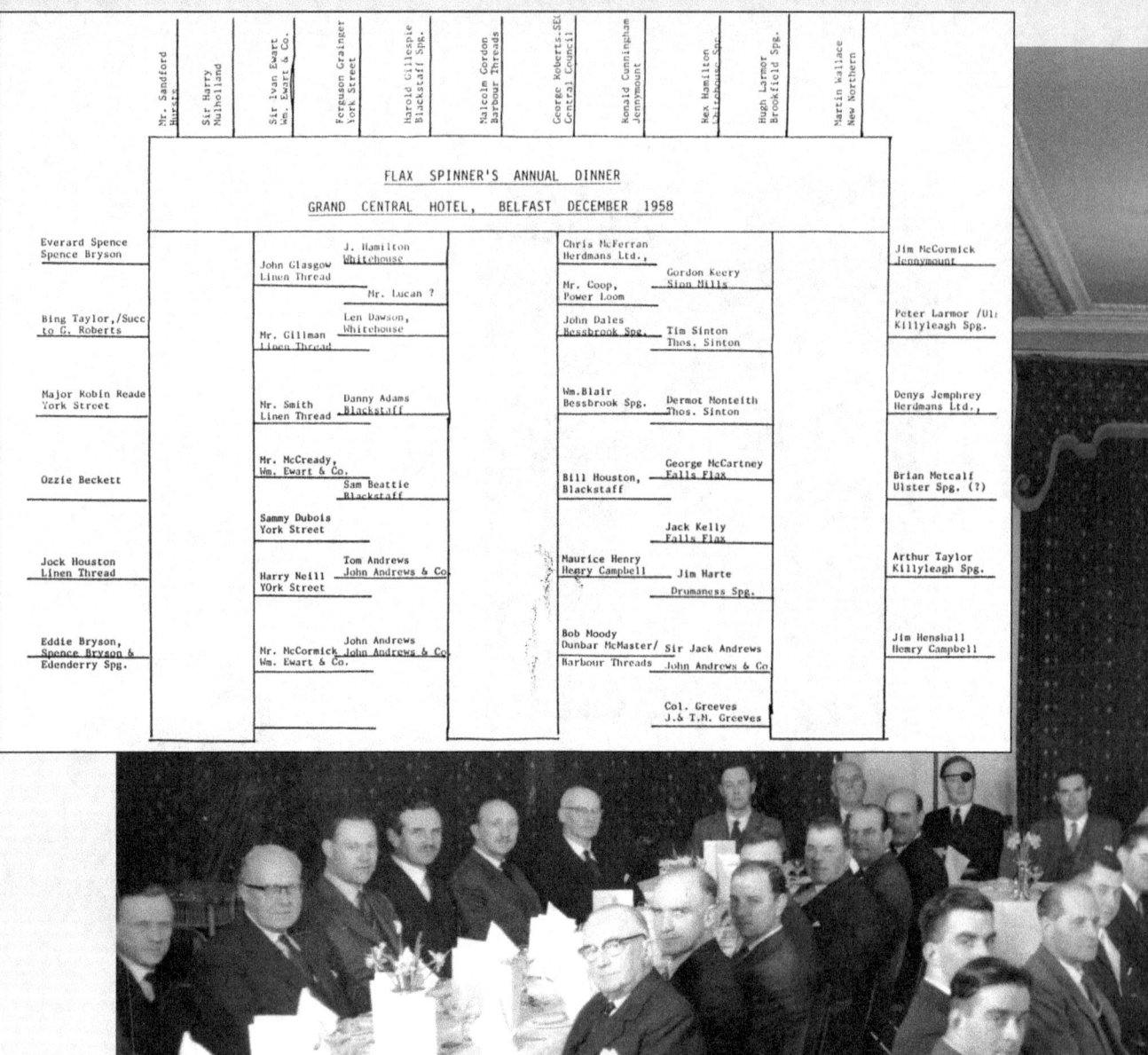

Flax Spinners Annual Dinner 1958,

6
NORTH EAST COUNTY DOWN

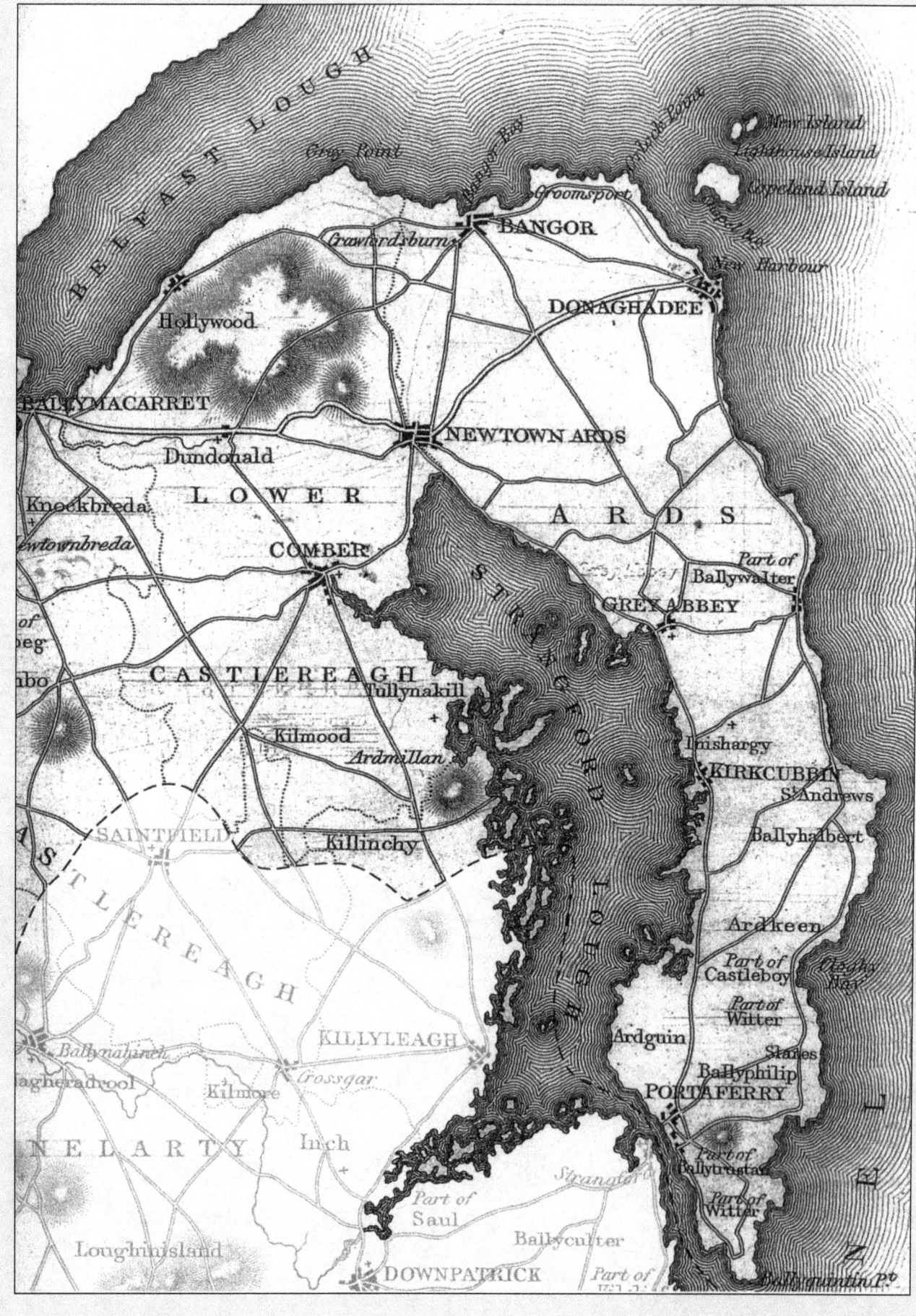

ANDREWS FAMILY TREE

This is an abbreviated family tree showing family members involved in flax spinning in Comber.

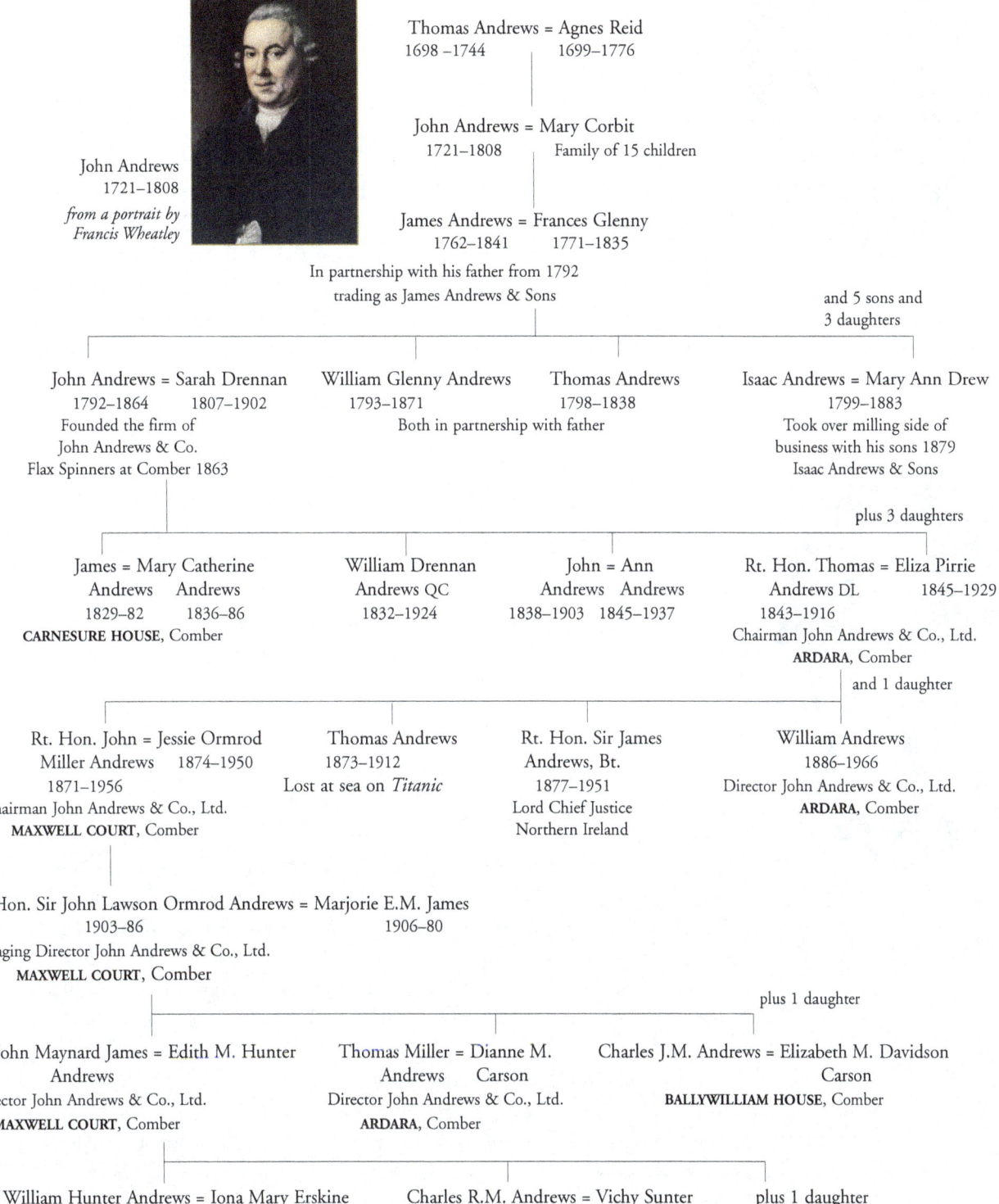

Thomas Andrews = Agnes Reid
1698 –1744   1699–1776

John Andrews = Mary Corbit
1721–1808   Family of 15 children

John Andrews
1721–1808
from a portrait by Francis Wheatley

James Andrews = Frances Glenny
1762–1841   1771–1835
In partnership with his father from 1792
trading as James Andrews & Sons

and 5 sons and 3 daughters

John Andrews = Sarah Drennan | William Glenny Andrews | Thomas Andrews | Isaac Andrews = Mary Ann Drew
1792–1864   1807–1902 | 1793–1871 | 1798–1838 | 1799–1883
Founded the firm of John Andrews & Co. | Both in partnership with father | | Took over milling side of business with his sons 1879
Flax Spinners at Comber 1863 | | | Isaac Andrews & Sons

plus 3 daughters

James = Mary Catherine | William Drennan | John = Ann | Rt. Hon. Thomas = Eliza Pirrie
Andrews   Andrews | Andrews QC | Andrews   Andrews | Andrews DL   1845–1929
1829–82   1836–86 | 1832–1924 | 1838–1903   1845–1937 | 1843–1916
CARNESURE HOUSE, Comber | | | Chairman John Andrews & Co., Ltd.
 | | | **ARDARA**, Comber

and 1 daughter

Rt. Hon. John = Jessie Ormrod | Thomas Andrews | Rt. Hon. Sir James | William Andrews
Miller Andrews   1874–1950 | 1873–1912 | Andrews, Bt. | 1886–1966
1871–1956 | Lost at sea on *Titanic* | 1877–1951 | Director John Andrews & Co., Ltd.
Chairman John Andrews & Co., Ltd. | | Lord Chief Justice | **ARDARA**, Comber
MAXWELL COURT, Comber | | Northern Ireland |

Rt. Hon. Sir John Lawson Ormrod Andrews = Marjorie E.M. James
1903–86   1906–80
Managing Director John Andrews & Co., Ltd.
MAXWELL COURT, Comber

plus 1 daughter

John Maynard James = Edith M. Hunter | Thomas Miller = Dianne M. | Charles J.M. Andrews = Elizabeth M. Davidson
Andrews | Andrews   Carson | Carson
Director John Andrews & Co., Ltd. | Director John Andrews & Co., Ltd. | **BALLYWILLIAM HOUSE**, Comber
MAXWELL COURT, Comber | **ARDARA**, Comber |

John William Hunter Andrews = Iona Mary Erskine | Charles R.M. Andrews = Vichy Sunter | plus 1 daughter
MAXWELL COURT, Comber

THE ANDREWS FAMILY
OF COMBER

John Andrews
1792–1864
*from a portrait by
Francis Wheatley*

James Andrews
1762–1841
*from a portrait by
Francis Wheatley*

The Andrews Family are very important in the industrial history of Comber, having arrived from Scotland and settled in or near Comber in the early seventeenth century. According to Lawlor the actual founder of the family was Thomas Andrews (1698–1744), who had a corn mill which was later changed to a flour mill. He had a son John (1721–1808), who set up the major family enterprises in the linen and milling trades in Comber, building his first wash mill, a low thatched building, on the site in 1745, and he also established a bleach green. The business flourished and in 1763, a year for which the records of his business have survived, John Andrews bleached 2,000 pieces of linen. Flour milling was becoming increasingly important in County Down, as a result of the bounties paid by the Irish Parliament, and in 1771 a flour mill was built in Comber by John Andrews on the site of the old wash mill with a new bleach works and beetling mill being erected alongside. John Andrews married Mary Corbitt in 1746, and had a family of fifteen children, his youngest son James (1762–1841) working with his father from 1792, and trading as John and James Andrews.

John Andrews died in 1808 and was succeeded by his son James during whose lifetime the business continued to expand under the name of James Andrews & Sons. He lived at 'The Old House', Comber, and married Frances Glenny of Newry, by whom he had nine sons and four daughters; of these the five youngest sons went into the legal profession attaining eminent positions. The four elder sons worked in the Comber business, which under their management developed and increased; John (1792–1864) and Isaac (1799–1883) were chiefly responsible for the linen trade of the firm while William Glenny (1793–1871) and Thomas (1798–1838) for the milling and bleaching sections. At the time of the American Civil War, 1861–65, when the demand for linen was high due to a lack of cotton, John, the eldest son, founded in 1863 with his sons, a new firm, John Andrews & Co., Flax Spinners, Comber, where they built a flax spinning mill in 1863–64. John Andrews married in 1826, Sarah, daughter of Dr William Drennan of Cabin Hill, Belfast, and by her had four sons, James (1829–82); the Rt. Hon. William Drennan (1832–1924), a Judge of the High Court of Justice in Ireland; John (1838–1903); and the Rt. Hon. Thomas Andrews, DL (1843–1916).

After the American Civil War there was a considerable slump in the Irish linen industry, and the linen sales and bleaching section of James Andrews suffered in the long depression. The Andrews family came to an arrangement by which Isaac and his sons bought out the interests of the other members of the family in James Andrews & Sons. According to Lawlor, Isaac and his sons then abandoned the linen section of James Andrews & Sons, closing the bleach works and the warehouse in 1872. The firm became Isaac Andrews & Sons in 1879, which was confined to the milling and grain trade, and in 1883, the year in which Isaac died, his firm purchased the old established Belfast Flour Mills in Percy Street, to which, after modernisation, it transferred the business from Comber.

The spinning mill, under the direction of Thomas Andrews of Ardara flourished, producing yarn of consistently high quality, the mill being enlarged in 1907, and he eventually became Chairman of John Andrews & Co., Ltd. However, the Rt. Hon. Thomas Andrews played a significant part in public life, becoming Chairman of Belfast & County Down Railway Co. from 1895. He was one of his Majesty's Deputy Lieutenants for County Down, and was made High Sheriff for County Down in 1912; he was also created Privy Councillor (Ireland) 1905, and was one of the Honorary Secretaries of the Ulster Unionist Council. In 1870 Thomas Andrews married Eliza, only daughter of James Alexander Pirrie, and sister of William James, who was to become Viscount Pirrie of Belfast, Chairman of the ship building firm Harland & Wolff, Ltd. They had four sons: (1) The Rt. Hon. John Miller Andrews, DL, MP, (1871–1956), who became Prime Minister of Northern Ireland, Managing Director of John Andrews & Co., Ltd.: (2) Thomas Andrews, (1873–1912) Managing Director, Harland & Wolff, Shipbuilders, Belfast, and Chief Designer, lost at sea by the foundering of the White Star liner RMS *Titanic* in 1912: (3) Rt. Hon. Sir James Andrews, (1877–1951), created a Baronet 1942, Lord Chief Justice Northern Ireland 1937–50: (4) William Andrews, (b. 1886), Director John Andrews & Co., Ltd., served in the First and Second World Wars.

John Lawson Ormrod Andrews, the son of John Miller Andrews, born 1903, was also a prominent politician. He succeeded his father as Unionist MP for Mid-Down in 1953 and held the seat until 1964, when he was elected to the Senate. However, he was also Managing Director John Andrews & Co., Ltd. from 1927, continuing the production of fine linen yarn in which he was joined later by his son John Maynard James Andrews. In the latter half of the twentieth century linen production in Northern Ireland substantially declined, and in 1997 the company ceased spinning flax, with the closure of the Comber mill.

However, Clatteringford, at Old Ballygowan Road, Comber, was established as a mail order business in the year 2000, being the retail division of John Andrews and Co., Ltd. Sales are based on designer knitwear made from natural fibres, and Irish linen in traditional and classic designs. With a family relationship to *Titanic* designer Thomas Andrews and an increasing interest in the *Titanic* brand, the company has sourced a range of table linen using the old patterns to the same specifications and design as was on the RMS *Titanic*. Customers are encouraged to visit the shop set up in the stables in a secluded courtyard at Clatteringford, to the rear of Ballywilliam House.

James Lawson Ormrod Andrews

MAXWELL COURT
COMBER

Maxwell Court is situated in its own considerable grounds on the outskirts of Comber. This is a large and mainly two-storey gentleman's residence, having a central gabled bay, single storey side wings, gabled dormers and oriels, and a large extension to the rear. The house has a late Victorian/Edwardian appearance but the main two and a half storey central section is originally a late eighteenth century building. There is evidence of a James Maxwell in Comber in 1767, since he was one of sixteen people offering a reward, and supporting John Andrews, when a notice was placed in the *Belfast News Letter* appealing for information on a robbery at the Andrews Bleach Green. (Andrews, *Nine Generations*) Lewis, in his *Topographical Dictionary of County Down* published in 1837, lists under gentlemen's seats in Comber, 'Maxwell Court of J. Cairns, Esq'. This house is also shown on the first Ordnance Survey map of County Down, published 1835. It would also appear that James Cairns had a working corn mill in the grounds of Maxwell Court, since in 1841 it was reported that in Comber there were two large corn mills – that of James Andrews & Sons in Mill Street and that of James Cairns at Maxwell Court (Comber Historical Society).

Maxwell Court came into the possession of the Andrews family through the will of John Miller, one of Comber's most distinguished citizens, who, for many years, was the owner of the Comber Distilleries, and who died in January 1883, aged 87. His will sets out the details of the property at Maxwell Court.

> **AUCTION SALES.**
> MAXWELL COURT, COMBER, COUNTY DOWN.
> ATTRACTIVE SALE OF
> CATTLE, VEHICLES, HOUSEHOLD FURNITURE, AND OTHER EFFECTS.
>
> I have been favoured with instructions from Major BAILIE to Sell by Public AUCTION, at his RESIDENCE, as above, on TUESDAY, 28th April, 1885, at Eleven o'clock a.m. sharp, HIS ENTIRE OUTDOOR AND INDOOR EFFECTS, comprising:—
> A single-barrel Duck Gun, eight-bore central-fire, by Powell & Son Birmingham, with all appliances.
> One very excellent b:y Cow, one Red Cow, in calf; Stanhope Wa nette, almost new, by Marshall, with portable seat and patent step; Wicker Dog Cart, by G. Barton & Sons, Carlisle; Spring Market Cart, in very good order; Gent.'s Saddles and Bridles, Car and Cart Harness, Oat Bruiser, Cucumber Frame and Hand Glasses, Garden Tools, Wheelbarrow, Lumber, &c., &c.
> HOUSEHOLD FURNITURE consists of—
> Dining-room—Chairs, in oak, upholstered in real morocco; Mahogany Pedestal Sideboard, Dinner Waggon, Marble Clock and Carriage Clock, Window Drapery, Poles, and Rings; Brussels Carpet, Skin Rugs, and Mats, Coal Vase, Fender, Fireirons. Drawing-room—Walnut Suite, of nine pieces; Loo Table, Occasional Table, Brussels Carpet, Rugs, Window Draperies and Poles, Fender and Steels.
> HALL AND LOBBIES.
> Hall Table and Stand, Oilcloth, Carpets, Stair Carpets and Rods, Mats, &c.
> Complete Furnishings of four Bedrooms and Dressing-room.
> Kitchen, Pantries, Culinary, and Cooking Utensils, Dinner War China, Flint, Glass, Dish Covers, and other usef Lots.
> On View day previo to Sale.
> Maxwell Court is only five minutes' walk from Comber Station.
> Terms—Cash, and 5 per cent. Auction Fees.
> **WALTER WATSON.**

I devise and bequeath to Eliza Andrews otherwise Pirrie wife of Thomas Andrews of Comber and to her heirs executors and administrators respectively for her sole and separate use independently of her husband and of his debts and engagements: All those lands houses mill and heridaments comprised in and conveyed to me by James Crea by deed dated the nineteenth day of March 1873 and commonly known as 'Maxwell Court' formerly occupied by my uncle James Cairns and recently by the said James Crea and also all mill gear machinery and working apparatus …

John Miller himself lived in a house called Aureen in Comber Square and appears to have let Maxwell Court to Major Bailie, since an auction notice of contents of the house was published for 28th April, 1885.

After the death of John Miller in 1883, in the ownership of the Thomas Andrews family, Maxwell Court was substantially enlarged by the addition of two single storey side wings and a large extension to the rear. According to the Street Directory for 1901 the Rt. Hon. John Miller Andrews was resident in Maxwell Court, perhaps after his marriage to Jessie Ormrod. He was followed in the house by his eldest son the Rt. Hon. Sir John L.O. Andrews, and following him in the twenty first century Maxwell Court continues to be occupied by members of the Andrews family (Comber Historical Society).

Maxwell Court doorcase
JFR

Sir James Lawson Ormrod Andrews, KBE, DL, was a memeber of both the Northern Ireland House of Commons and the Senate of Northern Ireland. He was knighted in 1983. He was the Managing Director of John Andrews & Co., Ltd. Jack Andrews is seen here sailing his yacht in Strangford Lough.

ARDARA
COMBER

Ardara is situated on the outskirts of Comber not far from Maxwell Court. This is a large two-storey house built in 1872 with later additions including curved and square bay windows. The roof is hipped and slated with projecting eaves, walls are smooth rendered with moulded details, and the windows have plain sashes. The three-bay entrance front has a central projecting square porch flanked on either side by paired semi-circular headed windows.

The Rt. Hon. Thomas Andrews (1843–1916) married Eliza Pirrie in 1870, and built Ardara in 1872, extending the house in 1904. Eliza Pirrie's brother was William, created Viscount Pirrie in 1906, the Managing Director of the Harland & Wolff shipyard in Belfast. Eliza Pirrie was also a niece of Agnes Pirrie, who married John Miller, owner of the Comber Distillery, and a prominent citizen in Comber (Comber Historical Society). Thomas and Eliza Andrews had a family of four sons and one daughter. The eldest son, John Miller Andrews (1871–1956), in addition to becoming Chairman of John Andrews & Co., Ltd., followed a political career occupying positions of responsibility in the Northern Ireland Cabinet, but ultimately he became Prime Minister during the Second World War.

Rt. Hon. Thomas Andrews, DL, 1843–1916

Andrews family. Thomas Andrews, designer, sits on the windowsill
PRONI D/3655/a/10

Aerial view of Ardara
PRONI D/3655/a/10

Thomas Andrews, Junior, designer
PRONI

However, their second son Thomas (1873–1912) was to achieve worldwide recognition as the ship designer of the *Titanic* for the White Star Line. After attending school at the Royal Belfast Academical Institution, Tom served an apprenticeship in the Harland & Wolff shipyard eventually becoming their Head of Design, and a Director of the company, of which his uncle, Viscount Pirrie, was head. Harland & Wolff constructed many ships for the White Star Line, including the *Oceanic*, *Olympic* and *Titanic*, which were amongst the largest ships of their day. Early in the year 1912, RMS *Titanic* left Belfast for Southampton, and its maiden voyage to America, with Thomas Andrews on board. After leaving Southampton the ship called at Cork on the south coast of Ireland, but when well into the journey to New York it collided with an iceberg on the night of Sunday, 14th April and sank to the bottom of the North Atlantic. Unfortunately, Thomas Andrews was not amongst the survivors, although there are stories of how he selflessly helped people to the lifeboats, only 712 passengers being rescued out of the 2,201 on board. The Thomas Andrews Memorial Hall was built in Comber almost opposite the Andrews Mill, and opened in 1915. It was erected by the people of Comber in memory of Thomas, who was greatly missed in the town evidenced by the sympathy shown to the whole Andrews family.

The third son of Thomas and Eliza Andrews was James (1877–1951), who had a distinguished legal career, becoming the Rt. Hon. Sir James Andrews, Bt., Lord Chief Justice of Northern Ireland 1937–51. Their youngest son was William (1886–1966), a Director of John Andrews & Co., Ltd., but who was also well known in cricketing circles, representing Ulster cricket many times, and on one occasion playing for Ireland.

RMS *Titanic* leaving Belfast Lough
PRONI D/3661/5888

BALLYWILLIAM HOUSE
COMBER

Ballywilliam House is situated a short distance from Comber, and within sight of Maxwell Court. This is an early nineteenth century house, built beside a flax mill, and mentioned in the Ordnance Survey Memoirs for the Parish of Comber as occupied by David Boyd in 1837. Ballywilliam House is a two-storey, three-bay house, of cream painted stucco with quoins, and a slated roof with tall chimneys at either end. A relatively modern flat roofed central porch, with side lights, has been added enclosing the original doorway, which has a spider web fanlight. The windows, which are Georgian glazed, are sashed and silled with a string course running level with and incorporating the sills of the second storey windows. There is a rear return which was added to the house between 1854 and 1858, being further extended *c.* 1925. A gate house to Ballywilliam House is situated at the entrance gates to the driveway and this may have been built *c.* 1854 to 1858 when there was an addition to the house.

Ballywilliam House is presently occupied by a member of the Andrews family, and in the rear courtyard there are stables where there is a shop selling linen goods, and named Clatteringford.

John M.J. Andrews marries Edith M. Hunter
PRONI D/3655/A/10/4171

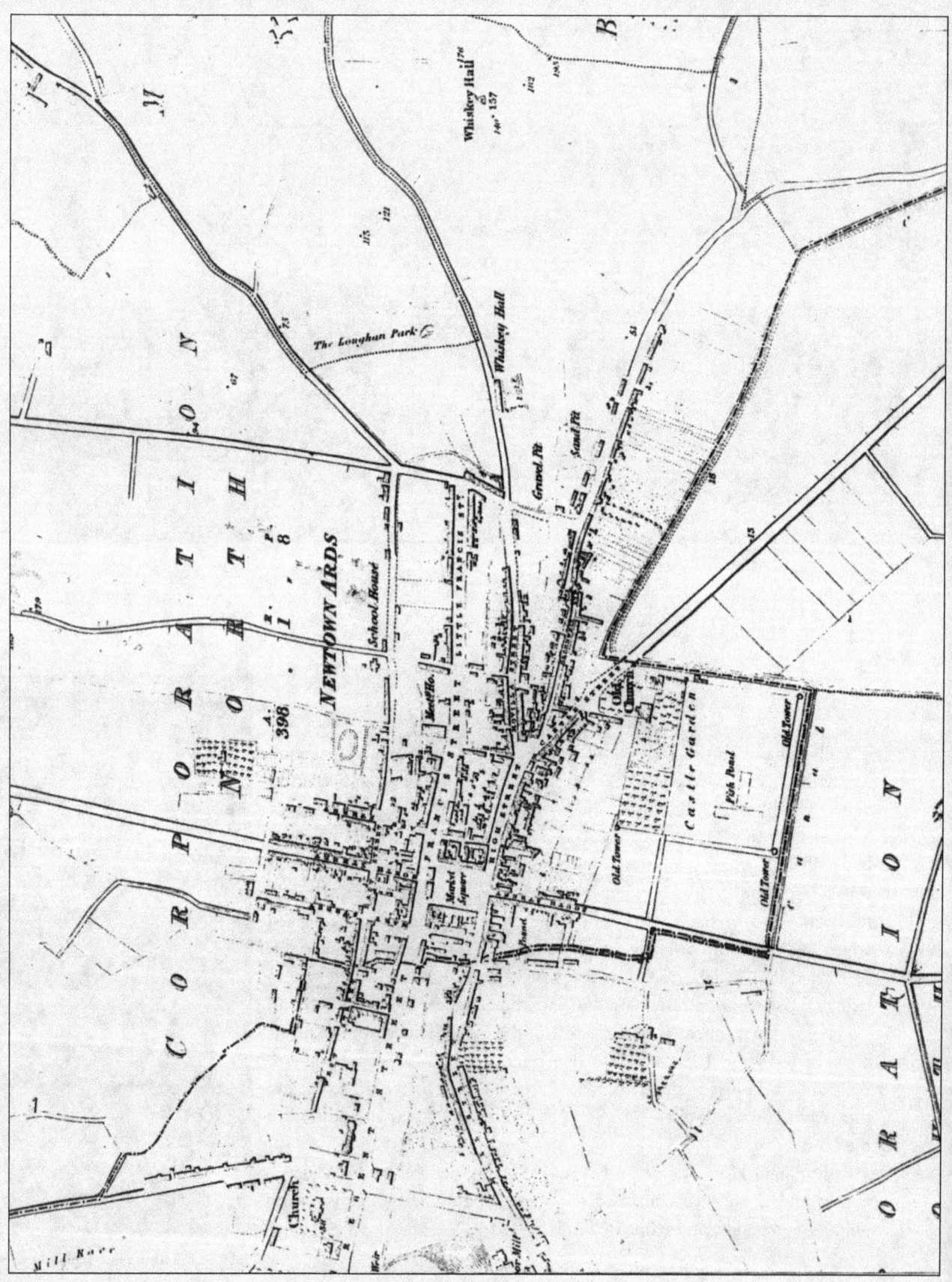

Newtownards *c.* 1835 showing Regent Street

REGENT HOUSE
NEWTOWNARDS

Regent House is situated in Regent Street, Newtownards, and is now in commercial occupation. This house was built about 1820, by the local brewer and maltster Peter Johnston, but by 1877 the house was occupied by George Walker who owned Castle Gardens Mill in Newtownards. This is a fine classical house of six bays and two storeys, the bottom storey of Scrabo sandstone ashlar, square channelled horizontally to the height of a first floor platband, and plain above. To the front there is a large projecting single storey portico which has paired Ionic columns with fluted shafts. The windows on each side of the portico are now of tripartite composition, although originally they were of the same size as those on the upper storey. However, there is a side entrance set in a segmental arched recess with a moulded archivolt, the door being in the Adam's style, with flanking side lights and a fanlight of spider-web glazing. The roof, which has a moulded cornice, is hidden behind a parapet, and no chimneys are now visible.

George Walker JP

In 1864 George Walker opened a spinning mill at Castle Gardens, Newtownards, spinning linen yarns for weaving purposes and thread manufacture. By 1901 the works had expanded and about 600 people, principally young women, were employed. In a booklet, published to celebrate their centenary in 1964, the directors state:

It is 100 years since the firm of George Walker & Co., Ltd., came into being. During this period we have been engaged in the spinning of flax yarns. We are one of a number of mills who make, amongst other goods, those yarns that go into the manufacture of Irish Linen. Ulster may be justly proud of her linen industry which has made her name famous the world over.

George Walker was still living in Regent House in 1889, but at the time of his death in 1911 his residence was Fern Bank, Knock, Belfast. The company eventually went into voluntary liquidation in 1972, with the consequent loss of over 200 jobs.

Regent House occupies an important place in the history of secondary education in Newtownards, since in 1928 Regent House School was opened in the premises. The property had been purchased in 1927 by the governors of a new co-educational secondary school, known as Newtownards Academy, and transferred to the Down Education Committee. By 1962 the premises were judged to be inadequate for the number of pupils, and the school moved to its extensive site on Circular Road, Newtownards, while still retaining the name Regent House School.

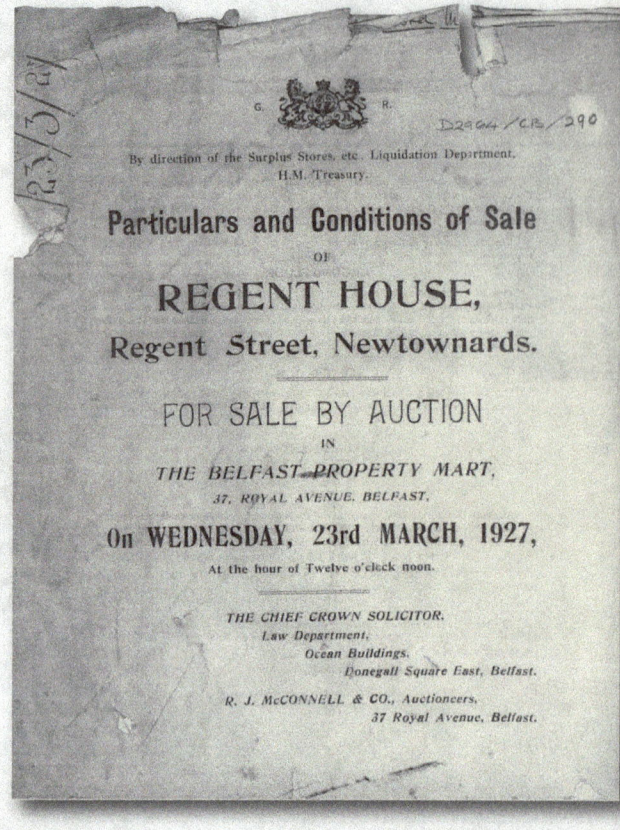

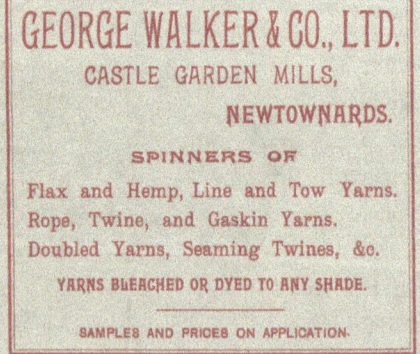

MILECROSS LODGE
NEWTOWNARDS

Milecross Lodge is situated off Bradshaw's Brae on the Belfast Road, Newtownards, the house being reached up a long winding avenue from the main road. Brett states, 'A simple, austere, but most attractive Quaker bleacher's house of the mid-eighteenth century, with extensive outbuildings, grounds, and beech walk, all in apple-pie order: from 1627 until 1885, seat of the Bradshaw family (of 'Bradshaw's Brae) until their unhappy downfall'. Milecross Lodge is a two-storey L-shaped house with five bays in each front, the walls being rough cast over bluestone, and entirely covered in well trimmed foliage. The garden front has a three light window at each end on the ground floor, with all the windows Victorian glazed, sashes and glazing bars being painted bright red, in contrast to the green creeper on the walls. There are two front doors; in the centre of the original front, looking out across the valley to Scrabo hill, there is a complex stone doorcase with triple keystone, but in the centre of the present entrance front, as with many early Irish Georgian houses, there is a simple stone Gibbsian doorcase.

According to Brett, the Milecross estate, until its sale in bankruptcy, comprised over 400 acres, on both sides of the Belfast Road, including both a bleach green and a bleaching mill.

Dr W.H. Crawford, in writing concerning 'Ulster Landowners and the Industry', states:

> The introduction of the weaving of diapers and damasks into north Down is ascribed to James Bradshaw, a Quaker from Lurgan who was persuaded by Robert Colville, the squire of Newtownards, to settle in that town in 1726.

Harris in his history of County Down in 1744 refers to Newtownards as being 'especially in repute for the sale of great quantities of fine diaper linen'. Additionally, in 1797 Robert Bradshaw described himself as a 'manufacturer and bleacher of fine linens and diaper upwards of forty years at Newtownards', though 'not in the trade now'. However, in the Valuation of 1834 the firm appears to have ceased work and the place is described as 'bleaching establishment long out of repair'.

In 1885 the Milecross estate was heavily in debt, and the Rev. Joseph Bradshaw, having been declared bankrupt, Milecross Lodge and the extensive garden were sold by auction. However, previously the bleachworks had been sold separately from the house and grounds, and was bought by Mr W. Sibbald Johnston, JP, who, in 1877, built a new and successful bleachworks at Kiltonga.

GLEN HOUSE
NEWTOWNARDS

Glen House is situated on rising ground at 2 Mountain Road, Newtownards, and is approached from the main road by an avenue 120 yards long, which is planted with trees and shrubs. This is a fine two-storey, three-bay Victorian house dating from *c.* 1870, which has a slated hipped roof, edged with red tiles and topped by two sets of chimney pots. There are two bay windows on the ground floor on either side of the front door, and a decorative platband runs across the front of the house: the stucco walls are painted white with decorative plasterwork around the front door and windows in dark green. In 1877 Glen House was occupied by Chas. C. Russell, a solicitor with a practice both in Belfast and Newtownards, who could be the builder of the property. However, by 1880 W. Sibbald Johnston, the owner of Kiltonga Bleach Works, was living in Glen House.

In the mid eighteenth century a bleach green at Kiltonga, owned by the Bradshaw family, was constantly used for the bleaching of fine linens, but after 1830 it fell into disuse. W. Sibbald Johnston bought Kiltonga in 1874, and by 1877 he had established the Kiltonga Bleaching Works on the outskirts of

Newtownards. The business gradually grew with the employment of 80 people for the bleaching of linen yarn, and later for the dyeing of the yarns. Latterly, in the twentieth century, Mr Johnston built a large residence at Kiltonga convenient to the works but this house has now been demolished. W. Sibbald Johnston was one of the most enthusiastic supporters for the establishment of the Scrabo Golf Club, whose links occupy a course over Scrabo hill. He became President of the Club in 1907/8/9, as is shown in the photograph which is wrongly labelled W.J. Johnston.

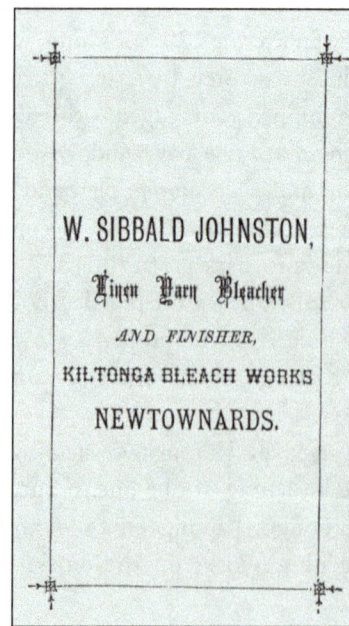

W. Sibbald Joh

MULHOLLAND FAMILY TREE

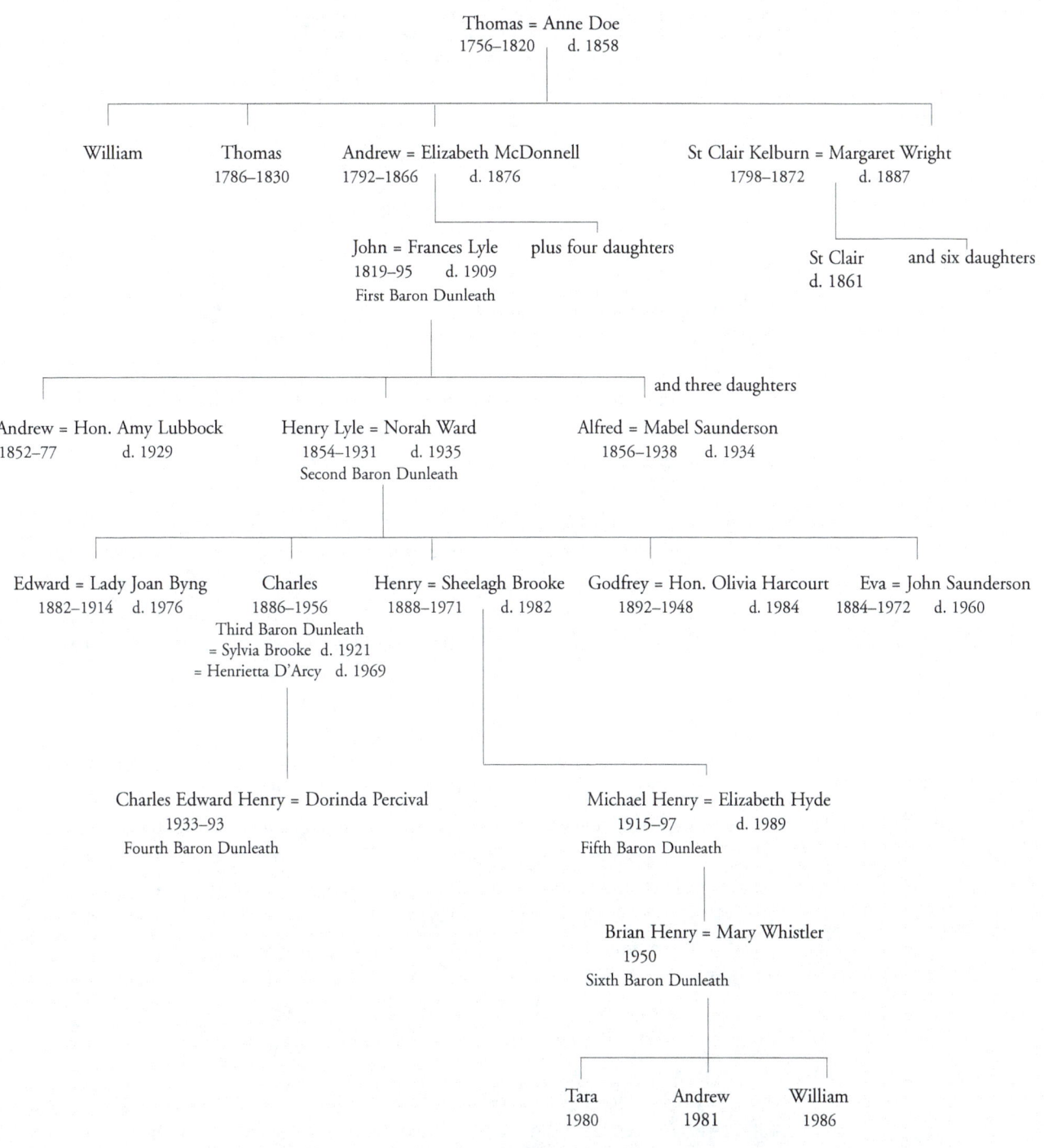

THE MULHOLLAND FAMILY
OF BELFAST

During the seventeenth century Ulster had a considerable linen industry but this was a domestic industry with spinning and weaving taking place mainly in farms and in villages, indeed it was dominated by the spinning wheel and the hand loom. In Belfast from the late 1770s mills began to be built for the spinning of cotton, and by 1825 there were about 20 cotton mills centred on the Smithfield area of Belfast, making the spinning and weaving of cotton the principal textile industry.

Thomas Mulholland (1756–1820), the founder of the firm that was to become York Street Flax Spinning Company, appears to have conducted a prosperous muslin manufacturing business in Belfast at the end of the eighteenth century. About 1815 the firm of McCammon, Milford & Bailey, cotton spinners of Winetavern Street decided to sell their mill. Thomas Mulholland entered into partnership with John Hind, who was the son of a prominent Manchester cotton spinner, to buy the Winetavern Street mill, and the new firm prospered. Thomas died in 1820 leaving five sons, Thomas (1786–1830), Andrew (1792–1866), John, William, who went to the West Indies, and St Clair Kelburn (1798–1872). The Winetavern Street mill succeeded so well that the firm acquired additional premises in Francis Street nearby, where they erected some of the newly invented power looms for weaving cotton. In 1822 the Mulholland brothers and John Hind erected what was at the time considered a huge cotton mill in the Point Field near York Street. John Hind superintended the technical side of the business, and the brothers Mulholland, the mercantile side.

In 1825 James Kay of Preston invented a wet spinning process in that he discovered that a thorough soaking in cold water made flax fibres more slippery so that they could be drawn by machinery into a very fine yarn. This led to Kay and others erecting a large wet-spinning mill at Leeds, which was quickly followed by others at Nidderdale. Subsequently the brothers Mulholland were much impressed by the steady increase in shipments of flax from Belfast consigned to Leeds and the corresponding growth in the imports of yarn from the same area. In Ireland the hand spinning industry was quickly being undermined by these imports, and great distress arose in many districts removing a prop from the rural economy.

Meanwhile in 1828, James Murland erected a wet spinning mill at Annsborough, Castlewellan, County Down, and was the first in Ireland to produce linen yarn in appreciable quantity by power spinning. It was found that a properly equipped spinning mill could produce yarn of better quality at a much lower price than could be made by hand.

Mulholland's cotton mill at York Street was destroyed by fire in the summer of 1828 but by then the firm had already realised that the competition of Lancashire and Glasgow, where raw cotton was imported direct, was steadily growing and they anticipated that cotton spinning in Ireland was doomed. On the other hand, the exports of flax from Ireland to England and the importation of the yarns to be woven in Ireland equally put English flax spinners at a corresponding disadvantage. The profits in prospect for Irish mills were very tempting since the flax and the market for yarn were in Ulster, whereas the English spinners had to pay freight both ways at a time when no railways and only sailing ships were available. The Mulhollands built a new steam power mill in York Street beside the ruins of the old mill and it started work in 1830. Andrew Mulholland employed the young architect Thomas Jackson, newly arrived in Belfast, to design the York Street Spinning Mills. The Francis Street mill continued operations until at least the 1840s.

On the death of Thomas Mulholland senior he left the business to his two older sons, Thomas and Andrew, providing otherwise for John, William, St Clair and their sisters. Thomas lived only to see the new flax spinning mill started, dying in 1830 unmarried. The business was ably carried on by his brother Andrew who continued to trade as T. & A. Mulholland, Muslin Manufacturers, Union Street, until about 1840 when he took his son John (1819–95) into partnership and the firm became Andrew Mulholland & Son. In 1846 Andrew Mulholland, having purchased the estate of Springvale, County Down, from the Matthew family, retired from the firm leaving John as sole proprietor. Andrew Mulholland added to the palatial residence at Springvale, then recently built by the Matthews, and now known as Ballywalter Park.

In 1852 the Mulhollands' great York Street mill employed 800 workers and had 16,000 spindles, spinning 700 tons of flax into yarn in a year. The Mulhollands made enormous profits from their wet spinning mill, and others were quick to follow, so that by 1850 there were twenty nine mills in Belfast spinning flax compared to only four spinning cotton. John Mulholland changed the name of the firm to the York Street Flax Spinning Company in 1851, and on becoming proprietor of the firm he took in as managing partner, his brother-in-law Nicholas de la Cherois Crommelin who retired in 1860, and was followed by Mr Ogilvie Blair Graham, a native of Belfast, who had acquired a fortune in New Orleans.

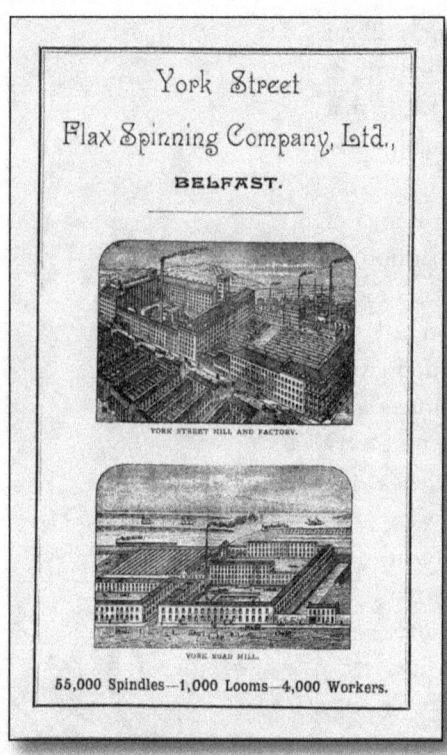

Linens rapidly took the place of cotton textiles when the American Civil War (1861–65) cut off the supply of raw cotton to Great Britain, and the Ulster linen industry expanded dramatically. John Mulholland, who had political ambitions, decided in 1864 to turn his firm into a Limited Liability Company, retaining a large holding of shares which eventually passed to his descendants, but meanwhile making immense profits in the American War boom. The Company extended its operations and opened branches in Paris (1870), New York (1871), London (1874), Berlin (1876) and Melbourne (1882). Expansion continued with new mills, and a weaving factory being built in York Street; other mills were purchased and the Muckamore bleachworks near Antrim was purchased in 1883 making the company totally vertically integrated.

In less than a century after Thomas Mulholland founded the firm, his grandson saw it achieve the position of the largest company of flax spinners, linen manufacturers and distributors in the world. After the formation of the York Street Flax Spinning Co., Ltd., John Mulholland sat as MP for Downpatrick from 1874 to 1885, having purchased from David Ker the Southwell (Downpatrick) estate. He was raised to the peerage in 1892 as Baron Dunleath, when he chose the title from the ancient name of Downpatrick, and was succeeded in 1895 by his only surviving son Henry Lyle, and thereafter by the third, fourth, fifth, and sixth barons.

York Street Flax Spinning Company was large enough to weather the many cyclical swings of the Irish linen industry through both the First and Second World Wars. Unfortunately, the York Street Mill was destroyed by German incendiaries in the blitz of Belfast, 4–5 May 1941, and was the largest fire ever seen in the city. However, after the war the York Street Mill was rebuilt but the linen trade decreased in the second half of the twentieth century as synthetic textiles took over and lifestyles changed. In the 1950s industrial consultants in 'Time and Motion' were called into the company to try and increase production but the real difficulty was that linen had gone out of fashion, and was also too expensive. The resolution to close the company was taken on 18 May 1961 and the York Street Flax Spinning Company was closed down on 1 February 1962.

BALLYWALTER PARK
BALLYWALTER

On the eastern side of the Ards peninsula, and just south of the village of Ballywalter, stands Ballywalter Park, once the home of Andrew Mulholland, proprietor of the York Street Flax Spinning Mill, Belfast. The estate has remained in the ownership of the Mulholland family, now the Barons Dunleath, for over 150 years, since it was bought from the Matthews family in 1846. At the time, the estate consisted of a demesne of about 250 acres, along with a Georgian house called Springvale. Andrew Mulholland found the existing house too modest, having recently become Mayor of Belfast, and he commissioned the architect Charles (later Sir Charles) Lanyon to build a house more in keeping with his status. The original Springvale House was not demolished but was included within the structure of the new house, construction taking about six years with completion around 1852. Brett states:

> Arguably the grandest of all the private Stately Homes, of north County Down – Ballywalter Park, in its present form, was built soon after 1847 to designs by Charles Lanyon for Andrew Mulholland.

Andrew Mulholland
COURTESY THE LORD DUNLEATH

According to Professor Alistair Rowan, writing about Ballywalter Park, County Down, in *Country Life*, 1967:

> Lanyon's scheme left Ballywalter as a new Italianate palazzo utterly different from its predecessor, though preserving much of the original building made into a regular block, and the entrance changed from south to east, where a Roman Doric porte cochere, four-square and solid, was added to the facade.

The roof finished by a modillion cornice, was raised an extra floor, and to the south and north two new single storey wings enclosed the composition. These were neatly designed with shallow segmental bows to the garden front and an abundance of High Renaissance detail.

Inside Lanyon turned the centre of the old house into one enormous hall that provided an opportunity for his most sumptuous and grandest manner. Sixty feet long and rising the full height of the building, it became the real core of the house.

Andrew Mulholland carried out extensive planting of the grounds at Ballywalter Park post-1846, and around 93,500 trees and shrubs were added in the first winter. Older shelter belts were retained as an important element in an exposed site, and others were planted for the present house. Development of the grounds has been continued over the years with the introduction of a collection of rhododendrons, which flourished in the first half of the twentieth century. The walled garden, contemporary with the present house, is cultivated, and a rose garden occupies the southern end of the garden. Mark Bence-Jones described the site in 1988 in *A Guide to Irish Country Houses*, 'The garden front of the house overlooks wide spreading lawns with paths and statues, beyond which is a notable collection of ornamental trees and shrubs.'

Ballywalter doorway
COURTESY THE LORD DUNLEATH

Andrew Mulholland married Elizabeth McDonnell in 1818, and they had one son, John, as well as four daughters. The family moved to Ballywalter Park in 1846, having previously lived in York Street, then later at Mount Collyer. Andrew Mulholland is perhaps best remembered in Belfast for having provided the Ulster Hall with its fine Grand Organ in 1862, giving the city a centre for musical concerts. He died in 1866, being succeeded by his son John, who assumed control of the family interests, not only the York Street Mills, but also the management of a substantial amount of land. John Mulholland was noted for his business and financial acumen which carried him well beyond the linen industry. Dr Elizabeth Malcolm writing on the Mulholland Family History comments:

> He was, for instance, involved in 1860 in advising the British government during negotiations with the French over an important commercial treaty regulating trade between the two countries – and, among various other provisions, lowering French duties on flax and linen.

The Drawing Room set for dinner
COURTESY THE LORD DUNLEATH

In 1874 John Mulholland stood as a Conservative candidate for Downpatrick, and was returned unopposed, retaining the seat until 1885, being a strong supporter of Tory policies. He was raised to the peerage in 1892, when he was created Baron Dunleath of Ballywalter, but did not live long to enjoy this status as he died in 1895.

C.E.B. Brett writing on Ballywalter Park in 2002 states:

> The house has endured threats of demolition, a serious fire, outbreaks of dry rot, and sundry other vicissitudes: it has had to endure also extensive re-wiring and, more recently, the modernisation of its plumbing arrangements in order to bring the bedrooms on the top floor back into use. However, it has been treated with affection and discretion, in somewhat differing styles, by its successive owners and occupiers.

The sixth Baron Dunleath has won praise for the recent fifty seven week programme of refurbishment and renewal at the house. In order to bring it into the twenty first century Ballywalter Park now has its own dedicated website featuring many aspects of its history and including interesting photographs.

The conservatory
COURTESY THE LORD DUNLEATH

CRAIGAVAD HOUSE
HOLYWOOD

Craigavad House, a restrained classical house on the shores of Belfast Lough, is now the club house of the Royal Belfast Golf Club, and is situated off Station Road, Craigavad, at the end of a long avenue. This house was built for John Mulholland, son of Andrew Mulholland, of Ballywalter Park, according to designs by Thomas Turner in 1852, whose drawings were discovered at Ballywalter Park in the late 1960s. Brett gives the following description:

> It is a fine cutstone two-storey mansion, five bays wide and four bays deep, with hipped roof and stone chimney stacks, standing on a splendid site at the top of a wooded and grassy slope descending to the shore of Belfast Lough. All the windows have segmental heads; the glazing pattern is unusual, Georgian upstairs and Regency below.

At the front of the house, which faces landward, there is a broad single storey projecting porch with Doric columns, and the seaward side has a large two storey projecting bay overlooking Belfast Lough. The interior of Craigavad House has as its focus a central hall, surrounded by an upper gallery, and top lit by a circular glass dome.

In 1866 John Mulholland inherited Ballywalter Park, on the death of his father, and he moved there, while renting out Craigavad House for some years until 1883, when the freehold was sold to Robert Kennedy. Eventually, after having a number of owners Craigavad House was sold in 1925 to the Golf Club.

Rear of Craigavad House overlooking Belfast Lough
JFR

Mount Randal by J.W. Carey

MOUNT RANDAL
BELFAST

Mount Randal is situated in Cranmore Park off the Lisburn Road in south Belfast, and is now Inchmarlo, the Preparatory School for the Royal Belfast Academical Institution. However, this is a house with a considerable history of connection both to the Irish linen industry and to RBAI, having been originally built by John Carlisle, who was Headmaster of the English School, RBAI, from 1861 until his death in 1884. The original name of the house was Cranmore, after the Cranmore woods nearby, and appears to have been built in 1879, first appearing in the 1880 Street Directory. James A. Bulloch of Bulloch Brothers, Linen Merchants in Belfast, occupied Cranmore from 1884 to his departure for Scotland in 1888, when the house was sold to Mr William Crawford, lately returned from Paris, where he was the principal representative of the York Street Flax Spinning Co., Ltd., Belfast. Mr Crawford renamed the house Mount Randal, having grown up near Randalstown in County Antrim, where his father the Rev. Alexander Crawford had been minister to the First Presbyterian Congregation.

John Carlisle built Mount Randal

Mr Peter Rankin has kindly supplied me with the following description of Mount Randal, which was the home of Sir William Crawford, his great-grandfather.

The architect of Mount Randal is not recorded, but the house is a substantially built and solid two-storeyed one, of which the entrance front faces north over lower ground towards Drumglass, the house of the Musgrave family. Built of coursed granite rough-hewn blocks with sandstone dressings, the house is Scottish Baronial in feel, the crow-stepped gables in which second-storey attic windows are set, the out-corbellings supporting canted bays merging upwards into square-cut gables, and the machicolated parapet tops to bay windows, over flat tripartite bays, and supporting the oversailing of the crow-stepped attic gables, all reinforcing the Scottish Baronial undertones. The interior contains generously-scaled rooms and circulation spaces, with extensive use of pine timber, and parquet flooring.

In 1908 Sir William Crawford, as he had become, extended the house at the back, southwards – a billiards room facing west and a conservatory facing east – the additions, in style and materials, replicating those of the original house, the architects being Young & Mackenzie of Belfast.

Mount Randal has since the 1930s been a preparatory school, Inchmarlo, to adapt to which use a number of further additions have been made.

Sir William Crawford
Oil painting by Dugdale, 1916

Directors of York Street Flax Spinning Co., Ltd., 1908

William Crawford returned to Belfast in 1888, after being elected to the Board of the York Street Flax Spinning Co., Ltd., and on the death of Mr R.H.S. Reade, DL in 1913 he was appointed Chairman, eventually retiring, due to ill health, in June 1918. His linen interests extended beyond York Street, and in 1894 he was president of the Linen Merchants' Association. Associated again with trade he was an energetic member of the Belfast Chamber of Commerce, and was elected president of that organisation in 1900. However, he was also closely identified with raising funds for the building of the Royal Victoria Hospital on the Grosvenor Road, Belfast, and for many years was chairman of the Committee of Management of the Hospital. In recognition of his services to the hospital, in June 1906, a knighthood was conferred on him on the recommendation of Mr Asquith's Liberal Government. Sir William Crawford

BELOW LEFT: Sir William Crawford with early motor car outside Mount Randal
BELOW: J.G. Crawford, his son, driving his car

J.H. Stirling, who succeeded Sir William Crawford in Mount Randal

died in 1922, and Mount Randal was sold to J.H. Stirling, who was another member of the Board of the York Street Flax Spinning Co., Ltd., so continuing the association of the house with the linen industry.

John Jamieson in his *History of the Royal Belfast Academical Institution, 1810–1960* states:

> J.H. Stirling, who died in office as Chairman of the Board of Governors, bequeathed his residence, Mount Randal, together with about six acres of ground, to Inst. The Board of Governors decided to convert the building into a Preparatory School and Inchmarlo opened in September 1935 in its new home, renamed Stirling House to perpetuate the name of the generous donor. There were excellent playing fields on the spot, as well as well wooded grounds which served both educational and recreational needs.

Since 1935 generations of young boys have enjoyed this house and its grounds.

MITCHELL FAMILY TREE

This is an abbreviated Family Tree referring only to male family members, some of whom were involved in the linen business.

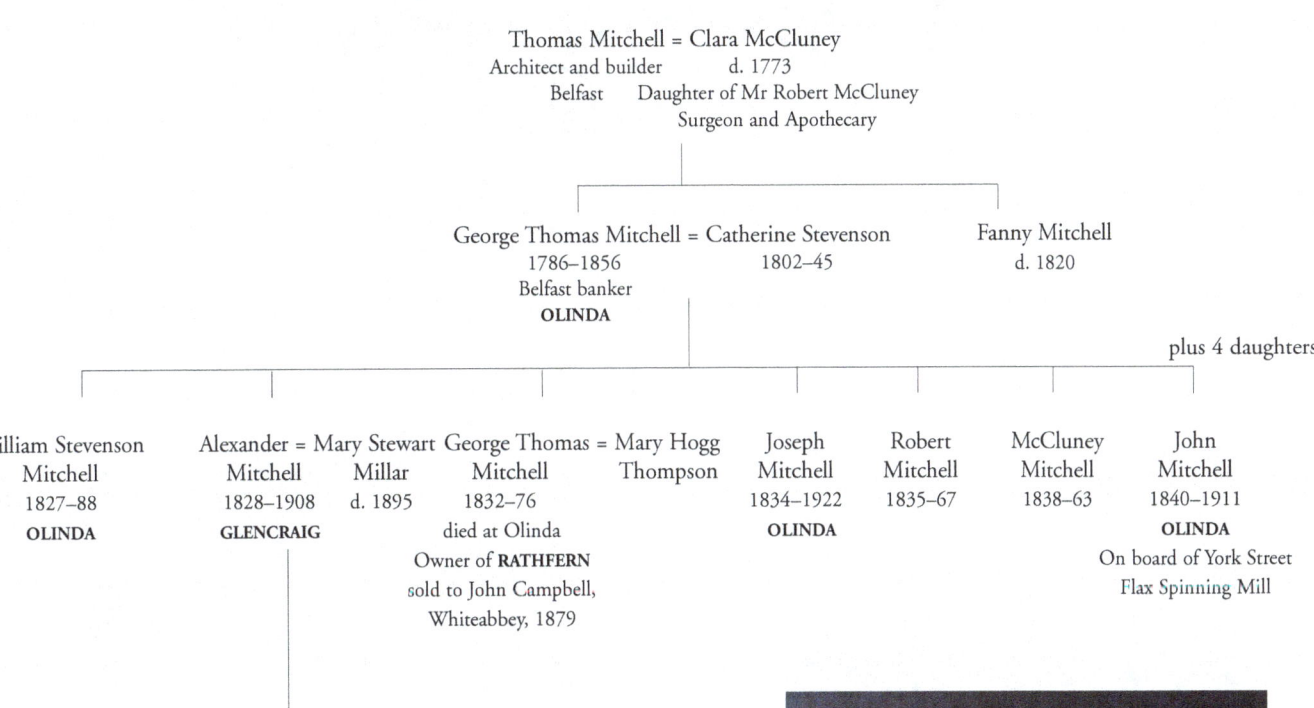

George Thomas Mitchell, 1786–1856

PRISCILLA CHADWICK

The Mitchell family coach

THE GREY HOUSE
CRAIGAVAD

This house was originally known as Olinda, when it was built by George Thomas Mitchell *c.* 1850, it sat on 30 acres of land close to the southern coast of Belfast Lough, at Station Road, Craigavad, Holywood. After 100 years of ownership by the Mitchell family Olinda was sold in 1950, and subsequently when a bungalow was built nearby in the grounds, named Olinda, the original property became known as 'The Grey House'. This is a three-bay, two-storey, with attic rooms and basement, classically styled nineteenth century house. The roof is hipped and slated, the eaves having a cornice, the stone built walls are smooth rendered with quoins, and the windows are sashed with moulded architraves. The porch, topped by a small balustrade stopping level with the

Front view of The Grey House
JFR

string course, has windows on each side and columns containing a niche at each corner. Olinda was advertised for sale in 1950 as having extensive stabling and out offices, but these would now have been converted to garages for cars.

George Thomas Mitchell, Esq., whose family originally came from Dublin, was firstly a Belfast merchant, but in 1831 he was appointed as one of the four directors of the Belfast Bank, remaining in this position until his death in 1856. For many years he was also treasurer of the Harbour Board (the present day Belfast Harbour Commissioners). In 1825 G.T. Mitchell married Catherine Stevenson, whose family traded as linen merchants. They lived at 6 Wellington Place, College Square, Belfast, and eventually, in 1852, three of their eldest sons, William S., Alexander, and Joseph, built premises in Flax Street, Crumlin Road, for flax spinning. The Mitchell Brothers added, in 1865, a power loom factory for the manufacture of linen. Their property on the Crumlin Road became known as Rosebank Mill by 1877, and the Henderson Directory 1880 recorded under Joint Stock Companies, 'The Rosebank Linen Co., Ltd.' Unfortunately, by February 1882 the Mitchell Brothers had become bankrupt, and both their town house at Wellington Place and their country house, Olinda, became owned by the bank. However, in 1883, Olinda was

Letter from the Rt. Hon. Sir Harry Mulholland

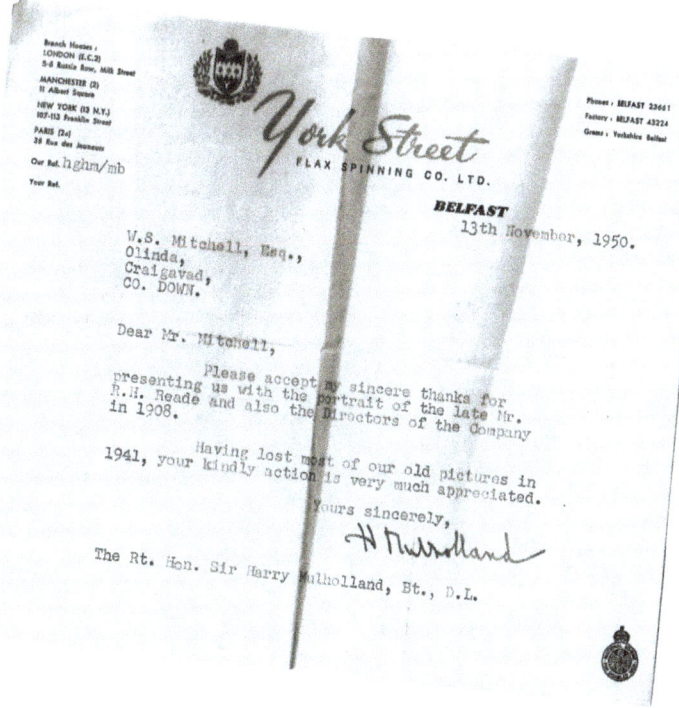

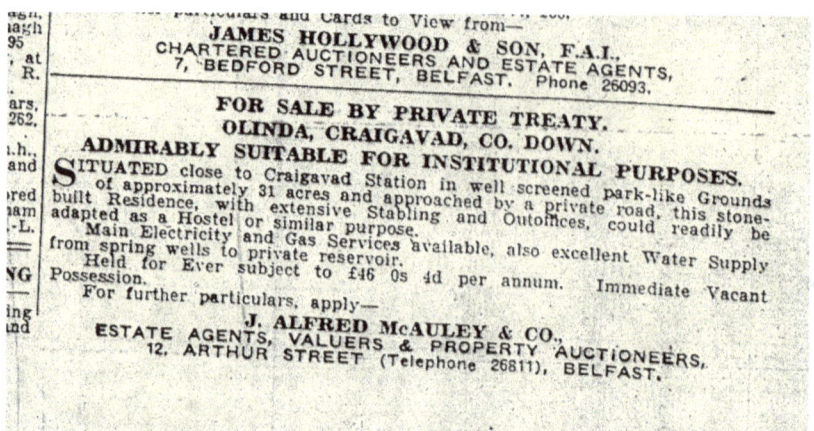

bought back from the bank by their youngest brother, John Mitchell, for the sum of £6,000.00.

According to an obituary published in the *Belfast News Letter* of April 10, 1911, John Mitchell inherited a great deal of the business capacity which had distinguished his father. Early in life he went out to India and there he amassed a substantial fortune. On his return to the north of Ireland he took a deep interest in public affairs as well as the work of various social and philanthropic agencies, and of the latter he was a most generous supporter. He served as a Grand Juror for County Down, and some years later he was appointed High Sheriff of the county, an office he filled with considerable success. John Mitchell was an enthusiastic member of the Coaching Club in London, and his teams were to be seen at the annual 'meet' in Hyde Park. He was one of the founders of the Soldiers' Home in Holywood, and was a liberal subscriber to the building fund. In addition to his many public duties he was one of the governors of Campbell College, and a director of the York Street Flax Spinning Company.

In his will John Mitchell left Olinda to his elder brother Joseph, and on his death, in 1922, the house was left to his nephew William Stephenson Mitchell, who eventually sold the property in 1950.

HURST FAMILY TREE

This is an abbreviated Family Tree referring only to male family members.

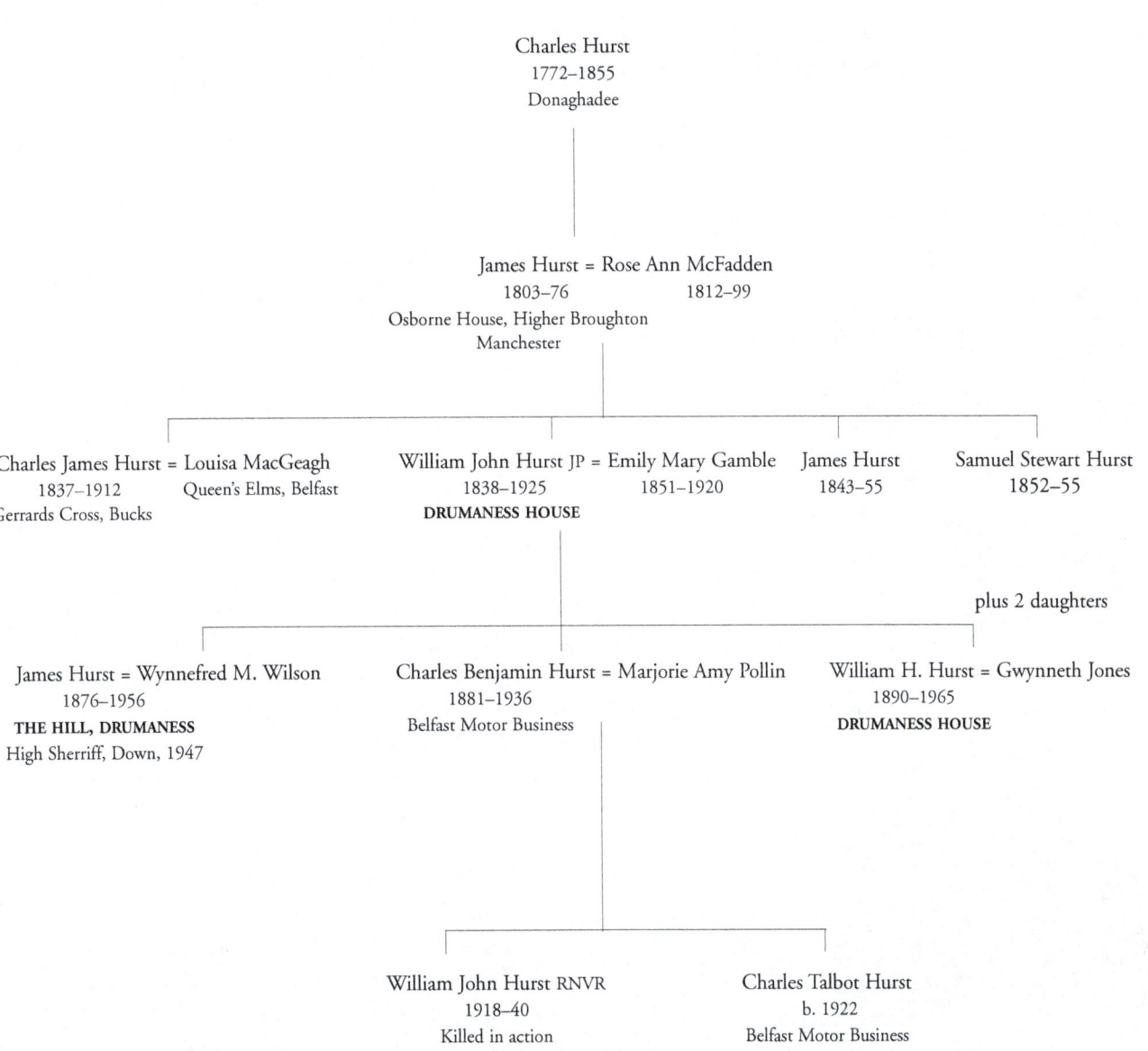

185

Hursts, Limited.
Drumaness Mills.
Ballynahinch,
Co. Down, N. Ireland.

10th January 1869

THE HURST FAMILY
OF DRUMANESS

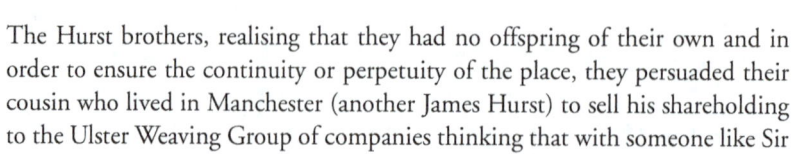

After the advent of the wet spinning process for flax, and its adoption by Murlands of Annsborough in 1828, the whole outlook on flax spinning changed. Many new mills sprang up in Ulster, and around 1850 William Davidson and Thomas Chermside, a Belfast spinner, built the Drumaness spinning mill. Drumaness is approximately two miles to the south of Ballynahinch and it developed as a mill village in 1850, after the opening of the spinning mill on the banks of the River Cumber. Prior to this date a bleaching green was sited north east of the new mill and in 1838 the business, owned by John Davidson, consisted of a beetling mill, a boiling house, an engine house, and a yarn drying house. There was a change of ownership of the mill in November 1856 when it was sold to James Hurst, a Manchester oil merchant, buying it for his son William John Hurst, who assumed responsibility for the running of the mill, making chiefly fine warp yarns. The original mill was stone built, only two stories high, but as the business prospered W.J. Hurst had the roof removed and added two more storeys in red brick.

William J. Hurst married Emily Mary Gamble in September 1875, and they lived at Drumaness House, a large Victorian house adjacent to the mill, which appears to have been demolished around 1980. Their son James entered the business as a young man, and on the death of his father in 1925 he took over the business, becoming managing director. He was joined at a later date by his brother William H. Hurst and they were joint managing directors until James's death in December 1956. Hursts Ltd. always had a reputation for good fine spun yarns. James Harte in a Living Linen recording LL1 R00/4 stated that in the early 1950s:

William and Mrs Hurst
COURTESY DOWN MUSEUM

> The Hurst brothers, realising that they had no offspring of their own and in order to ensure the continuity or perpetuity of the place, they persuaded their cousin who lived in Manchester (another James Hurst) to sell his shareholding to the Ulster Weaving Group of companies thinking that with someone like Sir

Graham Larmor at the head of it, that would ensure that the mill was continued ad infinitum. That, as it turned out, didn't prove to be correct. This cousin, as a matter of fact, held a fairly substantial number of shares, something approaching 50 per cent – not quite.

William H. Hurst died in 1965. Mr James Harte, who had joined the company in 1932 and was secretary from 1945, was appointed managing director in 1963. After James Hurst's death Ulster Weaving managed to increase their shareholding above 50 per cent, and later, after the death of W.H. Hurst, at a Hurst board meeting an announcement was made that the Ulster Weaving Company had taken the decision to close the mill at Drumaness and to transfer the machinery to the Killyleagh Flax Spinning Co., Ltd. Drumaness village lost its employment role in 1968, following the closure of the mill, and, today, it is largely a commuter settlement.

THE HILL
DRUMANESS, BALLYNAHINCH

The Hill was built by James Hurst (1876–1956) shortly after his marriage to Wynnefred Margaret Wilson in 1908. There is a prominent localised hill and ridgeline to the south west of Drumaness, which is topped by mature trees forming a backdrop of steeply rising land. The Hill faces south west, well sheltered by trees, and occupies an elevated site on the ridgeline, giving the house extensive views over the surrounding countryside. This is a two-storey, multi-gabled house, built in the Arts and Craft style, with a white stucco finish, and of a considerable size which originally incorporated staff quarters. The ground floor rooms have bay windows with slated roofs and the front door is recessed with a porch matching the bay windows.

The Hill was occupied by James Hurst until his death in 1956. His widow continued to live there until her death in the mid-1960s, and the house was sold in December 1968, after the closure of the Drumaness Mill.

HARMONY HILL
DRUMANESS

Harmony Hill is set on rising land in its own grounds, surrounded by trees, and not far from Drumaness village. This is a Georgian, two-storey, five-bay house with slated roof and shallow eaves, possibly built *c.* 1830 by John Davidson, who owned a nearby bleach green. The ground floor is rusticated with a platband at the front separating it from the first floor. The windows, which retain their glazing bars, are sashed and silled, with sills on first floor windows level with the string course. The door is set in a porch with Doric columns surmounted by a semi-circular fanlight of spider-web glazing. At the rear there is a single storey return which may be older than the main building, and also a courtyard with old stable buildings. In the sale advertisement of 1968 Harmony Hill was described:

> This comfortable four-bed roomed house, which has two spacious reception-rooms and a large and expertly modernised kitchen, combines elegance with all the amenities of a modern home.

Thomas Adamson

Harmony Hill was traditionally occupied by the Drumaness mill manager, who, from 1881–1919, was Thomas Adamson. On his return from fighting in the First World War, and after the death of his father, McConkey Adamson became the mill manager, living in Harmony Hill. He was followed by E.R. Sandford who had obtained a job as a trainee manager at Hursts, Drumaness, in 1947 after serving in the Royal Marines in the Second World War. Ernest Sandford was made mill manager in 1951, and lived with his wife at Harmony Hill until 1959 when he left the company.

BIBLIOGRAPHY

ANDREWS, SYDNEY, *Nine Generations: A History of the Andrews Family, Millers of Comber,* Edited by John Burls, Ipswich, 1958

ARMSTRONG, D.L., *The Growth of Industry in northern Ireland,* Oxford, 1999

ARMSTRONG, ROBERT, *Through the Ages to Newtownabbey,* Newtownabbey, 1994

ATKINSON, A., *Ireland Exhibited to England in a Political and Moral Survey of her Population,* 2 vols., London, 1823

BASSETT, G.H., *The Book of Antrim,* Dublin, 1888

BASSETT, G.H., *County Down, 100 Years Ago,* Belfast, 1988

BENCE-JONES, MARK, *A Guide to Irish Country Houses,* London, 1988

BLACKWOOD, R.W.T.H., MS, 'Genealogies', in Linen Hall Library, Belfast

BRADBURY, JOHN, *Celebrated Citizens of Belfast,* Belfast, 2002

BRETT, C.E.B., *Buildings of County Antrim,* Belfast, 1996

BRETT, C.E.B., *Buildings of North County Down,* Belfast, 2002

BURKE, *Landed Gentry of Ireland,* 4th edition, London, 1958

CARTER, H.R., *Linen, Hemp and Jute Trades' Directory,* Belfast, 1909

CARTER, WILLIAM, *A Short History of the Linen Trade,* Vol. ii, Belfast, 1952

CHAMBERS, GEORGE, *Faces of Change: The Belfast and Northern Ireland Chambers of Commerce and Industry,* Belfast, 1983

CRAWFORD, W.H., *The Hand Loom Weavers and the Ulster Linen Industry,* Belfast, 1994

CRAWFORD, W.H., *The Impact of the Domestic Linen Industry in Ulster,* Belfast, 2005

CROSSLAND, PROFESSOR SIR BERNARD & MOORE, JOHN S., *The Lives of Great Engineers of Ulster,* Vol. 1, Belfast, 2003; Vol. 2, Belfast, 2008

DAY, ANGÉLIQUE & McWILLIAMS, PATRICK (eds), *Ordnance Survey Memoirs of Ireland,*
  Vol. 2, *Parishes of County Antrim I, 1838–39,* Belfast, 1990
  Vol. 19, *Parishes of County Antrim VI, 1830, 1833, 1835–38,* Belfast, 1993
  Vol. 23, *Parishes of County Antrim VIII, 1831–35, 1837–38,* Belfast, 1993
  Vol. 29, *Parishes of County Antrim XI, 1832–33, 1835–39,* Belfast, 1995
  Vol. 35, *Parishes of County Antrim XIII, 1833, 1835, 1838,* Belfast, 1996
  Vol. 37, *Parishes of County Antrim XIV, 1832, 1839–40,* Belfast, 1996
  Vol. 7, *Parishes of County Down II, 1832–34, 1837,* Belfast, 1991

DEAN, J.A.K., *The Gate Lodges of Ulster, A Gazetteer,* UAHS, Belfast, 1994

DIXON, HUGH, *An Introduction to Ulster Architecture,* UAHS, Belfast, 1975

DIXON, HUGH, 'Honouring Thomas Jackson (1807–90) (architect)', *Proceedings and Reports of the Belfast Natural History and Philosophical Society,* 2nd series, Vol. 9, Sessions 1970/71–76/77

DUNLOP, DURHAM, *Life of W.J. Barre, Belfast*; a memoir of the professional life of William J. Barre, James Magill, 1868

GILL, CONRAD, *The Rise of the Irish Linen Industry*, Oxford, 1925

GIRVAN, W.D., ROWAN, A.J., & ORAM, R., *Historic Buildings, Antrim & Ballymena*, UAHS, Belfast, 1969

GIRVAN, W.D., & ROWAN, A.J., *Historic Buildings, West Antrim*, UAHS, Belfast, 1970

GREEN, E.R.R., *The Lagan Valley 1800–1850, a local history of the industrial revolution* London, 1949

GREEN, E.R.R., *The Industrial Archaeology of County Down*, Belfast, 1963

GRIBBON, H.D., *The History of Water Power in Ulster*, Belfast, 1969

HAINES, KEITH, *neither Rogues nor Fools: a history of Campbell College and Campbellians*, Belfast, 1995

HARRIS, W., *Antient and Present state of the county of Down*, Dublin, 1744, reprint, 1977

HILL, EDWIN DARLEY, *The Northern Banking Company Limited, 1824–1924*, Belfast, 1925

HORNER, J., *The Linen Trade of Europe during the Spinning Wheel Period*, Belfast, 1920

HAUGHTON, T.W., *Memoirs of the family of Haughton in Ireland*, Cullybackey, 1929

JAMIESON, JOHN, *The History of the Royal Belfast Academical Institution, 1810–1960*, Belfast, 1959

JOHNSTON, JIM, *A Well-Spun Thread: Memoirs from Mossley Mill*, Newtownabbey, 1999

JUPP, BELINDA, *Heritage Gardens Inventory 1992*, Belfast 1992

LARMOUR, PAUL, *Belfast: An Illustrated Architectural Guide*, Belfast, 1987

LAWLOR, H.C., 'Rise of the Linen Merchants in the Eighteenth Century', *Irish and International Fibres and Fabrics Journal*, Belfast, 1941–1943

LEWIS, SAMUEL, *Topographical Dictionary of Ireland*, London, 1837

McCALL, HUGH, *Ireland and her Staple Manufactures*, 2nd edition, Belfast, 1865

McCAVERY, TREVOR, *Newtown: A History of Newtownards*, Belfast, 1994

McCONNELL, JOHN, *The Braid Water Spinning Company Ltd., Ballymena, 1865–1998*, Ballymena, 1999

McCREARY, ALF, *A Vintage Port, Larne and its People*, Antrim, 2000

McCREARY, ALF, *Titanic Port*, Belfast, 2010

McCUTCHEON, W.A., *The Industrial Archaeology of Northern Ireland*, Belfast, 1980

McERLEAN, THOMAS, McCONKEY, ROSEMARY, FORSYTHE WES, *Strangford Lough: An archaeological survey of the maritime cultural landscape*, Belfast, 2002

McKINNEY, JACK, *Where the Six Mile Water Flows*, Belfast, 1991

McTEAR, THOMAS, Personal Recollections of the Beginning of the Century, in Ulster Journal Archaeology, Vol. V, 1898

MALLIE, EAMONN, & MACKIE, PADDY, *Kathleen Isabella Metcalfe Mackie, 1899–1996, The Life and Work of an Ulster Artist*, Belfast, 2009

MEGAW, JANE, *The Sun-Dialled Meeting-Houses Cullybackey*, Ballymena, 2004

MERRICK, A.C.W., & CLARKE, R.S.J., *Old Belfast Families and the New Burying Ground*, Belfast, 1991

PIERCE, RICHARD, & COEY, ALASTAIR, *Taken for Granted, a Celebration of 10 years of Historic Conservation*, Belfast, 1984

RANKIN, P.J., Ulster Houses Series Editor, *Ballywalter Park,* UAHS, Belfast, 1985
SHAW, WILLIAM, *Cullybackey, the Story of an Ulster Village,* Cullybackey, 1913
SMITH, F.W., *The Irish Linen Trade Hand-Book and Directory,* Belfast, 1876
STEVENSON, J., *Two Centuries of Life in Down, 1600–1800,* Belfast, 1920
TAYLOR, A.R., *Willowfield Parish Church, Belfast, 1872–1972,* Belfast, 1972
THOMPSON, HEATHER, *Weaving Webs of Wealth,* Antrim, 1982
WALKER, G.M., *George Walker & Co., Ltd., Newtownards, Northern Ireland, A Century of Flax and Hemp Spinning, 1864–1964,* Belfast, 1964
WALLACE, CRAIG, *Gardens in Mid-Antrim,* Belfast, 1960
YOUNG, R.M., *Belfast and the Province of Ulster in the twentieth century,* Belfast, 1909

PUBLIC RECORD OFFICE OF NORTHERN IRELAND
REFERENCES

Mackie Letter Heading D/1905/4/11
Rathfern, Whiteabbey, Sale in 1934 D/2964/CB/386
The Moat, Strandtown D/2964/CB/498
The Irishman, 29/11/1822, Auction of Moylena D/1216/1
Letter Heading, York Street D/2448/12
Linen Seal of 1799, Drumaul, Antrim D/1286/3/3
Sale of Incumbered Estates in Ireland, Estate of Galgorm D/3027/3/4
History of Frazer & Haughton Ltd. T/2062/3
Regent House, for sale by Auction, 23/3/27 D/2964/CB/290

PHOTOGRAPHS

Glenmmachan after the additions were finished, *c.* 1903/4 D/4185/A/1/6426
Wedding: Ewart – Greeves D/4185/A/1/15427
Lady Ewart, Lily Ewart, Warren Lewis, on steps of Glenmachan D/4185/A/1/16429
Tennis at Glenmachan in 1911 D/4185/A/1/11425
Lavens M. Ewart, Esq., J.P. (portrait) D/3563/13c/5645
Mackie Family at Hazelbank House with dogs D/1964/7/47/G396
Rathfern, picture of house D/2473/1/11c
Robinson & Cleaver, *c.* 1900 D/3598387
Muckamore, includes Ballycraigy, Map D/1326/35/26
Firgrove, Moylinny and Bank Engines D/1326/22/20
Muckamore, 6 Photos, Moylena House D/2760/2/2246
    Moylena Banks D/2760/2/2242
Larne, Co. Antrim, Drawing of bleach green, harbour and Inver House D/1129/138574
Andrews Papers, Thomas Andrews (Junior) D/36611/7889
    Including RMS *Titanic* leaving Belfast Lough D/3661/5888
    Andrews, Ardara (aerial view) D/3655/a/10/14146
    Thomas Andrews and Family D/3655/a/3/1/5
    Derry bride for MP's son D/3655/a/10/4171

INDEX

NOTE: a reference ending with 'p' denotes a photograph/illustration.

Abbeydene House, Newtownabbey, 63
Abbeydene *see* Lismara
Adair, Ian, 46
Adamson, McConkey, 189
Adamson, Thomas, 189
Africa, 26
Albert Foundry, Belfast, 24
Albert Street Works, Belfast, 23
Albert Street, Belfast, 23
Aldergrove, Co. Antrim, 71
Alexandra, Princess, 98
Alnick, Northumberland, 3
Altona, Strandtown, Belfast, 9, 10
America, Central, 26
America, North, 97, 121, 123, 129, 138, 158
America, South, 26, 81
American Civil War, 12, 109, 152, 170
Anderson, Samuel, 109
Anderson, William, 109
Andrews & Co., (Ltd.), John, 152, 153, 155p, 156, 158
Andrews & Sons, Isaac, 153
Andrews & Sons, James, 152, 154
Andrews Bleach Green, Comber, Co. Down, 154
Andrews Memorial Hall, Thomas, 158
Andrews, Eliza (née Pirrie), 153, 155, 156, 158
Andrews, Isaac (son of James Andrews), 152, 153
Andrews, James (son John Andrews and Sarah Drennan), 152
Andrews, James (son of John Andrews), 152
Andrews, John (son John Andrews and Sarah Drennan), 152
Andrews, John (son of James Andrews), 152
Andrews, John (son of Thomas Andrews), 151p, 152
Andrews, John Lawson Ormrod, 153, 155
Andrews, John Maynard James, 153, 159p
Andrews, Rt. Hon. John Miller , 153, 155, 156
Andrews, Rt. Hon. Sir James, 153, 158
Andrews, Rt. Hon. Thomas (son John Andrews and Sarah Drennan), 152, 153, 155, 156, 158
Andrews, Rt. Hon. William Drennan (son John Andrews and Sarah Drennan), 152
Andrews, Thomas (son of James Andrews), 152
Andrews, Thomas (senior), 152
Andrews, Thomas (*Titanic* designer), 153, 157p, 158
Andrews, William, 153, 158
Andrews, William Glenny (son of James Andrews), 152
Annsborough, Castlewellan, Co. Down, 169, 186
Antrim Hills, 6
Antrim, Co. Antrim, 19, 29, 40, 72, 74, 76, 81, 82, 84, 85, 87, 88, 89, 90, 91, 104, 110, 144, 170
Archaeological Survey of County Down, An, 30–31
Ardara, Comber, Co. Down, 153, 156, 157p
Ardmoulin House, Falls Road, Belfast, 37
Ards peninsula, Co. Down, 171
Ardvernis House, Glenarm, Co. Antrim, 115, 117

Armstrong, Robert, 24, 27, 51
Arthur & Co., 145
'Arts and Craft' movement, 33, 132, 188
Asquith, Herbert Henry, 178
Atkinson, A., 64, 74, 122, 144
Atlantic (North), 97, 158
Aureen, Comber, Co. Down, 155
Austria, 24

Bailie, Major, 155
Balee, Co. Antrim, 109
Ballinderry, Co. Antrim, 49
Ballyalton, Newtownards, Co. Down, 36
Ballyarnott Road, Aldergrove, Co. Antrim, 71
Ballyclare, Co. Antrim, 92
Ballycraigy [House], Muckamore, Co. Antrim, 64, 82, 83, 84, 85
Ballycraigy Manor, Muckamore, Co. Antrim, 83, 85
Ballyhenry, Mossley, Co. Antrim, 40
Ballymacarrett, Co. Down, 11
Ballymaclean, Belfast, 5
Ballymeaghan, Co. Down, 59
Ballymena, Co. Antrim, 40, 104, 107, 108, 109, 110, 111, 113, 121, 125, 128, 138, 142, 143, 144
Ballymena–Ballyclare–Larne railway, 82
Ballynahinch, Co. Down, 186, 188
Ballywalter Park, Co. Down, 169, 171–4, 176
Ballywalter, Co. Down, 171, 172, 173
Ballywilliam House, Comber, Co. Down, 153, 159
Balnamore Spinning Mill, Ballymoney, Co. Antrim, 109
Baltimore, USA, 108
Banford, Co. Down, 129
Bangor, Co. Down, 59
Barbour & Co., Messrs John (of Whitehouse), 49, 53
Barbour, Agnes, 49
Barney's Brae, Randalstown, Co. Antrim, 102, 103
Barre, William J., 59
Bassett, George Henry, 66, 93, 97, 99, 125, 142
Beck & Sons, J., 74
Beck, James, 74
Bedford Street, Belfast, 109
Belfast, 3, 4, 5, 6, 7, 8, 9, 11, 12, 13, 15, 18, 19, 23, 24, 25, 26, 27, 29, 30, 31, 33, 36, 37, 38, 39, 41, 45, 46, 49, 50, 52, 55, 56, 61, 62, 63, 64, 65, 66, 67, 72, 73, 84, 85, 87, 88, 90, 97, 109, 129, 139, 152, 153, 156, 158, 162, 165, 168, 169, 170, 171, 172, 175, 177, 178, 179, 182, 183, 184, 186
Belfast & County Down Railway Co., 153
Belfast and Northern Counties [railway] line, 56
Belfast Banking Company, 24
Belfast 'blitz', 170
Belfast Chamber of Commerce, 26, 46, 55, 56, 100, 109, 179
Belfast College of Technology, 24
Belfast Corporation, 18, 49

Belfast Flour Mills, Percy Street, Belfast, 153
Belfast Harbour Commission(ers), 26, 55, 183
Belfast Lough, 6, 29, 33, 61, 64, 175, 176p
Belfast News Letter, 37, 74, 105, 154, 184
Belfast Public Library, 49
Belfast Road, Antrim, 90
Belfast Road, Muckamore, 87
Belfast Road, Newtownards, 163
Belfast Steamship Company, Ltd., 56
Belfast Telegraph, 38, 82
Bell & Co., Richard & Jacob, 55
Bell, John L., 59, 60
Belmont Road, Belfast, 5, 7, 8, 45
Bence-Jones, Mark, 172
Berlin, Germany, 170
Bernagh House, The Grange, Co. Tyrone, 65
Bernagh, Strandtown, Belfast, 8
Bessbrook, Newry, 4, 23
Birnie, Thomas M., 122–3
Book of Antrim (Bassett), 66
Boomer & Co., James, 36–7, 45
Boomer, James, 37
Boyd, David, 159
Boyd, John, 43
Boyle, James, 88, 138
Bradshaw, Miss, 104
Bradshaw, Rev. Joseph, 164
Bradshaw, Robert, 164
Bradshaw's Brae, Newtownards, Co. Down, 163
Braid Water Spinning Company, Ltd., 109
Braid, River, 109, 111
Brett, C.E.B., 61, 75, 105, 115, 127, 128, 138, 140, 143, 144, 145, 163, 171–2, 173, 175
Briarfield, Randalstown, Co. Antrim, 101
Bridge Street, Ballymena, Co. Antrim, 121
Bristow, J.T., 55
Broadbent, Samuel E., 93
Brooke, Charlotte Ellen (wife of C.J. Webb), 97
Brookfield Linen Co., Ltd. (Brookfield Mill), 49, 50
Brooklands, Malone, Belfast, 67
Broughshane, Co. Antrim, 91, 108, 121, 138, 139
Brown Shipley & Co., 108, 121
Brown, Alexander (son of William Brown), 138
Brown, John A. (of Philadelphia), 121
Brown, William, 138
Browns of Broughshane, 108
Brown's Square, Belfast, 23
Buildings of County Antrim, 61, 105, 138
Bulloch Brothers, Linen Merchants, Belfast, 177
Bulloch, James A., 177
Burma, 26

Cabin Hill, Belfast, 7, 152
Cairncastle Lodge, Larne, 82, 85
Cairns Esq., James, 154, 155
Calwell, Rosemary, 103
Campbell College, Belfast, 7, 45, 184
Campbell, (Robert) Garrett, 38, 46
Campbell, Anna ('Nan'), 37, 46

Campbell, Anna (née McCullough), 40p
Campbell, Dermot, 38, 46
Campbell, Elizabeth, 44, 45
Campbell, Henry, 36, 37, 38, 43, 44, 45
Campbell, Henry & Co., Ltd., 37, 38, 40, 41, 45, 46, 47, 53, 56
Campbell, Henry James, 37, 45
Campbell, Howard, 38, 46
Campbell, James, 36, 37, 45
Campbell, John, 36, 37, 38, 39, 40, 41, 45, 46
Campbell, John (cousin of Henry Campbell), 45
Campbell, Lawford, 38, 46
Campbell, Lloyd, 38, 46, 56
Campbell, Michael, 36
Carey, W.J., 177p
Caribbean, the, 81
Carlisle, James, 49
Carlisle, John, 177
Carncairn Lodge, Broughshane, Co. Antrim, 91, 138–9
Carnkeeran (townland), Broughshane, Co. Antrim, 139
Carnlough Road, Broughshane, Co. Antrim, 138
Carnmoney, Co. Antrim, 28, 36, 40
Carnreagh, Annahilt, Co. Down, 11, 13
Carrickfergus, Co. Antrim, 64, 84
Carrickfergus Gaol, Co. Antrim, 128
Carrington-Viyella, 98
Castle Gardens Mill, Newtownards, Co. Down, 161
Castle Gardens, Newtownards, Co. Down, 161
Castle Place, Belfast, 63
Castle Upton, Templepatrick, Co. Antrim, 84
Castlewellan, Co. Down, 169
Caulfield, Colonel, 136
Chaine Memorial Tower, 81p, 82
Chaine, James (son of James Chaine), 82, 84, 85
Chaine, James (son of William Chaine), 82, 84, 85, 86
Chaine, Very Rev. John (Dean), 64, 81
Chaine, William (senior) (son of Dean Chaine), 64, 81, 82, 83, 84, 86, 88, 90
Chaine, William (son of James Chaine), 82, 85
Chaine, William (son of William), 82, 88, 89
Chambers, Dr George, 46
Charters, John, 19, 37
Cheltenham College, 52
Chermside, Thomas, 186
Cinnamond, William, 76
Circular Road, Belfast, 8
Circular Road, Newtownards, Co. Down, 162
Clady Bleach Works, Dunadry, Co. Antrim, 78
Clady Cottage, Dunadry, Co. Antrim, 77, 78
Clady House, Dunadry, Co. Antrim, 75–6
Clady Road, Muckamore, Co. Antrim, 77
Clady Water, Dunadry, Co. Antrim, 75, 76, 77
Clarendon, Mary Elizabeth, 18
Clarendon, V.F., 13p
Clark, Roland, 53
Clark, Sir George, 65
Clatteringford, Old Ballygowan Road, Comber, 153, 159
Cleaver, John, 62
Cloughfern Road, Whiteabbey, 42
Coaching Club, London, 184

INDEX

Coey, Alastair, 86
Cogry Flax Spinning Company, Doagh, 92, 93
Cogry House, Doagh, Co. Antrim, 92, 93
College Square (East), Belfast, 183
College Square North, Belfast, 37, 39
Colville, Rev. Dr Alexander, 110
Colville, Robert, 164
Comber Distilleries, 154, 156
Comber Historical Society, 154, 155, 156
Comber, Co. Down, 152, 153, 154, 155, 156, 158, 159
Comber Square, 155
Cooke, Frank, 109
Corbitt, Mary (wife of John Andrews), 152
Country Life, 171
Cowan & Co., William, 57
Cowan, John, 77, 78
Cowan, W.T. (son of John Cowan), 78
Cowan, William, 57
Cowdy, John R., 76p
Craig, John, 56
Craigavad House, Holywood, Co. Down, 175–6
Craigavad, Co. Down, 38, 45
Craigavon, Lord, 109
Craigs (townland), Co. Antrim, 127, 135
Cranmore (House), Lisburn Road, Belfast, 177
Cranmore Park, Lisburn Road, Belfast, 177
Crawford, J.G., 179p
Crawford, Rev. William, 138, 139, 177
Crawford, Sir William, 177, 178, 179–80
Crawford, W.H., 31, 164
Crea, James, 155
Creery, Henrietta de Salis (wife of James Chaine), 82, 85
Creeth, Mary, 55
Creighton, Agnes, 36
Crevilly Valley, Ballymena, Co. Antrim, 140, 143
Crommelin, Nicholas de la Cherois, 169
Cromore, Co. Londonderry, 62
Crookedstone, Aldergrove, Co. Antrim, 71, 72, 125
Crossland, Prof. Sir Bernard, 23, 26
Crumlin Road, Belfast, 12, 49, 50, 183
Crymble's [music shop], Wellington Place, Belfast, 33
Cuba, 81
Culcatta, India, 34
Cullybackey, Co. Antrim, 108, 113, 114, 115, 117, 119p, 125, 127, 129, 131, 132, 133, 135
Cumber, River, Drumaness, Co. Down, 186
Cunningham Memorial Church, Cullybackey, 117
Cunningham, Anne, 29, 117p
Cunningham, Barber, 72
Cunningham, Catherine (daughter of Samuel Cunningham senior), 115, 117
Cunningham, Jane (daughter of Samuel Cunningham senior), 115, 117
Cunningham, John (son of William Cunningham of Lisnafillan), 121
Cunningham, Josias (brother of Samuel junior), 72
Cunningham, Merchants, Josias & Barber, 72
Cunningham, Patrick, 71
Cunningham, Ronald Leslie Chaytor, 52, 53
Cunningham, Samuel, 108, 113, 115

Cunningham, Samuel (grandson of Thomas), 72
Cunningham, Samuel (son of Samuel), 72
Cunningham, Thomas, 72
Cunningham, William (son of John Cunningham), 125, 135
Cunningham, William (son of Samuel), 72, 115, 121, 125
Cunningham, William (son of William Cunningham of Lisnafillan), 121, 125, 135
Cupar Street, Belfast, 4
Curry's Bridge, Kells Water, Co. Antrim, 145p

Dalriada, Whiteabbey, Co. Antrim, 49, 50, 51
Dalrymple Graham & Co., 39
Darracq (car), 136p
Davidson, John, 186, 189
Davidson, William, 186
Davison, Augusta Mary, 121
Davison, John (of Raceview), 121
Dean, J.A.K., 6, 18, 42, 48, 50, 58, 62, 65, 90, 111, 113
Delaney, Mrs, 110
Deramore House, Bessbrook, 24
Derryvolgie, Lisburn, 13
Dickey, Adam, 105, 115
Dickey, John, 115
Dinsmore, John, 145p
Dixon and Co., Messrs Thomas, 85
Dixon, Hugh, 9, 33
Doagh Road, Whiteabbey, 42
Doagh Stream, Dunadry, Co. Antrim, 76, 81
Doagh, Ballyclare, Co. Antrim, 92
Donaghcloney, Co. Down, 13
Donegal Square East, Belfast, 61
Donegall Place, Belfast, 55, 62
Donegall Square Methodist Church, Belfast, 49
Donegall Square North, Belfast, 63, 66, 73
Donegall Square West, Belfast, 55
Dorma Old Bleach Works, 98
Down Education Committee, 162
Downpatrick, Co. Down, 170, 173
Drennan, Dr William, 152
Drennan, Sarah (wife of John Andrews), 152
Drogheda, Co. Louth, 23
Dromana House, Cullybackey, Co. Antrim, 135–6
Dromona & Main Ltd., 108, 136
Dromona (bleach green), Co. Antrim, 72, 108
Dromona Works, 136
Dromore, Co. Down, 100, 130
Drumaness House, Co. Down, 186
Drumaness Mill, Co. Down, 186, 188, 189, 190
Drumaness, Co. Down, 186, 187, 188, 189, 190
Drumglass (House), Belfast, 178
Drummaul House, Randalstown, Co. Antrim, 104, 106
Dublin, Ireland, 97, 183
Dublin Penny Journal, 111p
Duffin's Creek, Toronto, Canada, 55
Dugdale, Thomas Cantrell, 178p
Dumfries, Scotland, 23
Dunadry, Co. Antrim, 73, 76
Dundela, Co. Down, 59
Duneoin Road, Cullybackey, 125

Duneoin, Cullybackey, Co. Antrim, 72, 121, 125–6
Dungannon, Co. Tyrone, 3,
Dunleath, Barons, 170, 171, 173, 174
Dunlop, Durham, 59
Dunminning Bridge, Glarryford, 124
Dunminning Cottage, Glarryford, Co. Antrim, 124
Dunminning House, Glarryford, Co. Antrim, 109, 121, 122–3, 124, 125
Dunminning Road, Glarryford, Co. Antrim, 122
Dunmurry, Belfast, 52
Durham Street, Belfast, 62

Edinburgh, the Duke of, 13
Eisenhower, General Dwight D., 63
Elizabeth II, Queen, 13
Encumbered Estates Court, 111
Eves, Trevor, 4p
Ewart & Son (Ltd.), William, 12, 13, 18
Ewart, Frederick William, 13
Ewart, George Herbert, 12, 18, 46
Ewart, Gordon, 6p
Ewart, Helen Flora, 46
Ewart, James Mathewson, 12
Ewart, Lavens Mathewson, 12, 18
Ewart, Lily, 16p
Ewart, Richard Hooker, 12
Ewart, Sir W. Ivan C., 13
Ewart, Sir William (1817–1889), 12, 14, 56
Ewart, Sir William Quartus, 12, 17
Ewart, Thomas, 11, 13
Ewart, William (1759–1851), 11, 12
Ewart, William (1790–1873), 12

Falls Flax Spinning and Weaving Company, 37
Falls Road Mill, 37
Falls Road, Belfast, 4, 36, 37, 45, 56
Fenaghy House, Cullybackey, Co. Antrim, 72, 108, 113, 114, 115, 136
Fenaghy Road, Ballymena, co. Antrim, 115
Fern Bank, Knock, Belfast, 162
Fernshaw, Dungannon, Co. Tyrone, 4
Festival of Britain, 46
Fibres and Fabrics Journal, 105, 108, 128
Finlay, John, 61
Firgrove House, Muckamore, Co. Antrim, 90–91, 139
Firmount, Belfast, 12
First World War, 25, 38, 46, 97, 103, 130, 131, 153, 170, 190
    Somme 1916, 38, 97
Flax Advisory Board, 38
Flax Spinners Association, 47, 53, 146–7p
Flax Street, Crumlin Road, Belfast, 183
Flax Supply Association, 56
Forrest, Mrs, 14, 17
Forsythe, Wes, 31
Fortwilliam Park, Belfast, 56
Foster Green Hospital, Belfast, 12
Four Mile Burn, Dunadry, Co. Antrim, 76, 81
Fourth River Mills, Belfast, 4

France, 24, 55, 130
Francis Street, Belfast, 168, 169
Frazer & Haughton, Ltd., Messrs, 128, 129, 130, 131, 132, 133
Frazer, John W., 129

Gailey, John, 34
Gailey, Marcia, 34
Galgorm Castle, Co. Antrim, 108–09, 110–11
Galgorm Road, Ballymena, Co. Antrim, 110
Galgorm, Co. Antrim, 72, 108
Gamble, Emily Mary, 186
Gardens in Mid-Antrim, 114
George VI, King, 46
Germany, 24, 46
Giffen, Thomas, 126
Gihon, Grace (daughter of William Gihon), 121
Gihon, William, 121
Glarryford, Co. Antrim, 72, 121, 122, 124, 126
Glasgow, Scotland, 23, 169
Gledheather, Dunminning, Glarryford, 121
Glen House, Glenavna, Co. Antrim, 58
Glen House, Newtownards, Co. Down, 165–6
Glenavna House Hotel, 58
Glenavna House, Co. Antrim, 57–8, 59
Glenbank Bleach Green, 18, 19
Glenbank House, Ballysillan, Belfast, 12, 18, 19
Glenbank, Ligoneil, 12
Glencairn House, Broughshane, Co. Antrim, 108, 138, 139
Glenhurst, Muckamore, Co. Antrim, 86
Glenmachan [House], Strandtown, Belfast, 5, 9, 14, 16p, 17, 19
Glenmachan Road, Belmont, Belfast, 9
Glenmore, Lisburn, 4, 55, 65, 66
Glenny, Frances (wife of James Andrews), 152
Glenwherry River, Ballymena, Co. Antrim, 142, 144
Gotto, Christopher, 98, 101
Gotto, Felix, 101
Gotto, James Porter Corry, 97, 98, 101
Gotto, Rita Corry, 97, 100
Graham, Ogilvie Blair, 169
Grange, Co. Tyrone, 3, 65
Gray, James, 27, 29
Great Exhibition of 1851, 46
Green, E.R.R., 36
Greencastle, Co. Antrim, 36
Greenfield House, Kells, Co. Antrim, 144
Greenfield Mill, Kells, Co. Antrim, 145
Greenisland, Co. Antrim, 33, 99
Greenmount, Antrim, 90
Greer, Henry, 3,
Greer, Robert, 3,
Greer, Thomas, 65, 67
Greer, Thomas MacGregor, 65
Greeves & Co., T.M., 4
Greeves, Arthur, 5p, 8, 10, 16p
Greeves, Bertha, 5p, 6
Greeves, George, 5p
Greeves, Georgina (née Jackson), 7
Greeves, Greta, 5p
Greeves, Jackson, 5p

INDEX

Greeves, Jane, 65
Greeves, John, 4, 5, 6, 10, 65
Greeves, Joseph Malcomson, 5p, 8
Greeves, Lieutenant Colonel J.R.H., 4, 9p, 10
Greeves, Lillian, 5p, 6
Greeves, Ltd, J. & T.M.,, 4, 8, 10
Greeves, Margaretta, 6
Greeves, Owden Valentine, 4, 5p
Greeves, Rachel, 5p, 6
Greeves, Rachel (wife of Thomas Greeves), 4
Greeves, Thomas, 4
Greeves, Thomas Jackson, 4
Greeves, Thomas Malcomson, 4, 7, 10
Greeves, William Edwards, 4
'Grey House, The', Craigavad *see* Olinda
Griffith's Valuation, 135
Grimshaw, Edmund, 36, 39, 40
Grimshaw, Nicholas, 36
Grimshaw, Thomas, 36, 39
Grimshaw's Mill, 38
Grogan, Robert, 19
Grosvenor Road, Belfast, 178
Guide to Irish Country Houses, A, 172
Gunning & Campbell, Ltd., 36, 37, 39, 45
Gunning, Robert, 37, 45

Haines, Keith, 7
Hanna, John, 142, 143
Hanna, Robert, 90p, 91
Hanna, William, 142
Hanson Trust, London, 38
Harbour Board *see* Belfast Harbour Commission
Harland & Wolff, 7, 25, 153, 156, 158
Harmony Hill, Whiteabbey, Co. Antrim, 57
Harmony Hill, Drumaness, Co. Down, 189–90
Harperstown House, Cullybackey, Co. Antrim, 129, 130–31, 133
Harte, James, 186–7
Haughton & Co., Thomas, 129
Haughton, Elizabeth F., 121
Haughton, John Wilfred, 131, 133
Haughton, Lieutenant Thomas G., 130
Haughton, Samuel Gillmor, 132
Haughton, Thomas Wilfred, 121, 129, 130, 131, 132
Haughton, Wilfred James, 133
Hazelbank House (Hazel Bank), Newtownabbey, 27, 28, 29
Hazelbank Park, 29
Henderson's Directory, 74, 76, 183
Henshall, Colonel Louis Sydney, 38, 46, 47, 48
Henshall, Herbert, 38, 46, 47
Henshall, James, 38, 46, 47, 53
Herdmans Ltd., Sion Mills, 4, 38, 53
Heritage Newsletter (UAHS), 14, 17
High Street, Belfast, 63
Hill, John, 108, 127, 128
'Hill, The', Drumaness, Ballynahinch, 188
Hillmount (bleach works), 108, 129, 133
Hillmount House, Cullybackey, Co. Antrim, 121, 127–8, 129, 132
Hillmount Road, Cullybackey, Co. Antrim, 127, 129, 130, 133
Hillsborough, Co. Down, 11, 12

Hind and Sons, John, 62
Hind, James, 62
Hind, John, 62, 168
Hobart, Henry, 100, 130
Hollybrook House, Randalstown, Co. Antrim, 104, 105, 106
Holywood, Co. Down, 175, 182, 184
Hunter, Edith M., 159p
Hurst, James, 186
Hurst, James, (son of William J. Hurst), 186, 187, 188
Hurst, William H., 186, 187
Hurst, William John, 186
Hursts Ltd., 186, 190
Hyde Park, London, 46, 184

Impact of the Domestic Linen Industry in Ulster, The, 31
Inchmarlo Preparatory School, Belfast, 177, 178, 180
India, 26, 34
Industrial Development Board, 91
Invermuir House, Doagh, Co. Antrim, 92–3
Irish Builder, 5, 85
Islandreagh Bleach Works, 73
Islandreagh Dyeing and Finishing Company, 73–4
Islandreagh House, Dunadry, Co. Antrim, 73, 74
Islandreagh Road, Dunadry, Co. Antrim, 73

Jackson, Elizabeth Pim, 10
Jackson, Georgiana Eliza, 10
Jackson, Thomas, 5, 6, 7, 9, 10, 14, 37, 65, 113, 169
Jaffe Spinning Company, 25
Jaffe, Sir Otto, 25
Jamaica, 81
Jamieson, John, 180
Jemphrey, Denys H.L., 4, 46
Jennymount Flax and Tow Spinning Mill, 49, 52
Johnston & Sons, Ltd., Philip, 52, 53
Johnston and Carlisle, Brookfield Mills, 49
Johnston, Daniel (son of Philip Johnston), 49
Johnston, David Woods, 49
Johnston, Lieutenant William, 49
Johnston, Peter, 161
Johnston, Philip (son of Lieutenant William Johnston), 49, 50, 51, 52
Johnston, Samuel Alexander, 49, 51, 52
Johnston, W. Sibbald, 164, 165, 166
Johnston, William, 144
Jordanstown Road, Newtownabbey, 48, 50

Kay, James, 168
Kells Water (river), Ballymena, Co. Antrim, 140–41, 142, 145p
Kells, Co. Antrim, 142, 144
Kelly, W. Redfern, 85
Kelso, Isabella, 12
Kenbally, Broughshane, Co. Antrim, 138
Kennedy, Robert, 176
Ker, David, 170
Kilconway, Cullybackey, Co. Antrim, 133
Kildrum (townland), Kells, Co. Antrim, 140–41

Kildrum and Lisnawhiggle, Dyeing and Finishing Works of, 142–3
Kildrum House, Kells, Co. Antrim, 142–3
Killead Presbyterian Meeting House, 72
Killead, Co. Antrim, 72
Killleagh Flax Spinning Co., Ltd., 187
Killydonnelly (Beetling Mills), Co. Antrim, 136
Killyleagh, Co. Down, 30, 31
Killylodge, Glarryford, Co. Antrim, 136
Kiltonga Bleach Works, Newtownards, 165
Kiltonga, Newtownards, Co. Down, 164, 165, 166
Kintullagh, Ballymena, Co. Antrim, 109
Knock, Belfast, 162
Knockvar(r)e, Randalstown, Co. Antrim, 99, 100

Lagan Boat Club, 25
Lagan Valley, 36
Lagan, River, 25, 52
Lamb, Maria, 97
Lambeg, Lisburn, 55
Lancashire, England, 36, 46, 169
Landscape, Greenisland, Co. Antrim, 99
Lanyon and Lynn (architects), 62
Lanyon, Sir Charles, 61, 62, 113, 171
Larmor, Peter, 52
Larmor, Sir Graham, 186–7
Larne and Stranraer Steamboat Company, 82
Larne, Co. Antrim, 82, 85
   Larne Harbour, 82
Lawlor, H.C., 71, 74, 76, 83, 105, 108, 115, 125, 128, 152
Le Pan, Marianne (wife of William Valentine), 55
Leeds, England, 168
Lendrick, John, 73, 75, 127, 142
Lewis, C.S., 8, 16p
Lewis, Samuel, 154
Lewis, Warren, 16p
Liddells (of Donaghcloney), 13
Lindsay & Co., Ltd., James, 62
Linen Board, 11
Linen Directory (Carter), 78
Linen Merchants' Association, 109, 131, 178
Linen Trade Directory (F.W. Smith), 78
Lisburn Meeting of the Society of Friends, 55
Lisburn Road, Belfast, 177
Lisburn, Co. Antrim, 4, 11, 13, 38, 49, 55, 66, 97
Lismachan, Strandtown, Belfast, 5, 6, 7, 10
Lismara, Newtownabbey, Co. Antrim, 61–2, 63
Lisnafillan Bleach Works, Broughshane, 108, 115, 128
Lisnafillan House, Broughshane, Co. Antrim, 108, 121, 125, 135
Lisnafillan, Co. Antrim, 72
Little Lea, Circular Road, Belfast, 8, 16p
Liverpool, 45, 93
Lives of Great Engineers of Ulster, The, 34
Living Linen, 24, 25, 26, 46, 52, 186
London, England, 38, 106, 170
Lonsdale, Newtownabbey, 47, 48
Lorne, Craigavad, Co. Down, 38, 43, 44, 45
Lough Neagh, 71
Lowtown (linen bleach works), 115
Ludlow Corporation of Massachusetts, 34

Luke, James, 74
Luke, John, 74
Lurgan, Co. Armagh, 164

MacClure, Samuel, 73–4
MacClure, Samuel Arthur (son of Samuel MacClure), 74
Macedon *see* Hazelbank House
Macedon Point, Newtownabbey, Co. Antrim, 61
Mackie & Son(s) (Ltd.), James, 23, 24, 25, 26, 31, 34, 42
Mackie Engineering Works, Belfast, 27, 34
Mackey and Charters, 12, 18
Mackie, Frazer (son of James junior and E.S. (Lily) Pringle), 24, 25, 34
Mackie, Gordon, 26, 34
Mackie, Isobel (daughter of James junior and E.S. (Lily) Pringle), 24, 28p
Mackie, Jack (John Pringle) (son of James junior and E.S. (Lily) Pringle), 24, 25, 26, 28p, 31, 32
Mackie, James (1823–87), 23, 24
Mackie, James (1864–1943), 24, 25, 26, 28p, 34, 42
Mackie, James Alexander (Jim)(son of James junior and E.S. (Lily) Pringle), 24, 25, 26, 27, 28p, 33, 34
Mackie, Kathleen née Metcalfe, 31, 32
Mackie, Lavens Mathewson (son of James junior and E.S. (Lily) Pringle), 24, 25, 26, 28p, 42
Mackie, Michael, 25
Mackie, Michael F., 24
Mackie, Paddy, 24, 26, 31, 32
Mackie, Thomas, 19
Mackie, Thomas (Tom), 22, 26, 31
Mackie, Thomas Frazer, 28p
Mackie, W. Grenville (son of James junior and E.S. (Lily) Pringle), 24, 25, 33, 34
Magdalene College, Cambridge, 82
Main Works, Cullybackey, Co. Antrim, 136
Main, River, 72, 95p, 97, 105, 113, 114, 115, 121, 122, 124, 125–6, 127, 130, 133, 135, 140
Malcolm, Elizabeth, 172
Mallie, Eamonn, 24, 26, 32
Malone Golf Course, Belfast, 52
Malone, Belfast, 67
Manchester University, 24
Manchester, England, 78, 168, 186
Marietta, Barnetts Road, Belfast, 31
Masonic Order, 56
Maxwell Court, Comber, Co. Down, 154–5, 156, 159
Maxwell, James, 154
McCall, Mr, 104
McCammon, Milford & Bailey (cotton spinners), 168
McConkey, Rosemary, 31
McConnell & Co., R.J., 57
McConnell, Kennedy & Co., 4
McConnell, Samuel J., 109
McCullagh, Sir Crawford, 63
McDonnell, Elizabeth, 172
McErlean, Thomas, 31
McIlroy, John, 126
McLaughlin & Harvey, 33, 133
McLaughlin, E.F., 133

INDEX

McLaughlin, Priscilla Elizabeth, 133
McMeekin, Ivan, 92
McMeekin, Muriel, 92
McMeekin, Vera, 92
McMeekin, William, 92, 93
McNeill, John, 55
McTear, David, 28, 29
McTear, Thomas, 28, 29
McVickar, John, 135
Melrose Abbey, Scotland, 24
Meroc, Greenisland, Co. Antrim, 33, 34
Merville, Newtownabbey, Co. Antrim, 21p
Metcalfe, J.B.H., 4
Methodist College Belfast, 49
   Philip Johnston Mathematical Prize, 49
Milecross Lodge, Bradshaw's Brae, Newtownards, 163, 164
Milehess Mill, Volga, Russia, 25
Mill Street, Comber, Co. Down, 154
Millar, Jesse, 140–41, 143
Miller, John, 154, 156
Ministry of Agriculture, 91
Ministry of Aircraft Production, 26
Ministry of Supply, 26
Mitchell family, 41
Mitchell, Alexander, 183
Mitchell, George, 42
Mitchell, George Thomas, 181p, 182, 183
Mitchell, Jill, 52
Mitchell, John, 184
Mitchell, Joseph, 183, 184
Mitchell, William S., 183
Mitchell, William Stephenson (nephew of Joseph Mitchell), 184
Moat, The, Strandtown, Co. Down, 56, 59, 60
Moon, William, 93
Moore, Mr J., 98
Moravetz, Ludwig, 28p
Morris, William, 132
Morton, Mary, 3
Mossley House, Whiteabbey, 37, 39, 40
Mossley Mill, A Short History, 38
Mossley Mill, Co. Antrim, 36, 37, 38, 39, 40, 45, 46, 48
Mossley, Co. Antrim, 36, 37, 40, 41, 56
Mount Cashel estate, Kells, Co. Antrim, 145
Mount Cashel, third Earl of (Stephen), 108, 110, 111
Mount Collyer, Belfast, 172
Mount Colville, Ballymena, Co. Antrim, 110
Mount Randal, Belfast, 177–8, 179p 180
Mountain Road, Newtownards, 165
Moy, Co. Tyrone, 3
Moylarg (townland), Co. Antrim, 135
Moylena [House], Muckamore, Co. Antrim, 87, 88, 89
Moylena Bridge, Muckamore, Co. Antrim, 69p, 87p, 90
Moylinny [Cottage], Muckamore, Co. Antrim, 88, 89
Moylinny, Muckamore, Co. Antrim, 87, 90
Muckamore Bleach and Dye Works, 91, 170
Muckamore Bleaching and Linen (Green), 82, 86, 87, 90
Muckamore Bridge, 86, 88
Muckamore Cricket and Lawn Tennis Club, 91
Muckamore, Co. Antrim, 64, 69p, 73, 78p, 81, 82, 83, 85, 86, 90, 91

Mulholland & Son, Andrew, 169
Mulholland, Andrew (son of Thomas Mulholland), 168, 169, 171, 172, 175
Mulholland, Henry Lyle (second Baron Dunleath), 170
Mulholland, John (son of Andrew Mulholland), 169, 172, 173, 175, 176
Mulholland, John (son of Thomas Mulholland), 168, 169, 170
Mulholland, Mr, 37
Mulholland, Muslin Manufacturers, T. & A., 169
Mulholland, Rt. Hon. Sir Harry, 183p
Mulholland, St Clair Kelburn (son of Thomas Mulholland), 168, 169
Mulholland, Thomas (senior), 168, 169, 170
Mulholland, Thomas (son of Thomas Mulholland), 168, 169
Mulholland, William (son of Thomas Mulholland), 168, 169
Mulligan, Baldwin, 56
Munce & Kennedy, Messrs (architects), 52
Murland, James, 169, 186

New Orleans, USA, 169
New Street, Randalstown, 101, 104
New York, USA, 12, 108, 170
Newcastle, Co. Down, 82
Newry, Co. Down, 152
Newtownabbey Borough Council, 38
Newtownabbey Way, 29
Newtownabbey, Co. Antrim, 29, 47, 48, 50
Newtownabbey, Through the Ages to , 24
Newtownards Academy, 162
Newtownards, Co. Down, 44, 160p, 161, 162, 164, 165, 166
Newtownstewart, Co. Tyrone, 12
Nicholas Street, Dublin, 97
Nidderdale, England, 168
Nine Generations, 154
North Howard Street, Belfast, 36, 37, 45
Northern Banking Company, 55
Northern Counties Railway Company, 109
Northern Ireland Chambers of Commerce, 100, 109
Northern Spinning and Weaving Co., Ltd., 56
   New Northern Spinning and Weaving Co., Ltd., 56
Northern Whig, 19p

Oceanic, 158
Old Ballygowan Road, Comber, Co. Down, 153
Old Belfast Families and the New Burying Ground, 37
Old Bleach Carpet Factory, 98
Old Bleach Linen Company, Randalstown, 78, 97, 98, 100, 101, 102, 103, 104, 106, 121
Old Green Wollen Mills, 145
Old Holywood Road, Belfast, 14, 59
'Old House, The', Comber, 152
Old Manse Road, Glenavna, Co. Antrim, 58
Old Staffordstown Road, Randalstown, Co. Antrim, 99, 100
Oldstone Road, Muckamore, Co. Antrim, 86, 87
Olinda, Craigavad, Co. Down, 182–3
Olympic, 158
Ordnance Survey Memoirs, 28, 36, 40, 61, 64, 72, 76, 77, 83, 86, 88, 89, 113, 122, 125, 127, 135, 138, 140, 143, 145, 154, 159

Ahoghill, parish of, 113, 127, 135
Antrim, parish of, 84, 88
  Comber, parish of, 159
  Connor, parish of, 140
  Drummaul, parish of, 104
  Rasharkin, parish of, 122, 125
  Skerry, parish of, 138
Ormiston, Belfast, 7
Ormrod, Jessie, 155
O'Rorke, Daniel, 33
Owden, John, 65, 66–7
Owden, John (of Talbot House, Cuckfield, Sussex), 66–7
Owden, Margaret, wife of Thomas Greer, and daughter of John Owden 67
Owden, Sir Thomas Scrambler, 67

Pakistan, 26, 34
Paris, France, 170, 177
Patrick, Colonel John (1871–1937), 121
Patrick, Dr John, 121, 123
Patrick, Grace (wife of Oswald B. Webb), 102, 121
Patrick, Isabella (daughter of Dr John Patrick), 121
Patrick, John (1802–79) (son of Dr John Patrick), 109, 121
Patrick, John (1844–94) (son of John Patrick(1802–79)), 121
Patrick, Malcolm (son of John Patrick (1844–94)), 109, 121, 126
Peebles Hydro, Scotland, 24
Percy Street, Belfast, 153
Phenix, W., 4
Philadelphia, USA, 108
Pickering, Toronto, Canada, 55
Pierce, Richard, 86
Pigot's Directory, 76
Pirrie, Agnes, 156
Pirrie, James Alexander, 153
Pirrie, Viscount William James, 153, 156, 158
Point Field (York Street) Belfast, 168
Portadown Weaving Company, 4
Portglenone Road, Randalstown, Co. Antrim, 102
Portglenone, Co. Antrim, 81
Presbyterian Meeting House, Cullybackey, 115, 117
Preston & Sons, John, 109
Preston, England, 168
Pringle, Alexander, 24
Pringle, Elizabeth Sara (Lily), 24

Queen Street, Belfast, 37, 45
Queen's University of Belfast, 47

Raceview, Co. Antrim, 121
Randalstown, Co. Antrim, 78, 97, 98, 99, 100, 101, 102, 104, 105, 106, 121, 177
  First Presbyterian Congregation, 177
Rankin, Peter, 178
Raphael, John, 109
Rasharkin and Finvoy Yeomen, 136
Rathfern, Whiteabbey, 40, 41, 42
Reade, George Sturrock, 91, 137p, 139

Reade, R.H.S., 178
Red Cottage, Cullybackey, Co. Antrim, 132
Red Hall *see* Bernagh, Strandtown, Belfast
Redford, Grange, Co. Tyrone, 3
Redlands, Randalstown, Co. Antrim, 100
Reford, Joseph, 88
Reford, Lewis, 87
Regent House School, Newtownards, Co. Down, 162
Regent House, Newtownards, Co. Down, 161, 162
Regent Street, Newtownards, Co. Down, 160p, 161
Reynolds, Ivor, 98p, 104
Richards Brothers & Co., 55
Richardson, James Nicholas, 65, 67
Richardson, John Grubb, 4
Richardson, Son & Co., James N., 55
Richardson, Sons & Owden, J.N.,, 4, 55, 65, 66
Richardson's Linen Mill, Bessbrook, 23
Richardson's Warehouse, Belfast, 67p
Richhill, Co. Armagh, 55
Ringdufferin House, Co. Down, 30–32
Roberts, G.A.E., 53
Robinson & Cleaver Ltd., Messrs, 62–3, 73
  Irish Linen Warehouse, 63, 73
Robinson, Alexander, 136
Robinson, Edward, 62, 63
Robinson, Hugh, 136
Robinson, Stewart John, 135, 136
Roome, William J.W., 33
Rosebank Linen Co., Ltd., 183
Rosebank Mill, Belfast, 183
Rosemary Street, Belfast, 12, 49, 72
Ross, Bob, 103p
Rowan, Alistair, 171
Royal Belfast Academical Institution, 158, 177
Royal Belfast Academical Institution 1810–1960, History of, 180
Royal Belfast Golf Club, Craigavad, 175, 176
Royal Irish Constabulary, 13
Royal Irish Rifles, 130
Royal Marines, 190
Royal Victoria Hospital, Belfast, 178
Russell, Chas. C., 165
Russia, 24, 25

Sandford, E.R., 189
Sandhurst, Knock, Belfast, 56
Science and Technology Park, Antrim, 91
Scott, Robert, 18
Scrabo Golf Club, 166
Scrabo, Newtownards Co. Down, 161, 166
Scrimegour, James, 23
Seapark House, Carrickfergus, Co. Antrim, 64, 65, 67
Second World War, 26, 34, 98, 106, 132, 153, 156, 170, 190
  Dunkirk, 51
Shanoguestown Road, Dunadry, Co. Antrim, 75
Shaw, James, 5
Shaw, William, 135
Shore Road, Carrickfergus, 64
Shore Road, Newtownabbey, 33, 57, 61
Simmy Island, Killyleagh, Co. Down, 31

INDEX

Sinclair, Thomas, 19
Sion Mills, Co. Tyrone, 4, 38
Six Mile Water, Muckamore, Co. Antrim, 73, 76, 78p, 81, 86, 87, 89, 92
Sligo, Ireland, 55
Smith, F.W., 78
Smithfield, Belfast, 168
'Society for the Promotion and Improvement of the Growth of Flax in Ireland, The', 56
Society of Friends (Quakers), 3, 4, 5, 10, 55, 65, 97, 163, 164
Society of Friends School, Lisburn, 55
Soldier's Home, Holywood, 184
South and East Belfast Health Trust, 8
Southampton, England, 158
Southwell (Downpatrick) estate, Co. Down, 170
Springfield Road, Belfast, 24
Springvale (House), Co. Down, 169, 171
St Mary's Flax Mill, Drogheda, 23
Stanton, Aaron, 40
Stanton, Moses, 39–40
Staples, Sir Thomas, 136
Station Road, Craigavad, Co. Down, 44, 175, 182
Steen and Redford, 88
Stevenson, Catherine, 183
Stewart, Alexander George, 28
Stewart, Thomas Ludford, 64
Stirling House, 180, *see also* Inchmarlo
Stirling, J.H., 178, 180
Stone, Malcolm, 34
Stothard, Matthew, 48
Straidballymorris, Dunadry, Co. Antrim, 76, 77
Strand Spinning Company, 25, 34
Strandtown Villa, 6
Strandtown, Belfast, 5, 7
Strangford Lough, 30, 31
Stranraer, Co. Antrim, 82
Stuart Esq., Thomas, 64
Stuart Esq., William, 64
Swan, Hugh (junior), 76
Swan, James, 74
Swanage, Dorset, 33
Swann, Hugh, 75, 76
Sydenham District Tramway Company, 56
Sydenham Park, Belfast, 12
Sydenham, Belfast, 9, 14

Tait, J.F., 89
Talbot House, Cuckfield, Sussex, 66
Templemoyle House *see* Greenfield House
Templepatrick, Co. Antrim, 84
Textiles of Ireland, 53
Thailand, 26
Thistleborough, Glenavy, Co. Antrim, 81
Thompson, Heather, 81, 87
Thompson, James, 29
Thompson, John (of Greenmount), 90
Thompson, Mary (wife of Samuel Cunningham), 72
Three Acres, Dunmurry, Belfast, 52
Three Mile Water, Co. Antrim, 57, 58

Tinamara, Greenisland, Co. Antrim, 33
Titanic, RMS, 153, 158
Topographical Dictionary of County Down, 154
Toronto, Canada, 55
Tullylagan, Co. Tyrone, 65
Turkey, 25
Turner, Thomas, 50, 175
Tweskard, Strandtown, Belfast, 7, 10

Ulster Arcade, Donegall Place, Belfast, 62
Ulster Architectural Heritage Society (UAHS), 14, 40, 104, 110, 144
Ulster Automobile Club, 131
Ulster Bank, 36
Ulster Flax Spinners' Association, 38
Ulster Guides, 44
Ulster Hall, Belfast, 172
Ulster Journal of Archaeology, 29
Ulster Polytechnic, 51, *see also* University of Ulster
Ulster Tourist Board, 131
Ulster Unionist Council, 109, 153
Ulster Weaving, 52–3
Ulster Weaving Company, 187
Ulster Weaving Group, 186
Union Street, Belfast, 169
University of Ulster (Jordanstown), 50, 51
Upper Malone Road, Belfast, 52

Valentine, George , 55
Valentine, George (son of George Valentine), 55
Valentine, Ina, 56
Valentine, James W., 56
Valentine, Louis Augustus, 56
Valentine, Thomas (son of George Valentine junior), 55, 56, 59
Valentine, William (son of George Valentine junior), 55, 56, 57, 58
Valentine's Glen, Co. Antrim, 57
Valley Cottage, Crevilly Valley, Co. Antrim, 140–41
Vantona, 13
Victoria, Queen, 63

Wales, the Prince of, 38
Walker & Co., Ltd., George, 162
Walker, George, 161, 162
Wallace & Whittle (bleachworks), Muckamore, 81
Wallace, Craig, 114
Waring Street, Belfast, 36, 49, 55
Waringstown, Co. Down, 11
Webb, Arthur (son of W. Hubert Webb), 98, 106
Webb, Charles (son of W. Hubert Webb), 98
Webb, Charles James (son of William Webb), 97, 99
Webb, Dorothy (wife of Roy Webb), 104
Webb, Heather, 100
Webb, Messrs C.J. and R.T., 97, 101
Webb, Norman F. (Roy), 97–8, 104, 106
Webb, Oswald Brooke, 97, 102–03, 121
Webb, Patrick Brooke (son of Oswald Webb), 97, 98, 103

Webb, Richard, 97
Webb, Richard Thomas (son of William Webb), 97, 99
Webb, Rosemary, 103p
Webb, W. Hubert (son of C.J. Webb), 97, 100, 101
Webb, William (son of Richard Webb), 97
Wellington Place, Belfast, 33, 183
Well-Spun Thread, Memoirs from Mossley Mill, A, 46
West Indies, 168
Westminster, London, 12
Wetherall, Sarah (wife of George Valentine senior), 55
White Linen Hall, Donegall Square, Belfast, 1p, 66
White Star Shipping Line, 97, 153, 158
White, John, 138
Whiteabbey, Co. Antrim, 55, 57
Whitehall, Co. Antrim, 138
Whitehouse, Co. Antrim, 27, 28, 36, 39, 45, 55
Whittle, Jane (wife of William Chaine), 81, 83
Whittle, Maria (wife of James Chaine), 84
Wilkinson's farm *see* Moylena
Wilson, Dorothy Lyall, 132
Wilson, Wynnefred Margaret, 188
Wilson's farm *see* Moylena
Winetavern Street, Belfast, 168
Woods, Hester, 49
Woods, John, 126
Workman Clark & Co., Ltd., 65

York Road, Belfast, 49
York Street Flax Spinning Company, Ltd., 26, 53, 82, 86, 90, 91, 139, 168, 169, 170, 171, 172, 177, 179, 180, 184
York Street, Belfast, 37, 55, 168, 169, 170, 172
Young & Co., W.R., 109
Young & Sons, William, 108, 138
Young and Mackenzie (architects), 63, 178
Young, Arthur, 19
Young, Dr William (son of William Young), 108, 111, 128
Young, James, 108, 113
Young, James (son of William Young), 108, 128
Young, James and Robert, Linen Merchants, 111, 128
Young, John (son of James Young), 108
Young, Robert (son of William Young), 108, 127, 128
Young, Rt. Hon. George C.G., 107p, 109
Young, Rt. Hon. John, 108–09, 111
Young, Rt. Hon. William Robert (son of John Young), 109, 110p
Young, Samuel (son of James Young), 108
Young, William (son of James Young), 108, 113, 114, 129, 136, 138
Young, William (son of William Young), 108
Young, William Alexander, 109
Young, William L.R., 113p, 114